SURVIVING
SMALL
SIZE

SURVIVING SMALL SIZE

*Regional Integration in
Caribbean Ministates*

PATSY LEWIS

University of the West Indies Press
Barbados • Jamaica • Trinidad and Tobago

University of the West Indies Press
1A Aqueduct Flats   Mona
Kingston 7   Jamaica

06 05 04 03   5 4 3 2

CATALOGUING IN PUBLICATION DATA

Lewis, Patsy.
Surviving small size: regional integration in Caribbean ministates / Patsy Lewis

p. cm.

Based on the author's thesis (PhD – University of Cambridge, 1991)
under the title: The integration of the Eastern Caribbean through the OECS.
Includes bibliographical references.

ISBN: 976-640-116-0

1. O.E.C.S. (Organization) – History. 2. O.E.C.S. (Organization) – Public opinion. 3.
Leeward Islands – Politics and government. 4. Windard Islands – Politics and government. 5. Caribbean, English-speaking – Economic integration. 6. Caribbean, English-
speaking – Foreign relations. 7. Regionalism (International organization). I. Title.

F2011.L48 2002   320.97297 dc-21

Book and cover design by Robert Harris
Set in Plantin Light 10/14 x 27

Printed on acid-free paper.
Printed in Jamaica by Stephenson's Litho Press

for my parents, Owen and Perlyn Lewis,
siblings, Petipha, Earl and Selwyn,
husband, Brian Meeks,
and children, Anya and Seya

Contents

Acknowledgements

This manuscript began as a doctoral dissertation, completed in 1991 for the history faculty of Cambridge University, so my acknowledgements go back to the collection of data and the preparation of the dissertation. In producing the dissertation and then transforming it into a manuscript, I depended heavily on the support and cooperation of a number of people and institutions. I wish to express my deepest thanks to them.

This study took me to ten Caribbean islands, allowing me to experience the legendary hospitality of Caribbean people. I wish to express heartfelt thanks to the following people who took me into their homes: Eric and Jocelyn Bishop in Antigua, Sheila Beaubrun in St Lucia, Maralyn Balantyne in St Vincent, Anthony Gonsalves in St Kitts, Yvette Cross in Brussels, Violet Davis in Guyana, and my own family in Grenada. In each island, I found people always willing to lend support, particularly in identifying and establishing contact with important interest-group leaders. In particular, I wish to thank Irwin Laroque in Dominica, Cynthia Barrow in St Lucia, and Keith Joseph in St Vincent. I owe a special debt to Cynthia for allowing me to use her interview with Julian Hunte. I am also grateful to all my interviewees, a number of whom have since passed on, for their willingness to talk to me and for the openness of their views.

I also owe thanks to the staff of the Institute of Social and Economic Research (now the Sir Arthur Lewis Institute of Social and Economic Studies) at Mona, the OECS secretariats, and CARICOM. My thanks in particular to Ms Murray and Beverly, the librarians at CARICOM, and Gregory McPhail and Percival Marie of the Economic Affairs Secretariat in Antigua. I owe special thanks to Vaughan Lewis, then OECS secretary-general, and Professor Eddie Green, then director of the Institute of Social and Economic Research, Mona, for their assistance in offsetting some of the costs of data collection.

This study would not have been possible without the financial support of a number of institutions. These are Trinity College, the Cambridge Commonwealth Trust, the history faculty of Cambridge University (for awarding me the Holland Rose Fund), the Smuts Fund, and the Cambridge Board of Graduate Studies (for awarding me an Overseas Research Studentship), and the Institute of Social and Economic Research, Mona. I also wish to thank two regional airlines, LIAT and BWIA, for offsetting my travel costs across the region.

I am most grateful, however, to my supervisor, Professor David Fieldhouse, who was a constant source of support and encouragement and, ultimately, a friend. I am also grateful to Professors Alistair Hennessy and Anthony Lowe, my thesis examiners. I also wish to thank Dr Don Robotham, then of the University of the West Indies, Mona, for his role as my external supervisor for a year, and Dr Cowley, my college tutor at Trinity, for his efforts on my behalf. I am also grateful to Terrence Smith, my brother-in-law, and to my friends Alana Johnson and Rumina Sethi or taking time off from their own work to proofread and help me produce the dissertation. I am especially grateful to my friend Alissa Trotz for her encouragement and support.

I also wish to thank Professor Rupert Lewis, at the University of the West Indies, Mona, and Professor Hilbourne Watson, at Bucknell University, for their comments and recommendations for publishing this manuscript. I wish to apologize for not addressing their comments more frontally. I also owe thanks to my colleagues, Professor Neville Duncan and Dr Don Marshall, for their comments on some of the chapters. I particularly wish to thank Don, whose discussions with me on the regional integration project served to sharpen my focus and forced me to take account of issues I would otherwise have ignored.

Finally, I wish to thank Brian Meeks, my husband, for his love, support and sacrifice, and constant intellectual stimulation; my parents, Owen and Perlyn, and my sister, Petipha, for believing in me; and my children, Anya and Seya, for just being there.

Abbreviations

ACP	Africa, Caribbean and Pacific States
BVI	British Virgin Islands
CANA	Caribbean News Agency
CARICOM	Caribbean Community and Common Market
CARIFTA	Caribbean Free Trade Area
CBI	Caribbean Basin Initiative
CCL	Caribbean Congress of Labour
CDU	Caribbean Democratic Union
CSME	Caribbean Single Market and Economy
EAS	Economic Affairs Secretariat
ECCM	East Caribbean Common Market
ECDS	Eastern Caribbean Drug Service
EU	European Union
FTAA	Free Trade Area of the Americas
GDP	Gross domestic product
IMF	International Monetary Fund
LDC	Less developed country
LIAT	Leeward Islands Air Transport Service
MDC	More developed country
NAFTA	North American Free Trade Area
OECS	Organization of Eastern Caribbean States
RCA	Regional Constituent Assembly
RSS	Regional Security System
SCOPE	Standing Committee of Opposition Parties of the East Caribbean States (later changed to Standing Conference of Popular Democratic Parties of the East Caribbean States)
UNESCO	United Nations Education, Scientific and Cultural Organization
WISA	West Indies Associated States
WTO	World Trade Organization

THE EASTERN CARIBBEAN

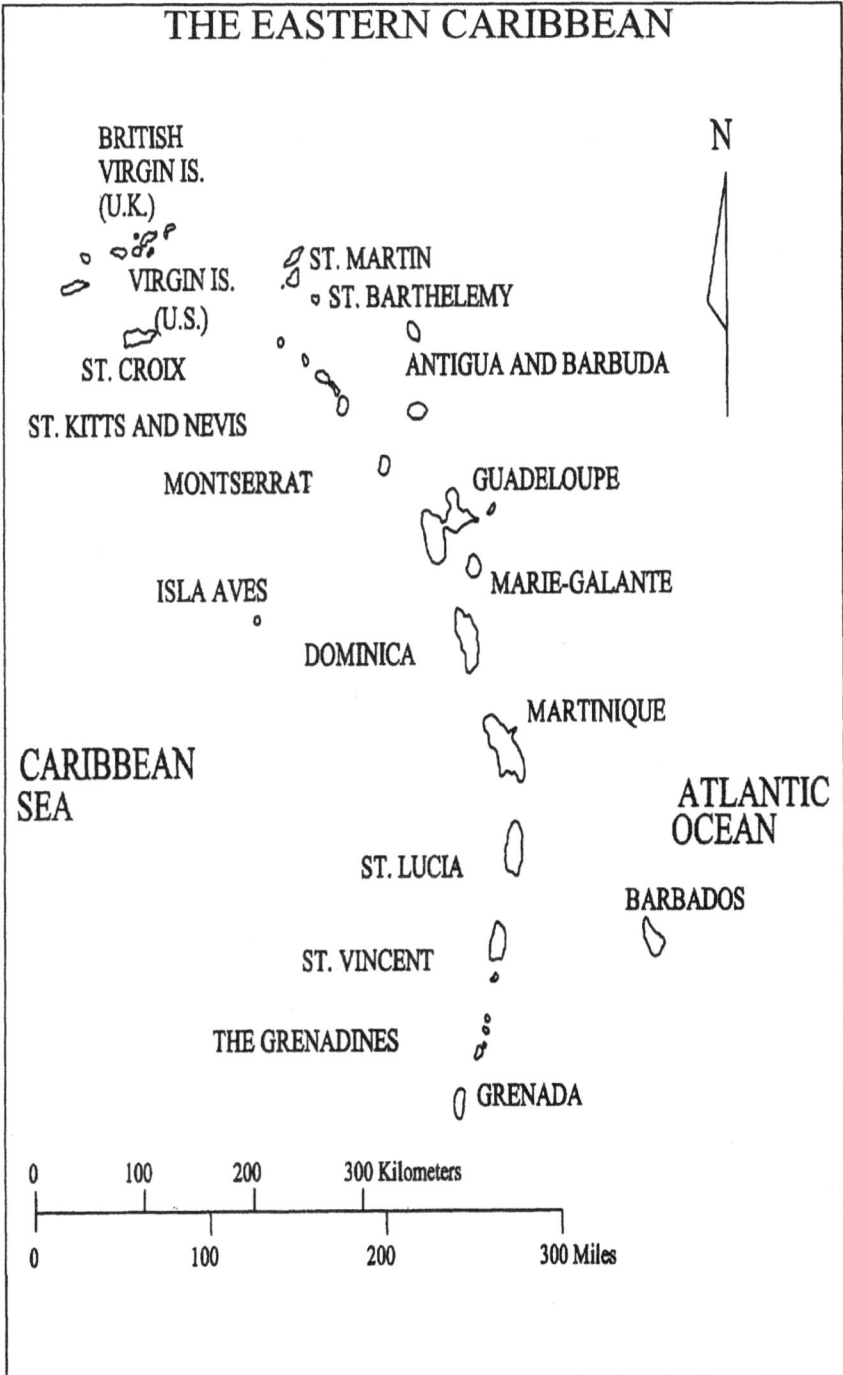

BRITISH
VIRGIN IS.
(U.K.)

N

ST. MARTIN
VIRGIN IS.
ST. BARTHELEMY
(U.S.)

ANTIGUA AND BARBUDA

ST. CROIX

ST. KITTS AND NEVIS

MONTSERRAT
GUADELOUPE

ISLA AVES
MARIE-GALANTE

DOMINICA

MARTINIQUE

CARIBBEAN
SEA

ATLANTIC
OCEAN

ST. LUCIA

BARBADOS

ST. VINCENT

THE GRENADINES

GRENADA

| 0 | 100 | 200 | 300 Kilometers |
| 0 | 100 | 200 | 300 Miles |

Leonard Notice

1

The OECS Political Union Initiative

To be or not to be a single nation.
> – James Mitchell, address at the eleventh meeting of the OECS Authority

Introduction

At a summit of heads of government of the Organization of Eastern Caribbean States (OECS) on 28 May 1987, St Vincent's prime minister, James Mitchell, called on fellow prime ministers to merge their countries into a single state. He argued that they had exhausted the possibilities of separate independence and the time had arrived for them to pursue their development by pooling resources to combat common problems. Six of the governments agreed to raise the issue at the national level but, from the onset, the Antiguan government rejected the proposal. Although by the end of the year all the islands of the Leeward grouping – Antigua and Barbuda,[1] Montserrat, and the Federation of St Christopher and Nevis[2] – had opted out of the initiative, the issue remained very much alive among the governments of the Windward chain – Grenada, St Vincent and the Grenadines,[3] St Lucia, and the Commonwealth of Dominica[4] – with a decision taken to test popular support for a political union.

The OECS political union initiative was precipitated by William Demas's statement in June 1986 that genuine independence for Caribbean countries could be realized only through a political union of the former members of the

West Indies Federation and Guyana – a movement which should begin with the OECS countries.[5] Demas's proposal was not new, as Caribbean spokesmen and intellectuals had made similar calls at various times. What was different was the response of some OECS leaders, led by James Mitchell, prime minister of St Vincent.[6] Following on Demas's speech, Mitchell declared his interest in pursuing a union with other OECS countries but said he would "wait to see what happened".[7] When "nothing happened", in his words, he broached the issue in September with other Windward Islands' leaders – Prime Minister Herbert Blaize of Grenada and Prime Minister John Compton of St Lucia – gathered in Washington for the annual meeting of the board of governors of the International Monetary Fund (IMF) and International Bank for Reconstruction and Development. Mitchell asked them to declare where they stood on union and demanded to know, in his words, whether "I had to plan for St Vincent and the Grenadines as a separate unit forever, or whether we could seriously be planning in the OECS together".[8] In response, Compton and Blaize expressed support and asked Mitchell to prepare a discussion paper, which he presented at the October 1986 heads of government meeting in St Lucia as "Thoughts on an East Caribbean Union".[9] Antigua's prime minister, Vere Bird, was absent from that meeting but the other leaders agreed to put the issue before their people and asked Compton, facing general elections the following April, to place it on his political agenda. They informed Antigua's deputy prime minister, Lester Bird, about their decision following an OECS meeting in Antigua on 29 November.[10] Thus the initiative was born.

Reactions to the Initiative

Governments

Prime Minister Bird, in his address to the November 1986 OECS summit, gave a cautious response, advising his colleagues to strengthen economic institutions and cooperation before considering political union. He suggested that they be guided by the European Community's experience, which illustrated that it was "more sensible to build up economic institutions before attempting common political institutions". He observed that European Community countries were "pooling wealth" while OECS countries were "pooling comparative underdevelopment"; and that despite the wealth of the former they had opted to postpone a political federation. He advised that the OECS countries would be "unwise not to do likewise".[11]

The proposed initiative faced a further hurdle following St Lucia's elections. The elections, which were held the following April (1987), resulted in Compton barely holding on to power with a one-seat majority. He went to the polls that same month, on 30 April, seeking a bigger mandate, but the results remained pretty much the same. Compton's narrow victory threw cold water on the initiative. He had raised the issue in his election campaign,[12] reportedly pledging that if his United Workers' Party was returned with a two-thirds majority, he would seek to amend the constitution to facilitate a political union with the other OECS countries.[13] Mitchell interpreted this result as a setback for the initiative,[14] though it is unclear why he did so. Presumably, he read Compton's "defeat" as suggesting that there was little popular interest in a political union. Despite this "setback" William Demas and Alister McIntyre urged him to pursue the idea.[15]

Mitchell put the issue formally on the regional agenda at the OECS heads of government meeting in Tortola in May 1987, nearly a year after Demas first mooted it. In his address at the opening ceremony, he declared that the issue before OECS leaders was to decide whether "to be or not to be a single nation".[16] He favoured rapid progress towards political union, urging a referendum by the end of 1987 on support for a "united state", followed by a draft constitution and a second referendum to approve the proposed constitution.[17] The six heads present agreed to mount "a process of [national] comprehensive consultation" and hold a referendum. They were to decide on "an appropriate question to be simultaneously put" before their people, and agreed that the OECS legal unit would prepare draft legislation for the referendum.[18]

A month later, when OECS heads were gathered in St Lucia for the Caribbean Community and Common Market (CARICOM) summit, six of them met and issued a communiqué on the initiative.[19] Although the Antiguan representative had participated in the meeting, when Vere Bird arrived he refused even to enter the discussions and, upon his return to Antigua, he declared his decision not to participate. He stated that Antigua was not interested in a political union since it represented a form of colonialism,[20] proposing, instead, closer cooperation among the Leeward Islands. In what appeared to be an alternative to an OECS political union, Bird suggested to St Kitts–Nevis and Montserrat that the Leeward Islands should set up a

"Council of Ministers" which would function at a deeper political level than the OECS.[21] Deputy Prime Minister Lester Bird claimed that "there is a feeling in Antigua and Barbuda frankly, that it would be easier right now to have a kind of a union of the Leeward Islands".[22] Prime Minister Kennedy Simmonds of St Kitts–Nevis stated definitively that the country was not going to "rush" into a union of the Leeward Islands.[23] Nevertheless, Lester Bird asserted that St Kitts–Nevis had accepted the idea, although it was not pursued directly because at the time St Kitts–Nevis was still exploring the broader political union initiative. According to Lester Bird, in that context "we didn't want it to be perceived that we were sabotaging the other situation" (a reference to the initiative). Lester Bird stated that his father, Prime Minister Vere Bird, had wanted Montserrat to enter into a federation with Antigua immediately.[24]

Antigua was thus absent from the initiative from the start. The subsequent OECS Authority meeting in November, in St Lucia, reviewed the activities which had been undertaken nationally to promote the idea; those present agreed, among other things, to accelerate the educational efforts in their countries. A special desk at the OECS was to be established for that purpose.[25] Prime Minister Bird was also absent from that meeting.

The initiative began without Antigua but, by the end of 1988, Montserrat and St Kitts–Nevis had joined Antigua in rejecting it. Montserrat, although still a British colony and therefore not in a position to take a unilateral decision on the matter, initially backed the idea. Chief Minister Osborne[26] also agreed to consult his people on their interest in forming a union with other OECS countries and, in an interview in June 1987, claimed that he had already initiated discussions with the political opposition.[27] His support for the union was short-lived, however. In April 1988 he joined Antigua in rejecting the initiative on the basis that his country was not interested in a political union that excluded Antigua.[28] Osborne's decision to withdraw was obviously influenced by Antigua's lack of interest, as suggested in his declaration that "Montserrat, as long as I am leader will not be part of it if Antigua is not coming because it probably would not be a real union".[29] He withdrew four days before the scheduled first meeting of a committee established to educate and consult Montserratians on their support for union.[30]

However, Osborne's position was not clear because, although rejecting the idea of union without Antigua, he maintained that Montserrat would be a part of closer political union "no matter what happens".[31] He stressed Montserrat's support for an OECS political union, pointing out that his country "has probably done more than any other Caribbean island in terms of fostering this union" by allowing people from other Leeward Islands and Dominica to enter Montserrat without passports and to work without work permits. Montserrat also permitted citizens from the OECS and CARICOM to be treated as nationals for immigration purposes.[32]

Prime Minister Kennedy Simmonds cautiously supported the idea at first, describing it in his address at the Tortola meeting as the "ultimate objective". He advised that while the leaders should "move forward with all deliberate speed" they should, nevertheless, "be careful to avoid undue haste". He warned that "the process of Regional Integration and Regional Co-operation should not be judged only on how quickly or, [sic] if at all, political union occurs".[33] Simmonds's response was viewed by some as lukewarm.[34] It therefore came as little surprise when the St Kitts–Nevis government, after briefly consulting different interest groups, declared in November 1988 that there was little popular support for an OECS political union.[35] St Kitts–Nevis differed from the other Leeward Islands, however, in attempting to solicit public opinion on the initiative.

The British Virgin Islands, an associate member of the OECS but still a British colony, had, like Antigua, asked not to be included.[36] Chief Minister Lavity Stoutt[37] said that while the British Virgin Islands valued its relationship with the OECS, political union was out of the question because of its peculiar relationship with the US Virgin Islands. The official currency of the British Virgin Islands was the US dollar, which it was reluctant to relinquish in favour of the Eastern Caribbean dollar, the common currency of OECS countries. Also, there was the issue of the free movement of people which would be inevitable in any political union. While the British Virgin Islands shared many common institutions with OECS countries,[38] Stoutt was afraid that, because of its small size, the British Virgin Islands could not accommodate immigrants from OECS countries.[39]

What began as a call for an OECS political union, therefore, had been reduced by the end of 1988 to a Windward Islands' initiative. Windward Islands' leaders were unable to pull along the Leeward Islands, and so decided at the fourteenth meeting of the Authority in November to pursue a political union among themselves.[40] At the fifteenth Authority meeting held in June 1989 in Antigua, they agreed to hold simultaneous referenda early in 1990 to determine whether their people supported the idea.[41]

Opposition Parties

The initiative caught opposition parties by surprise, but they recovered quickly and, by July 1987, had formed themselves into the Standing Committee of Opposition Parties of the East Caribbean States (SCOPE), led by St Lucia's opposition leader, Julian Hunte. SCOPE included most of the parliamentary opposition parties in the Windward Islands. SCOPE's primary objective was to ensure that governments adopted a "proper process of consultation" before deciding on the type of political union. Its first task was to seek an audience with OECS governments.

SCOPE supported a closer union in principle, but expressed concern about the "haste" with which it was being pursued.[42] Hunte wrote to Prime Minister Compton, then chairman of the OECS Authority, seeking discussion with the heads of government and presenting certain requests which SCOPE viewed as necessary to create a climate of goodwill within which to pursue the initiative.[43] These were: an end to "political victimisation"; media access, which they believed was severely constrained; permission to hold meetings in each other's territories without restrictions; and assistance to establish a secretariat. Hunte charged that Compton did not acknowledge his letter although Compton did meet with him later, at which point he raised SCOPE's concerns. Hunte also suggested that St Lucia needed to hold local elections as part of the process of discussion and consultation. Hunte advocated a regional, rather than a national, approach to the consultation process, involving SCOPE and the governments.

SCOPE's next meeting, in August, criticized the governments' failure to respond to Hunte's request for a meeting;[44] expressed support for a SCOPE secretariat; and recommended unrestricted travel within the region by opposition party parliamentarians and representatives, an assessment of the cost and benefits of union, and the creation of a "climate of good will" among governments and opposition parties.[45] SCOPE called on the governments to publish a white paper on their union plans, and undertook to commission a "detailed study of the technical implications" of the proposal. The meeting noted that the initiative had lost momentum and that the governments were "only interested in unity in so far as it entrenched them in power and marginalized the opposition". It noted what appeared to be an absence of consistency among the heads of government on matters such as the timetable for union and the method of consultation.[46] Hunte concluded that SCOPE was not prepared to support union on those terms.

SCOPE met in March 1988 and changed its name to the Standing Conference of Popular Democratic Parties of the East Caribbean, also called SCOPE. It continued to be critical of the initiative, commenting that public confidence in the leaders had been undermined by conflicts among OECS countries, particularly well-publicized disputes over competing boxing plants and "national" airlines. SCOPE charged that the attitudes and motivations of the leaders, as well as their failure to create a climate of goodwill with the opposition, had "seriously flawed the initiative", in a context where SCOPE had been prepared to support it.[47] No indication was given that SCOPE had withdrawn its support for the principle.

In June 1988 SCOPE tried to convene a broad-based conference in Dominica on OECS political union, backed by the University of the West Indies; but this failed, SCOPE members claimed,[48] when Dominica's prime minister, Eugenia Charles, indicated to the University of the West Indies her dissatisfaction with their involvement in what she saw as a partisan political affair. SCOPE then entered a period of inactivity, that ended when the governments breathed new life into the initiative with the establishment of a Regional Constituent Assembly (RCA) in 1990. In 1989, however, it appeared that the proposal for union of all OECS members was moribund, if not dead, leaving only the more modest possibility of a smaller union of the Windward Islands.

For a brief moment, therefore, between the end of the 1980s and the beginning of the 1990s, West Indian people had dangled before them the elusive prospect of a political union among some of their members. This book investigates the initiative as it was unfolding, providing a rare insight into the opinions and attitudes which influenced its outcome. There is little secondary data available on the initiative itself, so the book relies on a rich array of primary sources which include newspaper articles, OECS documents and, more importantly, interviews with over eighty leaders of elite groups throughout the OECS, including most OECS prime ministers and opposition figures. The issues which are central to this book are: what factors gave rise to the union proposal, and why did it have such limited results? More generally, what light does its failure throw on the wider question of possible obstacles in the path of proposed union or federations among the region's small states? The book investigates these question in detail, examining the considerations which influenced individual national governments, how they tested the reactions of their constituents, and why the eventual decision in the Leewards proved to be negative while that of the Windwards remained positive, although ultimately unsuccessful.

The International Context

In 1986, when interest was first shown in an OECS political union, independence was still a relatively new phenomenon for most. Grenada, which was the first to become independent (1973), had been independent for only twelve years; St Kitts–Nevis, the most recently independent nation (1983), for only three. The organization still had non-independent members: Montserrat, a full member, and the British Virgin Islands, with observer status. OECS states had emerged on the international scene in the wake of the oil crisis which put a brake on the development efforts of underdeveloped states, and in the final stages of the cold war in which the Caribbean, given its proximity to the United States and the presence of the Cuban revolution, had been assigned an important role. Their existence as formally independent states was conditioned by their need to satisfy the economic and social aspirations of people optimistic about the possibilities which political independence suggested, and by the international political context within which they were located. Grenada, inspired by the Cuban revolution and its promise of social justice and the transformation of traditional relations away from dependence on Britain and the United States, sought to forge new economic and political relations with Eastern bloc countries and the Soviet Union, and, to a lesser extent, with other "Third World" countries. For most other OECS countries, their developmental path proceeded within the traditional patterns of political and economic relations with the United States and Europe, and the use of their geographical proximity with the United States as leverage for economic assistance. These patterns were manifested in a reliance on the United States for aid and an inflow of concessionary funds from international financial institutions, and the importance of protective trade and aid regimes with Western Europe through the Lomé Conventions, from which Grenada also benefited.

By the mid-1980s, however, these traditional bases for development appeared shaky; impending changes in the international economy portended their destruction, even before the formal collapse of the Soviet bloc. By then

the effects of increased globalization, which some writers identified as intensifying in the 1970s and 1980s, were clearly in evidence. Specifically, the reach
of global capital and the shift towards technologically based industries which
were increasingly not location specific were already effecting changes in their
major trading partners[49] which held the seeds of their marginalization. From
the early 1980s there were already talks around transforming the General
Agreement on Tariffs and Trade to facilitate the increased liberalization of
trade; the European Community was engaged in plans to establish a single
market[50] to facilitate the free movement of goods, capital, services and labour,
in order to increase their global competitiveness; and the United States was
already in discussion with Canada and Mexico to form a free trade area.[51]

The European Community's transformation to a European Union (EU)
and single economic market was felt to be particularly threatening as it meant
the restructuring of economic relations to bring the policies of member states
into alignment, with immediate consequences for the banana protocols at-
tached to the Lomé Conventions. It was not immediately clear how this would
be resolved, but OECS states with a vested interest in the banana industry had
good reason to worry. In particular, the community was faced with reconciling
the protective banana regimes in place in several EU countries with the
open-market policies of members like Germany. Any new policy had to be
compatible with the General Agreement on Tariffs and Trade, which was
already being renegotiated in the direction of decreasing barriers to trade, and
take on board US hostility to such protective measures.[52] US negotiations to
form a free trade area with first Canada (the Canadian United States Free
Trade Area), then extended to Mexico (the North American Free Trade Area
[NAFTA]), also encouraged a degree of anxiety. This move suggested, in all
likelihood, a diversion of trade away from the region to Mexico, given the
possibilities there for cheaper labour and lower transportation costs because
of Mexico's closer proximity to the United States. This would leave US
concessions to the Caribbean region, embodied in programmes such as the
Caribbean Basin Initiative (CBI), hollow.[53] Already, by 1986, the United
States had scored a major success in its conflict with the Soviet bloc, beginning
with the Grenada invasion and what was perceived as a victory over the Soviet
Union and Cuba in the US sphere of influence, and the weakening of left-wing
forces internationally.[54] In the region, this was already manifested in reduced
financial commitments from the United States, the trend continuing after the
fall of communism in Eastern Europe.

The call for an OECS political union in the late 1980s, therefore, must be located against the backdrop of international developments at the time, and read as a response to the feeling of marginalization experienced by some member states. This is developed further in chapter 6, when the motivations of Windward Islands' leaders in pursuing the initiative are discussed.

Structure of the Book

The book investigates a number of themes. Chapters 2 and 3 are concerned with establishing the development of a subregional identity among OECS states, which made the formation of the OECS possible. They also lay the foundation for explaining the eventual split in support for the political union initiative between the Leeward grouping, on the one hand, and the Windwards, on the other.

Chapters 4 to 7 address the question of why the initiative developed when it did. They analyse the OECS economies, the organization's performance as a subregional integration mechanism, and point to possible factors that underlay the motivation for union. In so doing, these chapters try to contextualize the OECS experience within a body of work on integration movements, specifically in terms of the primary factors influencing interest in, and the success or failure of attempts at, political unions.

Chapters 8 to 10 present attitudes towards the initiative among leaders of specific interest groups across the OECS, in an attempt to understand the leaders' responses to the initiative, particularly the bases upon which they supported or rejected it. The primary groups represented here are political parties, trade unions, private sector organizations, and an array of social groups, including youth, women and church organizations. The leaders of these groups were targeted, primarily, on the premise that they would be able to provide some insight into the extent to which the initiative was discussed within their organizations and the response of their membership, but also on the grounds that their own responses to the initiative may well have influenced, to some degree, their organizations' formal position (to the extent that this existed) and the views of their membership.

The book concludes by locating the significance of a political union among either all or some of the OECS members within the framework of a broader regional perspective, and questioning the basis upon which political integration should be grounded.

CHAPTER

Caribbean Integration
From Federation to Regional Integration

This is no time for bickering
Political squabble or mudslinging
Politicians, be sensible, please
And build the prestige of the West Indies
 – The Roaring Lion, "West Indians Get Together"

The OECS initiative put political union on the agenda of the Commonwealth Caribbean in a serious way for the first time since the collapse of the ill-fated West Indies Federation in 1962. The Federation's demise, coupled with the failure of continued attempts to forge new unions among remaining units, seemed to have ended the prospect of political union in the Commonwealth Caribbean. Instead, the focus shifted to economic cooperation expressed in regional integration schemes, influenced by the European Community experience and similar attempts in Latin America and other parts of the developing world. The Caribbean Free Trade Area (CARIFTA) was formed in 1969, giving way to CARICOM in 1973. This movement sparked a parallel organization among the smaller, still colonial units of the Federation, with the establishment in 1967 of the East Caribbean Common Market (ECCM), forerunner to the OECS. Attempts to forge a political union among OECS member states thus brought the regional movement full circle to political considerations.

This chapter provides an overview of the historical sequence which accounted for the regional integration movement, identifies the various debates which influenced its shape, and examines the relationship between economic and political integration.

The West Indies Federation

The West Indies Federation, which lasted from 1958 to 1962, marked the first stage in the Caribbean integration process. It represented the fulfilment of both a long-standing goal of the British government, convinced of its potential for administrative efficiency, and a desire for political independence within the West Indies. In addition, the formation of federations represented a more general colonial approach geared towards creating viable units for political independence in the final stages of the decolonization process, reflected in the plethora of federations that sprang up in the colonies.

The West Indies Federation departed from earlier colonially motivated administrative movements in two ways: first, its focus was on political and economic gain rather than administrative efficiency; second, it was as much a result of Caribbean desire as of British convenience.[1] From the Caribbean's perspective it was the culmination of a movement directed towards self-government and political independence which treated federation as a route to political advance, in keeping with the prevailing view that viability was closely associated with size. From the perspective of the colonial power it was a means of creating a viable political unit which would be able to achieve independence, thus extricating Britain from a relationship that was no longer considered desirable. As Watts summed it up, for the British colonial government, " 'viability' became the prerequisite for self-government, and inter-regional unity the means".[2]

The ultimate failure of the West Indies Federation can be located within the broad political and economic gap which existed between its larger, more advanced units (Jamaica, Trinidad) and the smaller, less developed units of the Eastern Caribbean. On the political front, by the time the Federation was established, political advances had made national independence an achievable goal, separate from the Federation.[3] As Watts noted, rapid constitutional changes after 1944[4] undermined the federal movement, and these changes appeared to be retarding rather than advancing the movement for independence.[5] On the economic front, Jamaica and Trinidad were already pursuing development strategies based on establishing an industrial base which, at best, did not require a Federation and, at worst, was inhibited by it. These presented difficulties for the immediate inclusion of issues such as customs union and the financing of the Federal government. A temporary solution was found in the decision to postpone their consideration for five years after the Federation was introduced. Specifically, Trinidad with its wealthier, oil-based economy resisted freedom of movement, worried that an influx of labour from smaller territories would strain its economic and social infrastructure, while Jamaica, anxious to protect its fledgling industries, opposed a customs union. The smaller Windward and Leeward Islands resisted free trade without the free movement of labour, arguing that national income would be reduced if they were forced to discriminate in favour of goods from Trinidad and Jamaica. In addition, both Jamaica and Trinidad were expected to share the major part of the financial requirements of the union, a prospect that met with Jamaican hostility. Trinidad supported a strong central government with powers over taxation, customs and excise duties, education, and national economic policy as the appropriate framework within which to handle the development of the smaller territories.[6] Jamaica, to the contrary, preferred a looser political framework, optimizing sovereignty, allowing the nation to pursue economic development with minimal interference from a regional central government.

It is clear that the Federation did not present a coherent approach to economic development for its member states but became, instead, a theatre for the acting out of competing interests. The Federation's demise, a mere four years after its inception, was symptomatic of its inability to reconcile the national developmental desires of countries like Jamaica with the interests of the region as a whole; this failure was reflected in the absence of a regional development programme.[7] Further, the attempt to treat political considerations of government and constitutional development as separate from economic development, evident in the decision to postpone thorny economic issues, proved unworkable. With the Federation's collapse, following Jamaica's withdrawal after a referendum on the issue, as well as the failure of successive attempts to unite the remaining units,[8] attention turned to the difficulties of independent survival and the desirability of developing areas of mutual cooperation among the former members. This led to the formation of CARIFTA in 1968, which gave way to CARICOM in 1973. F.G. Carnell, writing in 1961, had predicted that new federal states might be attracted to a looser concept of federalism based on the attempts at Western European integration in the 1950s. He predicted that nationalism might be too strong in these states to allow federations to survive, and that they might be more receptive to regional integration which provided the means for securing international cooperation across national frontiers.[9]

Integration as a Route to National Development: Latin America and the Caribbean

The integration movement in the Commonwealth Caribbean was set squarely within broad debates on the modernization of "backward" economies and the role of industrialization in achieving development, a process equated with economic growth. This approach, popularized by W.W. Rostow, treated development, as occurring in advanced capitalist countries, as universally applicable regardless of historical particularities. Development, therefore, was a process that could be replicated in underdeveloped countries once certain prescriptions were met. Indeed, development strategies already being pursued by Jamaica and Trinidad in the decade before the Federation, modelled on the Puerto Rican industrialization programme, were influenced by this ap- proach. W. Arthur Lewis[10] embraced the Puerto Rican programme and adapted it to suit the Commonwealth Caribbean, advocating industrial devel- opment within a federal framework and customs union. Lewis, in keeping with the underlying assumption of the universal applicability of the modernization experience, argued for industrialization as a means of absorbing the surplus labour from agriculture which, as an economic strategy, could no longer provide the standard of living the population required.[11] He called for both the mechanization of agriculture to increase yields and release labour for more productive sectors, and a programme of industrialization to absorb this surplus labour.[12] He advocated an industrialization programme based on export, rather than import substitution, arguing that local markets were too small either to absorb production or to allow production on an economic scale. Industrialization was to be based on low wages, low power input, and foreign investors as providers of scarce capital and know-how.[13] Lewis assigned a leading role to the state, particularly in attracting foreign capital, providing infrastructure and introducing incentives. This required the establishment of a "development agency"[14] to identify potential industries, seek out manufac- turers, and advise government on the types of incentives to offer.

Lewis's concerns with development were mirrored in debates among Latin American *dependistas,* preoccupied with finding an industrial strategy for Latin America. Under the guidance of the Economic Commission for Latin America, and its director, Raul Prebisch,[15] Latin American countries were pursuing industrialization based on import substitution, in an attempt to break away from their status as suppliers of raw materials and the deteriorating terms of trade which resulted. Latin American *dependistas,*[16] however, departed from Lewis in recognizing that capitalist development was not necessarily open to developing countries. They made a direct connection between capitalism and underdevelopment, arguing that underdevelopment, in what they characterized as peripheral or satellite states, was the logical outcome of capitalist development in the core or metropole. They were particularly concerned with the role of foreign capital in the region's development and the shortcomings of industrialization which, by the 1960s, was perceived to have failed. Industrialization strategies based on internal markets were stymied by markets too small to allow for a transition to intermediate goods. Moreover, industrialization, while generating growth, did not directly address unemployment or issues of democracy and equity.[17] In response to small national markets, the Economic Commission for Latin America shifted its focus to the formation of regional economic integration schemes designed to provide enlarged markets, increase efficiency and strengthen bargaining power. This shift, while addressing issues of small markets, did not provide answers to questions of poverty, equity or democracy, viewed as failings of the earlier approach. The dependency approach, with its focus on the state and "national" development, did not take on board issues of which groups were privileged by the industrial process and what the interest of others in the integration process might be. Regional integration, therefore, was little more than a mechanism for facilitating economic measures, its appeal narrowed to a thin stratum of society.

In the decade of the Federation's collapse, therefore, several such schemes had been formed in Latin America.[18] Thus, the Commonwealth Caribbean's decision to channel their relationship through economic integration schemes was influenced both by the experience of Western Europe,[19] especially Britain's decision to join the movement, and by the existence of such schemes in Latin America and other parts of the developing world. The Commonwealth Caribbean's focus on its own development problems in the wake of the Federation's collapse, like that of the Latin American dependency school,[20] centred on internal and external structures affecting development, with the added dimension of small size. This inquiry gave rise to the birth of a group of economists, primarily functioning out of the University of the West Indies, who became known as the New World Group.[21] The dependency school's critique of Import Substitution Industrializaton provided the framework for the New World Group's critique of similar policies pursued in the Caribbean, with special emphasis on the role of multinational corporations (MNCs).

The group focused on the failure of the Import Substitution Industrializaton programme to reduce unemployment, its tendency to increase dependency through the activities of MNCs[22] in the extractive sector, and its role in enhancing agricultural dualism.[23] They were particularly concerned with its failure to address unemployment, initially its chief objective under Lewis's prescription. Rather than being labour intensive, as Lewis had prescribed, industries tended to be highly mechanized. In addition, the types of industries the programme attracted were "screwdriver-type" operations with little scope for transforming economies. Alister McIntyre,[24] examining relationships between political advance, economic growth and development, sought to differentiate economic growth from development, arguing that impressive growth rates in the 1950s had left the economic structure virtually unchanged. Caribbean countries thus remained "outstanding examples of dependent economies" in both economic and intellectual spheres. He argued that this type of dependence could be broken down by a shift in trade policy away from preferences which he viewed as furthering the "economic Balkanization" of the Caribbean, towards regional integration as a means for accelerating growth and decreasing dependence.

William Demas[25] extended this focus on problems of structural transformation of regional economies by adding the dimension of small internal markets[26] which, he argued, made it impossible for the countries to achieve self-sustaining growth as defined by Rostow.[27] By Rostow's prescriptions, such growth could be achieved only in countries with a large area and population. Demas extended the concept of self-sustaining growth to the structural transformation of economies of underdeveloped countries, reducing the dualism[28] that existed. This meant integrating domestic production structures, increasing the volume of foreign trade, and shifting the composition of imports from consumer goods towards intermediate and capital goods.[29] Holding to the tradition of industry as underpinning economic development he argued that, given the countries' small size, development could be realized only within the framework of regional integration, which would address issues of small markets and limited capital.[30] Like Lewis, Demas advocated an industrial strategy directed at external rather than internal markets. Such a strategy, however, required "building up" institutions to promote and finance exports of manufactured goods as well as regional forms of industrial planning.[31] In a strategy for more control over resources, Girvan and Jefferson[32] viewed regional integration as the key. They argued that perhaps the most decisive argument for integration was the possibility it provided for poor countries to pool bargaining power. In particular it was important, in a strategy designed to counter resistance from domestic and international institutions, to rationalize methods of resource allocation.

The primary focus of the New World Group represented a shift from the internal structural elements in the economy, evident in Demas's approach, to an interest in the external elements influencing Caribbean economies and the implications of this for their development. The group, led by Lloyd Best[33] working with Kari Levitt, developed the concept of the "plantation" as an approach to analysing the structure of Caribbean economies.[34] Best, in particular, rejected Demas's emphasis on the role of size in development, on the ground that he was "defining away" the possibility of development for small countries. Best viewed the structure of Caribbean economies and the role of innovation and technology as important factors in explaining Caribbean underdevelopment.[35] In essence, the structure had not changed much from the days of the plantation, when the region's economies were geared towards servicing the metropole. Production was still monocultural, largely based on export agriculture and, in the case of Jamaica and Guyana, on bauxite. The pattern of the old mercantilism was replaced by the "parent-affiliate" relationship of new enterprises in the mineral sector and in manufacturing. The result was an absence of linkages among the region's economies or even among the internal elements of the national economy. Best and Levitt identified a key role for indigenous initiative and technology in internal dynamic development, arguing that these were necessary to reduce the negative dominance of foreign technology and innovation and to break what they viewed as psychological dependence on developed countries.[36]

Despite the different emphases of Caribbean writers on this subject, the common element was the importance they placed on regional action as a tool for addressing Caribbean problems. These various approaches[37] were carried to the debate over the type of regional structures the Caribbean should embrace.[38] These included the European Community model, which sought expanded trade through the removal of tariffs and the formation of a customs union;[39] the free trade model modified to avoid its negative effects, thus focusing on distributive measures to reduce polarization; and a more far-reaching approach which attempted to tackle the problem of underdevelopment itself, advocating planning and programme development on a regional scale.

Caribbean dependency theorists, therefore, shared the Latin American *dependistas'* perspective of viewing national economies as part of an international structure influencing specific internal structures. Like their Latin American counterparts, they focused on altering these relationships in an effort to decrease dependence on developed countries by exercising greater control over national resources. They also shared the underlying assumptions of the modernizing project. Likewise, their treatment of integration as primarily a mechanism for economic development masked the interests which different social groups might have in the movement, and the need for distributive measures to redress imbalances not just between participating states, but between social groups. It also ignored the potential the movement might have for further democratizing these countries.[40]

Customs Union Theory and Developing Countries

The idea underpinning classical growth theories, that free trade norms operating within an integration arrangement necessarily resulted in development, continued to attract critique among many analysts. Critiques centred on the fundamental assumptions of customs union theory[41] and its applicability outside of Europe, especially given the divergent goals of such schemes in underdeveloped countries. In particular, Latin America's experience was important in this process, both because its schemes were considered the most advanced among developing countries, and because they influenced the Caribbean integration movement.

Traditional customs union theory assumed that union was more likely to have beneficial effects under the following conditions: the more competitive the structure of participating economies; the greater the differences in the cost of commodities actually produced prior to the establishment of the union; the larger the size of the union; the shorter the economic distance between member countries; the higher the level of pre-union tariff; the greater the degree of pre-union intercourse between participating countries.[42] This contrasted directly with the reality in underdeveloped countries of limited regional markets and little intraregional trade. Trade, which generally consisted of primary produce, comprised the bulk of gross domestic product (GDP) and was directed chiefly towards industrialized countries rather than regional partners. Such trade was inelastic and suffered from deteriorating terms. Given the low levels of intraregional trade, the economies of such countries could be considered neither complementary nor competitive,[43] although they competed with one another for export markets. Another feature of underdeveloped countries was that production was not subject to high tariff walls, so a removal of tariffs was unlikely to have significant impact.[44]

In Latin America and other developing countries regional integration was expected to produce gains beyond the international specialization and competitiveness which were expected from a freeing of the internal market, to achieving economic growth and development.[45] Integration's main virtue was the increased potential for industrial development it provided through wider markets. The mere freeing of intraunion trade was inadequate to ensure real development. In fact, among underdeveloped countries it could exacerbate developmental problems, leading to economic polarization between relatively more developed countries (MDCs) and less developed countries (LDCs) within the union.[46] This called for measures to protect the LDCs. Free trade was considered unlikely to have a significant impact on the direction of trade within the union[47] because, unlike Western Europe where a high volume of trade among participating countries existed prior to integration, most developing countries conducted the bulk of their trade with industrialized countries. Thus minimum trade between members of a region, coupled with low levels of manufacturing, meant that a free trade area was unlikely to increase intraunion trade significantly, or to change its structure and direction. Regional integration in developing countries, therefore, had to go beyond free trade, requiring more intervention and coordination of the activities of participating countries. Regional integration was attractive to developing countries because it offered opportunities for achieving economies of scale of production and, in particular, an increased market for manufactured goods. Thus the development of industry, even at the expense of efficiency, cost and international specialization, was justified to the extent that it promoted industrial development, saved valuable foreign exchange and transformed the structures of production.

In the Caribbean, debates surrounding the establishment of the regional integration project had supporters of the three schemes (customs union; free trade modified to address polarization; and emphasis on regional coordination and integration of production).[48] The private sector of the larger countries, such as Trinidad and Jamaica, favoured a free trade approach and the increased access to markets this would provide for their manufacturing industries. The economically weaker countries were worried about the negative effects of such a scheme, and sought protection from some of its ill effects. The third type of integration scheme, reflected in the Brewster/Thomas study[49] commissioned by regional governments, was supported by elements of the intellectual community, concerned with broader issues of underdevelopment and dependency. The eventual structure adopted reflected the type-two integration scheme, with the immediate removal of most barriers to trade and measures addressed at avoiding polarization. This led to the differentiation of the countries into two groups: the MDCs and the LDCs. The OECS was almost a natural offshoot of this process along the lines of the Andean group, where it was felt that a subgrouping of the weaker units was necessary to safeguard their interests. Despite CARICOM's emphasis on trade, however, there were attempts to broaden it beyond a free trade area by including the goals of foreign policy coordination and functional cooperation.

Thus regional integration, as developed to suit the needs of underdeveloped countries anxious to achieve economic "development", and as embraced in the Commonwealth Caribbean, was essentially directed at economic goals. Political action was subordinated to the economic process, and was important to the extent that it promoted functional goals. The Caribbean process did attempt to go beyond economic cooperation by including the coordination of foreign policy as one of the goals of CARICOM, in recognition of their weak bargaining power. The focus turned to pooling "sovereignty" to strengthen the bargaining position of otherwise weak countries, thus anticipating a greater degree of political coordination. Although CARICOM had mixed success on this score, it was carried into the OECS treaty and was an important aspect of their cooperation.

The move from federation to regional integration saw political union disappear from the formal goals of the regional integration process. And while CARICOM did aim at closer economic and functional cooperation, involving some political input, there was no conscious goal – and Jamaica had made its refusal to relinquish any aspect of its sovereignty quite clear – to transform this into a political union. Despite this, however, many of the earlier advocates of the Federation continued to hold to the ideal of a politically united Caribbean.[50]

Political and Economic Integration

The failure of many postcolonial federations, and the rise instead of organizations of regional economic cooperation, resulted in a concentration of debate on the relationship between political and economic integration. This debate was particularly relevant in the context of the *"dirigiste"* rather than liberal approach to economic integration that such schemes in underdeveloped countries were likely to take. Nevertheless, the debate had been important in the European context as well. Three broad schools[51] developed, attempting to explain the relationship between the two: the federalist, transactionalist and neofunctionalist approaches. The federalist and neofunctionalist models, in particular the criticisms to which the latter gave rise, provided useful attempts to identify the factors which influenced the movement towards a political union.[52] In attempting to understand the relationship between central government and local institutions, federal theory examined the factors which encouraged and inhibited the desire for union and which influenced its success. Its focus on these provided some meaningful illumination of the conflicts between national and regional goals. Likewise, neofunctionalism, with its focus on the relationship between elites and interest groups, highlighted some of the non-institutional factors influencing this process.

Federalism

Federal theory developed from the experiences of federations such as the United States, Canada, Australia and Switzerland, but was given new life in the postwar era when Britain and other colonial powers adopted this as the best method for political administration at the advent of independence.[53] In federations the economic issue went hand in hand with the establishment of political union, and usually involved the establishment of a customs union with free movement of factors of production. Wheare[54] identified the factors that favoured political integration as: military insecurity, the desire to be independent of foreign powers, the hope of economic advantage, geographical neighbourhood and the similarity of political institutions. Those that encouraged the desire for autonomy were: geographical distance, previous existence as distinct entities, differences of race, language, religion and nationality, a divergence of economic interests, and different political structures or laws. He argued that while the latter did not override the desire for political integration, they tended to lead to a preference for a federal type of government with autonomy for the units.

In older federations the need for military security was a key element in the desire to federate. Riker[55] viewed it as one of two essential factors: the desire to expand territory without the use of force, and to ready the government for some military or diplomatic threat or opportunity. Also important were the economic advantages federation offered. In newer federations the colonial power played the role of catalyst. The more homogeneous these factors, the more likely its success, although not all factors carried the same weight. Franck[56] introduced the role of political and popular commitment to the "federal ideal" as an important element in determining the success of post-colonial federations. He concluded that the failure of most postcolonial federations lay in the absence of commitment to the federal ideal. Boxill, writing on the Caribbean experience with both federation and regional integration schemes, follows this line of argument. He suggests that both processes suffered from the absence of a "conceptual framework", seeking to reproduce "integration as a system" rather than "as a route to ensure political and economic viability within the wider world system".[57] He goes further, to proclaim that one of the main reasons for the Federation's failure was that it was viewed as a "means of attaining self-government" rather than the "reproduction of the Federation as an end in itself".[58] The introduction of a federal ideal or ideology, especially Boxill's attempt to introduce the broader concept of a regional ideal into the economic integration process, is useful because by considering factors other than economic or technical dynamics driving the integration process, it seeks to move away from a bureaucratic functionalist approach to the process evident in integration theory. This exercise, however, is useful only to the extent that it does not seek to present such an ideology as an end in its own right, disembodied from concrete impulses in the economic, cultural and political realm underpinning interest in such movements. Such an elevation of ideology introduces a static element which does not reflect developments in any of the identified spheres which may weaken or strengthen interest in union or make it more or less likely to succeed. Nor does Boxill, in proposing ways in which such an ideology might be developed, suggest its content or what should inform such an ideology.

The federal model, with its emphasis on legal and institutional arrangements of government, is of limited value in a discussion of economic integration where political union is a long way off and may not even be the stated intention. Despite this, however, its focus on factors underpinning unit loyalties as opposed to regional desires is important in identifying the forces influencing postcolonial integration experiences. The main difficulty with the federal concept lies in its reverence of individual state sovereignty and its focus on preserving autonomy for unit action *vis-à-vis* the central authority. This is problematic in integration schemes in developing countries where effective integration might require significant government intervention to secure regional goals that might not necessarily initially benefit the nation state. In addition, attempts to maintain unit sovereignty may prove too expensive for tiny states that might be attracted to political union as a means of cutting administrative costs.

Neofunctionalism

Functionalist theory, associated with the work of David Mitrany,[59] developed in Europe in the aftermath of two world wars in the twentieth century. Its focus was on securing world peace through the development of international regimes based on common welfare interests as a means of reducing conflict among states. Success in early spheres of cooperation, not initially involving the realm of "high politics", would encourage further cooperation in other spheres. States would find it difficult to end such cooperation as it ultimately might prove more costly. Eventually, at the popular level, people would shift their loyalty from the state towards these organizations, weakening the power of the state and thus reducing the likelihood of war.

Neofunctionalism is rooted in the functionalist tradition of functional cooperation but, unlike functionalism which emphasized international cooperation, it focused more narrowly on economic integration. Neofunctionalism, associated with Ernst Haas's work on European integration,[60] focused on the relationship between competing elites and interest groups and was best expressed in what became known as the Haas-Schmitter model. Haas and Schmitter[61] attempted to use this approach to analyse the potential for success of integration schemes in developing countries. They were concerned with the politicization of the process, as economic integration required increased political compliance. Haas and Schmitter[62] treated the relationship between economic and political integration as a continuum, since there were political implications in most movements towards economic integration. They attempted to separate the process of integration from the end product of political union. The model identified three categories of variables, or "functional equivalents", to calculate the progression from economic to political union. The "background conditions", such as the size and power of units, the rate of transaction among them, and elite complementarity, fell within the first category. The second comprised the conditions at the time of economic union, which included the level of commitment to political union. This led to a differentiation between "built in" or "automatic" integration,[63] and negotiated integration.[64] The third range of variables, the "process conditions", involved the decision-making style which developed among the actors once they confronted one another regularly in implementing their economic union.[65] These variables were the basis for a grading system to determine whether an integration scheme was likely to make the transition from economic integration to political union.

This model was criticized, particularly by economists involved in analysing the Latin American and African experience. Wionczek[66] criticized the notion of automaticity as being more applicable to economically advanced regions where objectives were clearer and democratic forces counteracted vested political and economic interests. Nye[67] questioned Haas and Schmitter's treatment of the relationship between integration and political union as a continuum, their characterization of integration as gradual politicization, and the applicability of both concepts to underdeveloped countries. He argued that the concept of "gradual politicization" was irrelevant to underdeveloped countries whose political structures were characterized as "over politicized". This politicization was likely to restrict the opportunity for autonomous bureaucrats to advance integration in "non-controversial spheres". In this context, the role of the regional bureaucrat was likely to be restricted.

Nye's attempt to apply the model to the East African Common Market found that its relevance was limited. It was difficult to separate "high politics" from technical economic cooperation in underdeveloped countries where political leaders viewed governmental power as a means for effecting rapid economic and social change. He found that in the East African experience, there was a high degree of economic integration spillover and spill-back into political integration. The approach, with its functionalist bent, placed too little emphasis on conscious political action whereas, in underdeveloped countries, the political elite was intent on using the powers of the state to create a national society. The model also ignored the international environment within which the process was taking place, ignoring possible "catalysts" in encouraging the transition from economic to political union. Nye identified these as outside actors or events which would provide the will power to leap from the "brink to the other side". He identified economic aid as a possible catalyst in the contemporary environment, given the dependence of underdeveloped countries on the outside world.[68]

Although the experience of regional integration movements was not sufficiently well established to make the Haas-Schmitter approach an appropriate model to produce generalizations on the potential for success of all such movements, the model did point to some important indicators of success and failure. In particular, the background conditions such as size and degree of transaction, as well as the other variables which would derive largely from the experiences of political and economic integration, provided a useful indicator of the type of difficulties which such movements faced. Although Nye argued that the prominent role given to technocrats was likely to be much less in underdeveloped countries, their role in advancing the process requires analysis. The model could be further criticized for its elitist character, restricting integration largely to a tiny, unrepresentative bureaucratic elite as opposed to more broadly based social movements. Nye's critique did lead to the identification of "catalysts" which allowed for a level of unpredictability in the integration process, and it remains to be seen whether, in fact, there were any such catalysts operating in the OECS experiment.

Analysis of the Haas-Schmitter approach must be placed in the context of the type of integration schemes adopted. The liberalist free-trade type was likely to require less political involvement, particularly at the outset. The politicization of the process was likely to be a more gradual affair along the lines envisaged by Haas. While, as the European Community experience suggested, even limited integration schemes involved increased political action and coordination over time, politicization was likely to be more immediate in more *dirigiste*-type schemes. If such schemes endeavoured to reduce the effects of distribution and allocation among participants, political considerations were likely to come to the fore immediately. In the CARICOM region the functionalist approach, which involves a gradual move from economic to political action, might well prove inadequate to overcome insularity, which might require a more direct commitment to political goals early in the process.

In discussing the relationship between political and economic integration, it is worth noting, as Nye and Haas and Schmitter pointed out, that there were few, if any, examples of regional economic cooperation preceding the formation of a political union. Usually, political union included measures to effect economic integration at the same time. In some regional integration schemes there were cases where political action was provided for in order to facilitate economic integration. Also, as in the case of the European Community, provisions were made for the implementation of large political institutions such as a European parliament, and the coordination of foreign policy. Further, the European integration experience had shown that closer economic integration meant more relinquishing of political power, as in the instance of the Exchange Rate Mechanism, which restricted governments' control over monetary policy.

The real difference between political and economic integration can be regarded as one of emphasis. In political integration the main impetus was political, for a variety of reasons, of which economic factors were an element, but not the totality of the desire to integrate. In economic integration, on the other hand, the focus was on economic considerations, with political action playing a secondary role, that of providing the basis for propelling economic integration. In both cases the focus could shift, disrupting the process. For example, while political gains might be the primary motive for a union, the incompatibility of economic issues might rise to the fore after union was achieved, disrupting the union itself. There are many experiences, particularly in postcolonial federations, to illustrate this. The West Indies Federation found that while political union was premised on the desire for political freedom, by the time union was achieved it was no longer necessary for political development, since this was possible outside of it. More importantly, the units could not accommodate their economic interests, which by then had become primary, within a joint political structure. Hence we see them settling for a process of economic integration which involved a slow, uncertain, uneven process of relinquishing minimal power to enhance the economic integration effort. In this context, one could treat CARICOM's aspirations for the coordination of foreign affairs and closer cooperation in the political sphere either as sentimental remnants from the federal ideal of a West Indian nation, or a realization of the interconnectedness of economic and political spheres.

Specifically, access to markets, investment funds, financial resources and economic aid required a strong political presence in the international arena, that was likely to be enhanced through common action.

Economic integration was primarily concerned with advancing economic interests; it focused, therefore, on issues likely to disrupt that process. These included the size and development of participating units, benefits accruing to various units, and measures to safeguard the interest of the less developed units. A shift in focus to political integration was likely to occur when more political action became necessary to effect deeper economic integration. Hence, the political mechanisms for facilitating economic integration would become paramount. The importance of politics in advancing narrower goals of economic integration was evident in the CARICOM experience in the 1970s, when governments responded to the international oil crises by introducing protective measures at the national level which nearly brought regional trade to a standstill. The situation was aggravated by the existence of different ideological perspectives, which in turn influenced both the economic policies pursued and the interpersonal relationships among regional prime ministers.[69]

Any analysis of the two processes reveals some basic similarities and underlying concerns, particularly in ensuring that some participants were not neglected. Both are engaged in balancing the interests of individual units with what is perceived to be that of the whole. In the case of political integration, it is the federal or unit government versus the states or regions; in economic integration, the tension is between national and regional interests. While the motives behind economic integration are fairly straightforward and clearly defined – that is, greater economic strength, viability or self-sufficiency, and increased economic weight in the international community – those behind political integration are not as straightforward and have generated a large body of writing. In particular, there has been considerable interest in federal unions. This is because this type of arrangement highlighted the tensions described, which ultimately influenced the decision to adopt a federal model rather than some other type of government. It was the form of political institution which the colonial powers, chiefly Britain, favoured in the period leading up to independence. This form would have been attractive for uniting disparate units that had objective commonalities but were inclined to separateness by a long history of fragmentation. This fragmentation, of course, was fostered by the colonial experience, giving rise to what were then viewed as nonviable units. In examining the attempts in the Eastern Caribbean to transform the relationship between the OECS countries into a political union, the experience of federation, particularly what Watts described as the "New Federations", is helpful. The OECS attempt should indicate whether there had been a shift in the balance of some of the factors or variables.

Conclusions

It is possible to identify some common failings running through the various debates on economic and political regionalism. Caribbean and Latin American dependency and federal theorists share a focus on the state as the primary unit of analysis, largely ignoring the role of specific interest groups, political constituents and so forth in the process. This focus, particularly among dependency theorists, is mirrored in an assumption of a "national" interest which integration advances and which benefits all. The analysis does not shift to questions of the content or validity of a national interest. This becomes particularly problematic when "national development" is premised on an industrial process that may well privilege a few groups over the majority. The dependency school's insight into the failure of ISI strategies to eradicate unemployment and address issues of democracy and equity did not lead to prescriptions for how these should be addressed by the industrial process or integration schemes. The Caribbean school perpetuated this failing with its focus on the state. The neofunctionalist school, while attempting to broaden the focus of analysis beyond the state to interest groups, repeats this failing with its tendency to locate the motor of integration in the technocratic/bureaucratic realm, ignoring possibilities for popular action to influence the process. All these approaches, therefore, suffer from a low democratic content, failing to move beyond bureaucratic and grand nationalist projects of development to find both a popular interest and operating space for groups not directly involved in this process. In the absence of such a perspective, the debate remains stilted.

These debates, occurring as they did in the 1960s and 1970s when optimism was high that underdeveloped countries could realistically break out of a cycle of dependency, appear to suggest that economic integration within existing capitalist structures was adequate to effect development. This entire approach has to be reopened and its underlying assumptions questioned. Since then, these processes have been exposed to a number of developments in international capital which have changed both the character and the content of such schemes. The 1980s, in particular, have seen a rebirth of regional integration schemes developing in tandem with the broad move, reflected in the establishment of the World Trade Organization (WTO), towards global free trade – its main expression being NAFTA, and a reinvigorated European Union.

This is also reflected in a perceptual shift in the original premise of integration arrangements in developing countries observed earlier. Regional integration schemes, particularly in the Caribbean and Latin America, are now being reconstructed, bringing them back into line with classical economic growth theory, which holds free trade to be the underlying basis for economic growth and development. Under this process, existing integration schemes are being incorporated into larger hemispheric bodies, along the lines of the Free Trade Area of the Americas (FTAA), where their markets are expected to be completely open to penetration from more competitive North American firms. This represents a complete turn-around from the original conception of such schemes in Latin America and the Caribbean, where regional firms of a similar size were provided a protected environment geared at increasing their competitiveness against US- and European-based firms. These developments suggest that debates about the goals of integration schemes for developing countries are more relevant than ever. And while issues of democracy do not ensure the economic viability of such schemes (either of the older or newer variety), they become particularly important if the schemes are really to serve some developmental end. In small Caribbean countries, it is particularly important that the region's participation in a wider FTAA, or a post-Cotonou reciprocal Regional Economic Partnership Agreement with the European Union, be open to discussion, especially in terms of goals. Central to this must be an analysis of how such schemes are likely to affect the economies and societies of these countries, especially the relationship of people to existing political structures. Such debates must allow for a popular construction of the type of society Caribbean people wish to cultivate, and the elements of the current society worth preserving. This would provide as good a basis as any other for the region's participation in such schemes.

3 Caribbean Integration and the OECS's Formation

We are a group of people conscious of our handicap in the development stakes. We are a group of people proud to belong to the West Indian heritage. We see our destiny as being unmistakably entwined with our other Caribbean partners, but in the same breath, I must warn that we are a people with dignity and a feeling of equality. Although historical circumstances have forced us into a grant-in-aid complex, we are now determined to extricate ourselves from the role of international beggars.

> – Sir Eric Gairy, address at the seventh conference of
> CARICOM Heads of Government

The OECS's formation by CARICOM's LDCs speaks to a perceived speciality of interests *vis-à-vis* the rest of the Caribbean community. There were two movements behind the OECS's formation: the historic experience which forged administrative and other links, and their experiences within both the West Indies Federation and the regional integration movement. The OECS's formation, however, based as it was on an acceptance of common interests, must not be allowed to obscure differences between the two groups of islands – the Windwards and Leewards – which formed the organization. This chapter traces the development of the subregional integration process, the factors influencing it and the effects of the broader regional integration experience in consolidating the movement.

Political Background

The OECS was formed in 1981 among Grenada, Dominica, St Vincent, St Lucia, St Kitts–Nevis, Montserrat and Antigua. St Kitts–Nevis and Antigua were still Associated States of Britain, and Montserrat was a British colony. By 1983 all, save Montserrat, had become independent.[1] The British Virgin Islands, still a British protectorate, was granted observer status in 1986. The OECS embraced all those states within CARICOM classified as LDCs except Belize. When the OECS was formed, these states had in common a number of key institutions: notably a common currency, the East Caribbean dollar; a common currency board, the East Caribbean Currency Authority, which was upgraded to a central bank; a unified judiciary with a court of appeal based in Grenada; and their own economic cooperation arrangement in the ECCM. They also had some experience of shared, though limited, diplomatic representation abroad, and some organization at the governmental level in the Council of Ministers. The OECS brought together these various elements of cooperation into a treaty.

The OECS's formation marked a qualitative stage in the regional integration movement, representing the formal differentiation of interests between the smaller Windward and Leeward Islands within the broader Commonwealth Caribbean integration movement. The basis for this differentiation was their minuscule size, poor resource base and relative poverty. It was the culmination of a long process that forced them to recognize a commonality of interests and served to develop what was considered to be an Eastern Caribbean identity. This process had begun with their colonial experience which, while contributing to their notorious insularity, nevertheless led to the development of common features that facilitated their integration. Their experiences in the broader integration movement, however, beginning with the West Indies Federation, had the greatest impact on consolidating their identity by forcing them to recognize their common problems.

The Windward and Leeward groups had the common experience of British rule which, in keeping with the British quest to unify the islands for administrative purposes, served to develop some links between them. On the other hand, their categorization into these two groups also reflected subtle differences arising from a longer period of British control over the Leeward Islands, which numbered among its earliest colonies; the Windward Islands came into its possession much later in the eighteenth and nineteenth centuries. The legacy of this colonial past was evident in the French-based creole which was still widely spoken in Dominica and St Lucia, and in the French names and many aspects of French creole culture manifest in these islands.

In the Leeward Islands, in particular, common links go back to the seventeenth century and British attempts to administer the area as a federation. These resulted in two federations from 1674 to 1798, and 1871 to 1958.[2] The latter was dissolved to allow them to enter the West Indies Federation as separate units. The Windwards shared a common governor, with the seat of government first in Barbados from 1833 to 1842, then in Grenada. Therefore, British attempts to forge administrative links encouraged a fair amount of movement between islands. However, while there was movement throughout the entire Windward and Leeward region, there was more interaction among the Windward Islands and their neighbours in Trinidad and Barbados, which were at various times linked by administrative arrangements. Likewise, there was more movement between the Leeward Islands and their more northerly Caribbean neighbours. Dominica was unique in belonging to both of the administrative groupings at different times, which meant that it had more interaction with the Leewards than did the other Windward Islands. Nevertheless, there was adequate evidence of this interaction, fostered by colonial administration, which encouraged movement of the educated elites to seats of government bureaucracy, schools, and so on and which was strengthened during the postindependence period. Such movements, often leading to the establishment of filial connections across islands, have encouraged the notion of an Eastern Caribbean identity. Some of these relationships were evident at the level of political and bureaucratic leadership, and obviously fed into the political union initiative. For example, St Vincent's prime minister, James Mitchell, and St Lucia's prime minister, John Compton, were said to be cousins, while Noel Venner, secretary of the St Vincent National Advisory Committee on Political Union in the Eastern Caribbean, and Dwight Venner, former director of finance in the Ministry of Finance in St Lucia, and a member of the St Lucia Independent Committee for OECS Political Unity, were father and son. In any event, Mitchell spent part of his childhood in St Lucia when his stepfather moved there with his mother to take up a job as comptroller of customs.[3] He also held his first job there teaching chemistry.

The basis for an Eastern Caribbean identity was even stronger among the offshore dependencies of many of these islands. From Grenada's Carriacou or Petit Martinique, St Vincent's Union Island, Bequia, and Petit St Vincent were a stone's throw away. Carriacouans seeking hospital treatment found it easier to travel by fishing boat to St Vincent, via its dependency Union Island, than to go to Grenada. The beat of a party in Petit St Vincent is audible from Petit Martinique, merely a fishing boat ride away. The fairly rigid immigration system which the main islands operated hardly seemed to exist among their dependencies, and it was easy to cross from Union Island to Carriacou without suffering the formalities of immigration and customs. This contributed to the existence of a thriving smuggling industry which carried these islanders all the way to the northern Caribbean, with St Bartholomew becoming more familiar to a Petit Martiniquan smuggler than Grenada, his own mainland.

Despite this, the legacy of division remained obvious, manifested most vividly in their communication problems and the structure of their economies. The prohibitive cost of air travel between the islands had a negative effect on intraregional travel. At the extreme end it was cheaper to fly to Miami or Canada from Jamaica than it was to fly to Grenada. And during the late 1980s, while British Airways offered a direct weekly flight between Grenada and England, travellers between Grenada and Jamaica were forced to stop over in Trinidad or Barbados. This was a general Caribbean feature, where communication with North America was easier than within the region, and the islands found it easier to trade with Europe and the United States than with one another. This was a direct result of British mercantile policies in the Caribbean, which discouraged inter-island trade in favour of trade with the metropole.

The actual integration experience played an important role in formalizing inter-island relationships. However, it must be said that even before the Federation there was a tendency for the smaller territories to be viewed as one group; this was evident in the strong opinion which held that they should first federate and then enter the Federation as a single unit.[4] They themselves appeared to appreciate the need for a common union, and even organized a conference on closer union of the Windwards and Leewards in 1947, precipitated by concrete moves towards the formation of the West Indies Federation.[5]

The Federation was important in delineating, for the first time, the interests of the Windward and Leeward groups from those of their more prosperous neighbours – Barbados, Trinidad and Jamaica. This was made poignantly evident in the rows between Trinidad and Jamaica (which ultimately contributed to the Federation's collapse) over financing development in the Windward and Leeward Islands. These conflicts served to highlight the small size, poor resource base and resulting limited prospect for development of the small Eastern Caribbean islands. This was particularly evident when, upon the Federation's collapse, they were forced to continue in an essentially colonial arrangement with Britain, while Trinidad, Jamaica and tiny but more prosperous Barbados proceeded to full independence. Various unsuccessful attempts at unity after this served to consolidate the perception that their destiny ultimately lay in some form of union among themselves. These included Eric Williams's offer of the prospect of a unitary statehood with Trinidad, discussions between 1963 and 1966 over the mechanics of a "Little Eight" federation with Barbados, and an aborted attempt at federation with Guyana in 1971.[6]

Most of the Windward and Leeward Islands entered an Associated Statehood arrangement with Britain in 1967; this lasted until they became independent, beginning with Grenada in 1974 and ending with St Kitts–Nevis in 1983.[7] While bringing the islands self-government, this arrangement left Britain in charge of foreign affairs and security.[8] It was based on the conviction that they could not be viable independent units, although it did provide for separate independence.[9] This period, nevertheless, was directly responsible for the development of concrete structures and a framework for cooperation, and laid the basis for their postindependence relationship.

The West Indies Associated States (WISA) Council of Ministers was formed in 1966,[10] followed by the ECCM in 1968. They shared an East Caribbean Tourist Association, joint diplomatic missions to the United Kingdom and Canada, and a common West Indies Associated Supreme Court, set up under the Associated Statehood agreement; the headquarters of the court, along with the Legal and Judicial Services Commission, was in Grenada. The supreme court, which also served Montserrat and the British Virgin Islands, consisted of a court of appeal and a high court of justice.[11] After Jamaica, Barbados, and Trinidad and Tobago established their own central banks upon leaving the Federation, the East Caribbean Currency Authority was established in 1965 to replace the British Currency Board, which administered a common currency under the Federation. The East Caribbean Currency Authority issued and regulated the Eastern Caribbean dollar; it was transformed to the East Caribbean Central Bank for the independent OECS countries in October 1983.

Economic Integration and the LDC/MDC Divide

CARIFTA's formation was significant to the Associated States on two counts: their classification, with Belize, as LDCs, with special compensatory measures to avoid polarization; and the establishment of their own common market structure, the ECCM. These features of the integration movement were important in further defining their place within the region, and in encouraging them to develop mechanisms to enhance their strength. Their classification within CARIFTA as LDCs, as opposed to the MDCs, and the special measures to which this gave rise, reflected an attempt to avoid the economic polarization which other such movements in Latin America and Africa had experienced, resulting from the freeing of trade. In both cases dissatisfaction with benefits accruing to weaker members placed stress on the movement.[12] Special concessions designed to reduce the negative impact of a free trade area on the LDCs included giving them a twenty-year period within which to open their markets, in contrast to the five years allowed the MDCs; longer periods for removing duties on goods on the Reserve List of commodities not immediately subject to free trade; and a Caribbean Development Bank with provisions for soft loans to establish industries within the LDCs. Article 39 of the CARIFTA agreement allowed the LDCs, with the council's approval, to protect their industries against corresponding industries in MDC countries, even where these were first established in the MDCs. An agricultural marketing protocol, intended to benefit the more agrarian economies of the LDCs, was agreed to as a mechanism by which the secretariat could allocate markets for agricultural commodities among the territories. In the scheme for harmonizing fiscal incentives to industry, the LDCs were to be allowed more generous incentives. Despite these "special" measures, CARIFTA was little more than a free trade area, with the LDCs viewing it as a mechanism for their exploitation by the MDCs.[13]

The very decision to launch a free trade area contributed to a further differentiation between the Eastern Caribbean states and their more developed neighbours. In anticipation of CARIFTA they formed their own subregional grouping, the ECCM, in April 1968, acceding to CARIFTA as a group in July of that year. This decision to form their own economic arrangements is instructive. The ECCM was more than a means of improving their bargaining position against the larger territories and maximizing CARIFTA's special concessions; it represented a tighter, more desirable scheme than CARIFTA offered.[14]

The ECCM agreement was the instrument around which the WISA states were organized. It established the WISA Council of Ministers, which comprised a ministerial representative from each member state,[15] and a secretariat to monitor the application of the agreement. It therefore provided the basis through which their economies could be integrated. Its stated aim was "to establish the foundation of a closer union among the peoples of the East Caribbean", and to ensure their economic and social development "by eliminating the barriers which divide them". The ECCM agreement was amended marginally to reflect their status as independent countries, and was included as part of the OECS treaty. Its substance therefore remained unchanged. The ECCM treaty sought to create a common market by going beyond the creation of a free trade area to measures designed to integrate their economies. There were thus two main elements: the elimination of trade barriers, and the development of common policies in targeted areas. Provisions for integration were ambitious; they involved, among other things, the establishment of a common customs tariff, the harmonization of investment and development policies, and the coordination of currency and financial policies and infrastructural development, all within three years, and a common agricultural policy within two. In addition, the states were to adopt common commercial policies towards third countries, and harmonize tax policies and incentive legislation. An important element of the treaty was the commitment to developing a common industrial policy to establish and distribute industries "equitably" among member states, "so as to facilitate complementarity [and] avoid unnecessary duplication", and to encourage import substitution manufacturing.

In 1973 CARIFTA was upgraded to CARICOM, with a common market including a common external tariff, areas of functional cooperation, and provisions for coordinating foreign policy.[16] CARICOM's formation was prompted by LDC discontent with their failure to benefit substantially from the creation of a free trade area.[17] The catalyst, however, was provided by the European Community's acceptance of Britain's bid for membership, which strengthened the LDCs' bargaining position.[18]

CARIFTA's transformation to CARICOM involved the implementation of other aspects of the Georgetown Accord establishing CARIFTA, namely the implementation of a common external tariff, associated with which was the adoption of a uniform regional policy on "tax holidays". While the MDCs largely supported a common external tariff from which their manufacturing sectors would benefit, the LDCs, wary that this would widen the gap between themselves and the MDCs, were reluctant to support it. They expressed their concerns in a paper, which Montserrat submitted to the Eighth Heads of Government (Commonwealth Caribbean) meeting, pointing to the dangers of polarization and calling for more emphasis on their development. It called, among other things, for a scheme for allocating industries to the LDCs and for mechanisms to ensure equitable distribution of trade benefits.[19] The MDCs made few concessions to these demands. They agreed to establish a Caribbean Investment Corporation by 1 June 1973; to implement the harmonization scheme on the same day; to establish a regional commission by May 1974 to monitor standards and pricing; and to review these mechanisms yearly at the Heads of Government Conference.[20] Most LDC countries signed the scheme without delay, except for Montserrat and Antigua, which did so later.[21]

CARICOM faced persistent charges throughout its existence from within both the MDCs and the LDCs of failing in its duties as an instrument of regional integration. Its performance and the factors affecting it have been discussed at length elsewhere, and are only briefly examined here.[22] CARICOM was beset by crises almost immediately. The first occurred in the 1970s in the wake of the first international oil crisis, precipitating trade wars between the major traders among the MDCs, but also affecting the LDCs with their smaller input in the CARICOM market. At a period when criticism of CARICOM was at a premium, Austin Bramble, Montserrat's chief minister, declared it to be "a meaningless voice", and asserted that "if it is going to continue as it is going, then, it would make absolutely no difference whether it breaks up or not".[23]

During this time CARICOM leaders failed to meet; the Heads of Government mechanism was therefore unable to function, weakening its institutional capability to deflect the crisis. The crisis, as well as CARICOM's failure to bring obvious benefits to the LDCs, contributed to a view that the organization had been of little benefit. Lestrade,[24] reviewing the LDCs' experience, described their attitude towards CARICOM as "unfavourable". He noted a tendency to consider it an MDC institution, which he attributed to the integration movement's inability to positively affect the LDCs. They received few benefits from the special concessions. In particular, they were not successful in establishing an industrial base, although Lestrade noted that in this they shared the blame in failing to honour protection arrangements after Article 56 protection had been sought and received.[25] It is therefore difficult to ignore the part played by the LDCs, by putting the interests of their own private sectors before the goals of subregional integration, in reducing even the limited potential for success of the few industries which were established. Their very poverty and the competitive nature of their economies meant that, within CARICOM, they did not always give one another the kind of support that was important in presenting a common front.

At the point of independence the LDCs were faced with the decision of whether to continue areas of cooperation developed during the period of Associated Statehood. They first faced the question in 1974 when Grenada became independent. Grenada remained a member of the WISA council and, on gaining independence, all the remaining islands decided not only to continue with the arrangement but to strengthen it. This indicated that, despite limited success in integrating their economies, cooperation in other spheres remained valuable. WISA's importance to its members was best illustrated by the decision of Grenada's People's Revolutionary Government to maintain its relationship with the group, even in the face of initial hostility from the other members. The WISA group's response to the revolution in Grenada showed an appreciation of the importance of their common institutions and spheres of cooperation. Some WISA states[26] sought Britain's intervention to restore democratic rule, while the council attempted to block Grenada's currency supply from the East Caribbean Currency Authority and removed the supreme court, whose headquarters had been in Grenada, to St Lucia. Grenada retaliated by withdrawing from the subregional court and setting up its own embassies, which it had begun to do after independence. The WISA group accepted Grenada, eventually, after the new government had received widespread international support, and accommodation by other CARICOM governments. Although relations remained strained, the WISA states and Grenada were able to find a basis for accommodation under the weight of shared problems.[27] Grenada's decision.to remain in the arrangement after the revolution suggests how interdependent the countries had become, and the importance which they placed on maintaining and strengthening economic, political and social relations.

The demise of the Grenada revolution in 1983 after Prime Minister Maurice Bishop was killed, and the OECS action in inviting US intervention, marked a new phase in the subregional integration movement. Despite sharp political differences with Grenada's People's Revolutionary Government, WISA had been able to agree on wide-ranging areas of cooperation, best expressed in the OECS charter. Cooperation was limited, however, in the areas of defence and foreign affairs. All OECS states, except Grenada and Montserrat (because of its status as a British dependency) went on to sign a separate memorandum of agreement on security with Barbados.[28] Cooperation in foreign affairs, particularly in presenting a common position on international issues, was nearly impossible.[29] These difficulties were greatly reduced when Grenada was brought back into the "democratic" fold following the US invasion. The post-invasion period saw a group of OECS leaders who were ideologically similar, and who shared a cosy relationship with the United States, strengthened by the decision to invade Grenada, taken in contravention of CARICOM's decision not to intervene.[30] Ironically, one could argue that the decision to intervene, disregarding the principles of sovereignty and self-determination, was at the same point an indicator of a new high-water mark in the forging of a common subregional identity and polity.

The contemplation of a single OECS state by some OECS leaders marked the beginning of a new phase in the broader regional movement, that had its roots in a changing international climate of reduced commitment to the Caribbean. This was suggested by the European Community Single Europe Act with the likelihood of reduced UK commitment, and the US/Canada/Mexico free trade initiative, coupled with a cut in financial commitment from the United States. While some OECS countries responded to these developments by calling for a political union, CARICOM's response was to renew its commitment to establishing a truly common market by agreeing to the creation of a single market by 1993. This was to be preceded by the implementation of the revised common external tariff and rules of origin; the harmonization of fiscal incentives; the establishment of a regional stock exchange in Jamaica, Barbados and Trinidad;[31] and the removal of all remaining barriers to intraregional trade.[32] The governments also agreed to consider transforming the common market into a monetary union[33] and, importantly, pledged to adopt steps on the political front, some of which were likely to have a greater popular effect. These included the decision to establish an assembly of CARICOM parliamentarians (at Trinidad's request) as a consultative body to influence the integration process; to remove job restrictions on certain categories of CARICOM workers; to formulate a list of distinguished persons who would become Caribbean nationals; and to produce a CARICOM passport. The Kingston summit of August 1990 also turned its attention to the establishment of a regional security mechanism to assist member states in "clearly defined situations which threaten their sovereignty".

The OECS

The main impetus underlying the OECS's formation was a feeling of fragility arising from what its member states perceived as a "hostile world environment"[34] insensitive to the needs of small states, which led them to believe that cooperation was necessary to strengthen their bargaining power *vis-à-vis* other states. Perceptions of insecurity arising from an awareness that they were unable to influence international developments were expressed in the observation by Grenada's prime minister, Herbert Blaize,[35] that they were "being focused on by hungry outside worlds", and in the suggestion by St Kitts–Nevis's prime minister, Dr Kennedy Simmonds,[36] that they needed to "hold firmly together" to "withstand the buffeting of a hostile economic environment over which [they had] no control". The OECS, therefore, was expected to increase their visibility and strengthen their prospects for survival. St Lucia's prime minister, John Compton, argued that the OECS "had gained renown and . . . respect" in the international community[37] and had increased the visibility of islands not known individually.[38] A number of OECS figures argued that the organization was necessary to strengthen their prospects for survival. Blaize[39] argued that their only chance for survival was through common action, as "individually and separately we are doomed to failure", while Compton[40] argued that joining forces was the only way to achieve "prosperity" for their people given their small markets. Vaughan Lewis, OECS director-general, argued that such cooperation was a prerequisite for maintaining their sovereignty.[41]

The driving force behind the OECS's formation, as these comments show, was the desire to strengthen bargaining power *vis-à-vis* other states in the international system. This was laid out in the charter's preamble, where the WISA council of ministers agreed to "establish[ing] and strengthen[ing] common institutions which could serve to increase their bargaining power as regards third countries or groupings of countries". This arose from the realization that, although independent and accepted by the international system as states in their own right, on their own they probably could not guarantee the rights and fulfil the obligations arising from their participation in the international system. They therefore saw an organization such as the OECS, through which they could "promote co-operation" (Article 3 [1a]) and "unity and solidarity" (Article 3 [1b]), as important in defending their "sovereignty, territorial integrity and independence" (Article 3 [1c]).

The OECS charter[42] sought to bring together areas of economic cooperation already occurring and codified under the ECCM, and cooperation in foreign affairs which occurred in a limited way through the WISA council of ministers. Many OECS objectives, therefore, were reflected in the ECCM charter, and included coordinating and harmonizing economic activities, currency and central banking, customs and excise, investment, agricultural development, and infrastructure.[43] The charter went beyond ECCM goals in a number of areas, extending economic integration to include cooperation in areas external to the economy but which, nevertheless, affected economic performance. This included coordinating, harmonizing and pursuing joint policies in "International Trade Agreements and other External Economic Relations", "Financial and Technical Assistance from External Sources", "International Marketing of Goods and Services including Tourism", and "External Transportation and Communications including Civil Aviation" (Article 3 [2]). These reflected the wider scope which independence provided to influence economic development, as well as recognition of the centrality of external factors to their economic fortunes. The charter also expanded cooperation to include "Matters relating to the sea and its resources", "Tertiary Education including University", "Statistics" and "Scientific, Technical and Cultural Co-operation". It formalized and expanded upon cooperation in foreign affairs and was committed to coordinating, harmonizing and pursuing joint policies in "External Relations including overseas representation" (Article 3 [1]). The inclusion of the judiciary as an area for common action represented the codification of what already existed, arising from the Associated Statehood experience when they shared a common judiciary. The really novel aspect of the treaty was the inclusion of "Mutual Defence and Security" as an area for cooperation, reflecting an awareness of the limitations small island states experienced in safeguarding their sovereignty.

The OECS countries' decision to set up structures for carrying out joint activities, and specifying the relationship between the various institutions, represented an advance in the integration movement. The OECS Authority was the supreme decision-making body, comprising the heads of government.

It was responsible for the "general direction and control of the performance of the functions of the Organization" (Article 6 [4]) and was vested with the power to take decisions on all matters within its competence. It was also empowered to establish new institutions as necessary, to conclude treaties or other international agreements on the organization's behalf, and to enter into agreements with other international organizations and countries. The Authority was also responsible for the organization's financial affairs. It met yearly,[44] and the position of chair was rotated every year according to alphabetical order. There were three committees under the Authority chaired by the ministers responsible for the charter's three main areas of cooperation: economic, foreign affairs, and defence and security. The foreign affairs committee was charged with "the progressive development of the foreign policy of the Organization and for the general direction and control of the performance of the executive functions of the Organization in relation to its foreign affairs" (Article 7 [4]). The charter (Article 11) allowed the countries to establish and maintain joint overseas diplomatic or other representation, and to accredit one representative to one or more states, international organizations or conferences. The committee was expected to advise the Authority on the selection of heads of diplomatic or other joint missions.

The defence and security committee was responsible for defending their territorial integrity by seeking to coordinate strategies for collective defence against external threats. Invoking the rights under the United Nations charter for "individual or collective self-defence" (Article 51 of the United Nations charter), OECS countries sought to assist one another in the face of external threats, even though the countries assisting were not themselves under threat (Article 8 [4]). The foreign affairs and defence and security committees were responsible to the Authority, and could act only on matters referred by the Authority. They were also restricted to making recommendations directly to the Authority. Their decisions, however, were binding on subordinate institutions unless the Authority determined otherwise. The economic affairs committee was responsible for economic matters, the most important of which was to oversee the implementation of the ECCM agreement and matters arising from it (Article 9).

OECS governments, while recognizing the need for close cooperation on key issues, were careful to construct the charter in such a way as to retain the principle of sovereignty, thus allowing individual governments to determine the extent of their cooperation. For decisions to be binding, therefore, the charter required unanimity (Article 6 [5]), which meant an affirmative vote by all members present and voting, and ratification by members not present.

The OECS's administrative arm was the central secretariat, headed by a director-general, appointed by the Authority for a period of four years. The director-general was responsible to the Authority and any other committees or institutions of the OECS (Article 10 [4]). The director-general was also expected to administer OECS diplomatic and other missions (Article 11). Although the charter mentioned only a central secretariat, the OECS had two secretariats. The main OECS secretariat or headquarters was based in St Lucia, while a secondary secretariat, the Economic Affairs Secretariat (EAS), which previously administered the ECCM, remained in Antigua. Both were answerable to the secretary-general, who was based in St Lucia.

The OECS treaty provided that membership was open to all former WISA states, even though a number were still not independent. It entered into force once it had been ratified by the independent countries of the WISA group. The non-independent countries were given full membership and allowed to accede to the treaty once they became independent. They were exempted from participating in defence and security matters and foreign affairs, which would have been the responsibility of the British government[45] (Article 23). Provisions for nonparticipation in these areas, however, were open to all members. Finally, the treaty could only be amended by a unanimous vote of the Authority (Article 25).

The Functioning of the OECS

Three main principles guided the OECS's functioning: a common approach to problems requiring countries to pool resources in seeking solutions; a united front to third countries and organizations, thus strengthening their bargaining power on common issues; and harmonizing policies, legislation and rules in order to facilitate economic cooperation and integration. The OECS secretariats played a pivotal role in this.

The Eastern Caribbean states benefited from presenting a united front. In particular, it strengthened them *vis-à-vis* other states. This was important in enhancing their position within CARICOM, particularly in channelling much-needed funds their way, and in securing funding in the international arena from donor agencies and countries, by submitting projects for the subregion. The principle of harmonizing legislation and rules, as far as possible, was based on the fact that for agreements and decisions made at the Heads of Government level to be effectively carried out in member states, there needed to be a high degree of commonality in the relevant rules and regulations in the countries. A common approach to problems took the form of implementing collective projects, generally administered by the EAS and the OECS secretariat.

OECS activity can be categorized under two broad headings, economic and functional cooperation, which were administered by the EAS and the OECS secretariat in Antigua and St Lucia, respectively. On the economic front, they operated what the EAS described as common trade policy systems, with a common external tariff and common rules of origin, and protection for their own enterprises through a system of quantitative restrictions.[46] They operated an industry allocation scheme which was inherited with the ECCM, developed new projects, and attempted to harmonize regulations and laws in key sectors of the economy. They also cooperated on a wide range of issues which included foreign representation, drug procurement, education and fisheries.

Administratively, the central secretariat was divided into a number of departments and units. The central secretariat had a legal unit, a sports desk and a special projects unit, and was headquarters to a variety of projects. The EAS, which was responsible for matters of cooperation arising from the ECCM agreement, was divided into two operational sections, one focusing on trade and economic policy, external economic relations, and statistics, and the other on sectoral policy and planning. Additionally, units were set up at the EAS at various times to administer special projects. In addition to secretariats in St Lucia and Antigua, the OECS had projects based in other countries. These included a fisheries unit in St Vincent and the Eastern Caribbean States Export Development Agency in Dominica. Since its establishment in 1981, the OECS bureaucracy had expanded rapidly to reflect increased areas of cooperation. At the EAS and the central secretariat, expansion tended to reflect the development of new projects.

The OECS functioned at two levels. First, the secretariats responded to requests and directives from the Authority and other committees recognized by the charter. Second, the OECS bureaucracy itself served to deepen the integration process by initiating action. Therefore, while member states helped to shape the organization's activities, the OECS bureaucracy, in its turn, contributed to the integration process by exercising initiative in trying to maximize avenues for further cooperation. The working of the OECS was not limited to the political leadership through the Authority and committees, but involved an ever-increasing complex of organizations and committees at the national and regional levels. Although the charter suggested a structure where decisions were made at the top and flowed to subordinate organs, the actual process was influenced very much at the national level through the bureaucracy. In addition, OECS politicians were influenced by national sectoral interests, particularly by the private sector, which traditionally had the ear of government.

The OECS gave rise to a number of regional groups, emerging primarily in an *ad hoc* fashion, which tended to mirror the economic, foreign affairs, and defence and security committees, although there were no formal regulations governing their functioning. Such organizations were formed at the level of the regional bureaucracy, which both carried out OECS instructions and influenced the making of OECS policies.[47] For example, the development of an OECS tourism sector plan precipitated the formation of a council of ministers responsible for tourism. There was a legal affairs committee that worked closely with the OECS legal unit, and a treaty committee was formed in Antigua in response to the unit's work. OECS programmes, particularly those geared at harmonizing policy and regulations, required participation from national bureaucracies, leading to meetings of customs officials, senior trade officials, directors of civil aviation and others. In this way, members of the national bureaucracy were able to influence the organization's activities and policy.

Authority meetings, usually held prior to CARICOM Heads of Government conferences, provided a forum for defining a common OECS position, which increased their negotiating strength in the twelve-member CARICOM community. This unified approach was recognized as being the basis for a strengthened OECS position within CARICOM.

Conclusions

The administration of the Commonwealth Caribbean during the colonial period contributed to the development of different levels of affinity among the former British colonies, evident in the Leeward and Windward groups of islands. Although they developed as two relatively distinct administrative groups during colonialism, the Windwards and Leewards found, in the federal and postfederal periods, that they shared common objective features and problems which made it imperative for them to act together. Their cooperation was also catalysed by fears of being swallowed up, arising from their experiences with the Federation and subsequent attempts at union with Barbados and Trinidad. Most importantly, the period of Associated Statehood, during which they developed and shared common organizations and institutions, assisted in developing what was recognized as an "Eastern Caribbean" identity.

The OECS's formation marked a new and dynamic phase in the history of the tiny Eastern Caribbean countries, moving them from the position of reactors to one in which they sought to take the initiative in addressing their own developmental problems. It also successfully enhanced their position in the broader regional integration movement. However, it was precisely because of the insularity which colonial rule encouraged, with its failure to develop communication links among Windward and Leeward Islands, that one can expect their integration process to be a rough one.

4 OECS Economies in the 1980s

The OECS countries are supported heavily by foreign flows. Foreign official grants, concessionary loans, net private transfers from abroad and the subsidy contained in the protected prices received for bananas and sugar together amount to about 25 per cent of their total GDP. . . . Any abrupt reduction in foreign flows would exert a dramatic impact on their economies.

– World Bank, *Long-Term Economic Prospects of the OECS Countries*

Introduction

OECS countries, who had been viewed by other members of the Federation as a possible drain of federal resources, and characterized within the economic integration process as LDCs, emerged from the decade of the 1980s (when most became independent) with far more impressive economic performances than their MDC counterparts. Their economic performance went against regional trends of devaluation and low, even negative growth,[1] with average growth rates for 1981 to 1988 ranging from a high of 7.7 per cent in St Lucia to a low of 4.5 per cent in Grenada. This is to be compared with an average of 1.2 per cent for Barbados, and 1.6 per cent for Jamaica (Table 4.1). By 1992, all OECS countries were being ranked by the United Nations Development Programme's *Human Development Report* as middle-income countries,

Table 4.1   Growth Rates for Selected CARICOM Countries, 1980–1989
          (at constant prices)

	Barbados	Belize	Antigua	Grenada	Jamaica	St Kitts	St Lucia	St Vincent	Trinidad
1980	4.3	2.4	6.7	–	-5.4	3.9	-1.0	3.3	-6.5
1982	-5.0	-0.8	0.4	5.3	0.5	6.8	3.2	5.1	4.0
1983	0.4	0.8	6.9	1.4	2.3	-1.1	4.1	5.8	5.2
1984	3.6	0.8	7.5	5.4	-0.9	9.0	5.0	5.3	-7.1
1985	1.2	2.3	7.7	4.9	-4.6	5.6	6.0	4.6	-4.5
1986	5.1	1.5	8.4	5.5	1.9	6.3	5.9	7.2	-1.0
1987	2.5	5.0	8.8	6.0	5.2	6.8	2.0	5.7	-6.1
1988	3.5	7.6	7.6	4.3	1.5	4.7	5.0	8.4	-4.7
1989	3.5	14.7	5.9	5.7	6.5	6.7	4.6	7.2	0.7
Average	2.1	3.8	6.7	4.8	0.8	5.4	3.9	5.8	-2.2

Source: United Nations, Economic Commission for Latin America and the Caribbean, *Review of Caribbean Economic and Social Performance in the 1980s and 1990s* (Port of Spain, Trinidad: Caribbean Development and Cooperation Committee, 1999), 9, Table 1.

with Grenada, Antigua and Dominica achieving higher rankings than Jamaica, and all being ranked above Guyana (Table 4.2). The World Bank noted that the "significant gains in the standard of living" achieved by OECS countries in the 1980s were "despite external vulnerability, declining terms of trade, inclement weather, and fluctuations in the growth performance of the world economy".[2]

As the World Bank suggested, despite their economic performance, OECS economies rested on a precarious foundation. They remained underdeveloped economies,[3] based in most instances on a single crop or industry, subject to additional constraints to economic development arising from their minuscule size.[4] Their relative economic prosperity could be explained by a heavy reliance on grants and concessionary loans, net private transfers from abroad, and preferential access and protected prices for bananas and sugar under the Lomé agreement; together, the World Bank estimated these to amount to 25 per cent of total GDP.[5] By the mid- to late 1980s, OECS countries were already being threatened with a reduction in concessionary financing because

Table 4.2   HDI Ranking for CARICOM Countries, 1991

Country UNDP	HDI Ranking
LDCs	
Belize	67
OECS	
Antigua/Barbuda	46
Dominica	53
Grenada	64
St Kitts/Nevis	65
St Lucia	68
St Vincent/Grenadines	79
MDCs	
Bahamas	28
Barbados	22
Guyana	89
Jamaica	59
Trinidad/Tobago	39

Source: *UNDP Human Development Report* (New York: United Nations Development Programme, 1991); *Caribbean Development Bank Annual Report 1988* (Bridgetown, Barbados: Caribbean Development Bank, 1989), 15.

of their status as middle-income countries, a diversion of funds towards newly emerging states in Eastern Europe, and a reduction, at best, in protection and access to the European market (see Table 4.3 for basic statistics). They were confronting a paradox where their successful economic performance was partly based on concessionary financing which they were in danger of losing because they were performing too well.[6]

Economies of the Windward and Leeward Islands

Agriculture

A glance at OECS economies in the mid-1980s showed a general divergence between the primarily agricultural Windwards and the more service-based Leewards. The economies of the Windward Islands were based on export

Table 4.3   OECS: Selected Indicators 1987

Country	Size (km²)	population (1987)	GNP per capita 1987 (US$)
Antigua	440	77,093	2,540
Dominica	750	81,185	1,440
Grenada	345	94,118	1,340
Montserrat	102	11,900	3,506
St Kitts/Nevis	269	44,000	1,700
St Lucia	616	142,342	1,400
St Vincent	388	113,000	1,000
BVI	153	12,197	7,581

Sources: Population and size data from OECS Economic Affairs Secretariat, *OECS Statistical Pocket Digest 1987* (St John's, Antigua: OECS Secretariat, 1987); GNP per capita, except for the British Virgin Islands (BVI) and Montserrat, World Bank, *World Development Report 1989: Financial Systems and Development World Development Indicators* (Oxford: Oxford University Press, 1989), 230, Box A.1, Basic Indicators for Countries with Populations of Less Than One Million; GNP per capita Montserrat, East Caribbean Central Bank research and information, East Caribbean Central Bank, St Kitts; GNP per capita BVI, BVI Development Planning Unit, *BVI National Account Statistics 1984– 1989*, no. 2 (Tortola, BVI: Development Planning Unit, c.1990), 31.

agriculture with bananas, in all except Grenada, playing a dominant role. In 1987 agriculture accounted for 29.9 per cent of GDP in Dominica, 20.8 per cent in St Vincent, and 18.8 per cent in Grenada, while in St Kitts–Nevis it accounted for only 9.4 per cent, in Antigua 4.68 per cent, in Montserrat 4.3 per cent, and in the British Virgin Islands 3.63 per cent.[7] Export agriculture was particularly important to the Windwards which, except for Grenada, remained largely dependent on the export of bananas to the United Kingdom.[8] In Dominica, the banana industry provided 70 per cent of foreign exchange earnings;[9] in St Vincent it earned 27 per cent of total export revenue, falling from 40 per cent in 1979;[10] and in St Lucia it accounted for 50 per cent of domestic exports and occupied 86 per cent of arable land.[11] In St Lucia, coconuts were the second major export crop.[12] In St Vincent, ground provisions contributed 37 per cent of export revenue.[13] Although agriculture constituted 95 per cent of Grenada's export sector, production was more

Table 4.4   OECS Banana and Sugar Exports (as Percentage of Domestic
Exports),1977–1979 and 1985–1987

	Dominica Bananas	Grenada Bananas	St Lucia Bananas	St Vincent Bananas	Total Banana Producers	St Kitts– Nevis Sugar
1977–79	56	20	48	41	41	70
1985–87	64	18	67	36	50	43

Source: World Bank, *Long-Term Economic Prospects of the OECS Countries*, report no. 8058–CRG
(Washington, DC: World Bank, 1990), 48, Table IV.3.

diversified, based on nutmegs, bananas and cocoa. In St Kitts–Nevis, agriculture had largely given way to tourism and manufacturing. Export agriculture, dominated by sugar, accounted for only 8 per cent of GDP.[14] In Antigua, export agriculture centred mainly around winter vegetables. While Grenada and St Kitts–Nevis had been diversifying away from bananas and sugar, the reverse was true for the Windward Islands, whose dependence on bananas in the 1980s had increased over the 1970s (Table 4.4), due to increased production spurred by higher prices on the UK market.[15]

The heavy reliance of the Windward Islands on the banana sector had important consequences for their economies. By 1986, governments of the Windward Islands were facing the likelihood of loss, or serious erosion, of their preferential access to the British market, when the Single Europe Act came into force in 1992. They feared that the industry, based on small peasant plots generally located on hilly slopes and thus vulnerable to hurricanes and high winds, bruising and diseases, would be unable to compete with Latin American bananas grown on large plantations with cheaper labour. Given the importance of bananas in all the islands except Grenada, these countries faced a social and political crisis if the industry were to be destroyed. In particular, this prospect posed a threat to the security of existing governments which had benefited politically from the banana boom in the 1980s. Neville Duncan located the industry's importance to the Windward Islands in these terms:

> The special arrangements [banana, sugar and rum protocols] have maintained thousands of jobs in the Caribbean and have underpinned the very economic life of several Caribbean states. They have produced substantial and vital foreign exchange earnings without which many of these countries would have been unable to adequately house, feed and clothe their populations. . . . Whether a significant

proportion of the population of these countries experience privation or some measure of material goods satisfaction depends upon these factors. The reproduction of culture therefore depends upon such considerations.[16]

Tourism

In most OECS countries tourism emerged as an important economic activity, even challenging agriculture for dominance in some of the Windward Islands. In St Lucia it was the main foreign exchange earner, bringing in twice as much money as bananas – US$41.1 million from tourism in 1984, as opposed to US$20.4 million from bananas.[17] In Grenada tourism was also the major foreign exchange earner, earning some US$28.2 million in 1988, slightly edging out the major export crops – nutmegs, cocoa and mace – which together contributed US$22.2 million.[18] Tourism dominated the Antiguan economy. It had grown in importance to St Kitts–Nevis, because of a deliberate government effort to diversify away from sugar. Tourism also played an important role in Montserrat's economy, as in the British Virgin Islands where, with the financial services sector, it was the main contributor to economic growth. Despite agriculture's dominance, tourism was still important to St Vincent's economy. In Dominica the tourist industry was still largely undeveloped, a result of poor infrastructure and few white sand beaches. Given tourism's potential as a means of generating quick income, governments placed increasing importance on its development, and its role was likely to increase, especially among the Windwards. In particular, the Vincentian government saw tourism's development as a means of tackling high unemployment levels in the Grenadines.[19]

Manufacturing

Despite attempts in the 1960s and 1970s to encourage industrial investment throughout the region, and the introduction of the CBI in the early 1980s, manufacturing in the OECS was rudimentary, centred around agri-processing. The industry was developed largely along the import substitution model within the framework of two protective schemes: the Regional Industrial Programme under CARICOM and the ECCM's Industry Allocation Scheme. The ECCM scheme protected approved industries within the OECS, while the Regional Industrial Programme, which was not restricted to OECS states, provided protection within the wider CARICOM market. Under the ECCM scheme, members were prevented for a five-year period from granting fiscal incentives to competing local enterprises, and were to allow free and unrestricted access to their markets for the products of approved industries, in an effort to prevent inter-island competition.

In St Lucia manufacturing contributed 7.86 per cent to the GDP in 1987,[20] largely due to the development of the garment industry and the establishment of a number of assembly-type operations.[21] Dominica's manufacturing industry centred around soaps and oils from coconut, contributing 6.60 per cent to GDP; it was the second highest foreign exchange earner.[22] In Grenada manufacturing, which centred around rum production, aerated beverages, retread tyres, garments, wheat bran and other light industries, was of increasing importance, amounting to 5.37 per cent of GDP in 1987.[23] Although St Vincent had a light manufacturing industry based on arrowroot by-products,[24] beer and tennis rackets, manufacturing contributed as much as 15.58 per cent to the GDP in 1987. In Antigua the manufacturing sector contributed 3.69 per cent to the GDP; it was based mainly on garments, paints, household appliances and (more recently) some agri-processing. Manufacturing in Antigua suffered from high tourism wage levels which squeezed out manufacturing firms, contributing to a decline in this sector's contribution to the GDP. The World Bank predicted that this downward trend was not likely to be reversed.[25] In St Kitts–Nevis manufacturing contributed 5.96 per cent to GDP in 1987; it centred around sugar and enclave industries, which included electronics and data processing firms, and garment production. Despite the increasing importance of manufacturing, however, its development within a framework of protective markets in the OECS countries led the World Bank to characterize industries as uncompetitive and "unsuitable for adapting to changing economic circumstances".[26]

The ECCM's Industry Allocation Scheme was considered problematic and was the subject of constant review by the OECS.[27] It suffered from a number of difficulties: the perception that the allocation of industries was influenced more by political than economic considerations of comparative advantage; the absence of support mechanisms to help implement and monitor industries; and the absence of penalties against governments violating its provisions.[28] Recommendations included a coordinated approach to creating an industrial infrastructure to provide support services, strengthening market protection measures, agreeing on criteria for selecting projects for allocation, and calling on member states to observe rules governing the scheme. The programme was supported on the marketing front by the Eastern Caribbean Investment Promotion Service and the Eastern Caribbean States Export Development Agency, established in 1987 and 1989 respectively. The OECS hoped to increase the sector's competitiveness by strengthening the export capability of local manufacturers through the Eastern Caribbean States Export Development Agency, and seeking overseas investments through the Eastern Caribbean Investment Promotion Service.

Unemployment

Unemployment has always been a focus of government policy in the Caribbean. The whole industrialization attempt was premised on the need to reduce the high levels of unemployment which characterized the Caribbean. In most CARICOM countries unemployment was a major problem. In Jamaica, for example, it was estimated to be as high as 30 per cent in the 1980s.[29] In the Windward Islands it remained a significant problem. Dominica's unemployment rate in 1987 was 15 per cent (although some estimated it to be as high as 50 per cent), Grenada's 18 per cent, and St Lucia's and St Vincent's 20 per cent (Table 4.5). Labour force projections for St Vincent suggested that the unemployment rate would grow at 2 to 3 per cent per year until the year 2000.[30]

Table 4.5   OECS: Unemployment and External Debt

Country	Unemployment[a] % (1986)	External Debt US$m[b] (1987)	External Debt per[b] % of GDP (1987)
Antigua	20[c]	249.6	90.6
Dominica	15	64.8	51.2
Grenada	18	76.1	50.7
Montserrat	14	n/a	n/a
St Kitts/Nevis	20	22.1	20.8
St Lucia	20	40.7	19.4
St Vincent	25	37.2	26.1

Sources: [a]Adapted for US International Trade Commission no. 1920, December 1986, as cited in *Caribbean Business*, 24 September 1987; [b]World Bank, *Long-Term Economic Prospects of the OECS Countries*, 261, Table 8.1. [c]This figure is questionable, since all reports and immigration trends suggest a high level of employment. When I visited Antigua in 1989, there were indications that people were employed in more than one job at a time, and I was even offered a job for the short time I was there.

The situation was very different in the Leeward Islands, where a shortage of labour was calculated to be a significant constraining factor in economic performance. In Antigua this was expected to hamper growth in both manufacturing and agricultural sectors. Antigua's labour shortage encouraged significant immigration from the other islands, particularly Dominica, Montserrat and St Kitts–Nevis. The World Bank predicted that in St Kitts–Nevis labour shortages limited the prospects for the development of the garment and sugar industries.[31] The Caribbean Development Bank reported that nearly 61,000 tonnes of sugar cane were not reaped in 1988 because of a shortage of labour.[32] Montserrat also had low unemployment figures, although the Caribbean Development Bank suggested that there was evidence of a high degree of underemployment. As in Antigua, labour had crucial implications for continued growth in the British Virgin Islands. Lack of manpower, and in the case of the financial sector lack of trained manpower, had been felt in most industries and was expected to be a major constraint to growth. Despite this labour imbalance between the Leeward and Windward Islands, the World Bank identified restrictions placed on the movement of labour between member states as an important factor in limiting economic development and hindering the emergence of an integrated OECS market.

At the end of the 1980s, therefore, OECS economies remained fragile, premised on one or more primary activities: agricultural production for export, and services, primarily tourism. Manufacture was rudimentary and uncompetitive, directed at narrow national or regional markets, and dependent on high tariffs for survival. OECS economies remained characterized by the absence of sectoral linkages among major sectors – agriculture, tourism and manufacturing – which had been identified by the dependency school in the 1960s. The reliance on export agriculture and the consequent neglect of domestic agriculture led to the importation of food, both for local consumption and to sustain the tourist industry. This resulted in the haemorrhage of vital foreign-exchange earnings from the agricultural and tourism sectors. In addition, despite OECS attempts to reduce barriers, many countries continued to operate restrictive legislation against nationals of member states. A notable example of this was the aliens landholding laws in place in most OECS countries, which proscribed land ownership even to nationals of other member countries.

Economic Cooperation

Economic cooperation among OECS countries, therefore, was geared at addressing some of the more competitive aspects of their economic relations. The ECCM's primary aim was to create a common market among OECS countries by removing internal barriers to trade, including restrictions on the movement of people, capital and services, and adopting common policies to countries outside the area. The OECS charter introduced additional areas of cooperation that included the international marketing of goods and services, external transport and civil aviation, statistics and audit, and procuring financial and technical assistance from external sources. By 1988 the OECS had been able to eliminate most barriers to trade, and the countries operated a common external tariff, common rules of origin, and a common trade policy which included quantitative restrictions to protect particular industries. This was to be formalized by the institution of an OECS regime of quantitative restrictions to establish rules and conditions for protecting industries. Under the CARICOM Common Fiscal Incentives to Industry legislation OECS countries operated common fiscal incentives *vis-à-vis* foreign enterprise,[33] and in the mid-1980s they were considering establishing common incentives for agriculture and tourism.[34]

The goal of the free movement of labour was more difficult to achieve, despite the obvious need for labour in the Leeward Islands. At the fourteenth Authority meeting (Antigua, 1989), some of the heads of government agreed to facilitate intra-OECS travel by removing passport requirements for nationals of member countries, simplifying immigration forms, and treating OECS nationals as locals for immigration purposes. However, none of these measures was implemented. Freedom of movement was viewed as an important element in gaining popular support for OECS integration and in contributing to a sense of community, but this was hampered by the sensitivity which surrounded the issue, particularly after the experience of the West Indies Federation. Governments, while attracted to the concept, were generally unsure of the actual consequences.

OECS Attempts to Address Economic Problems

Greater progress was made at the regulatory level, where laws and regulations were introduced to harmonize and coordinate policy in such areas as taxation, incentives and customs, facilitated by a legal unit established at the OECS headquarters in 1984. Efforts were made towards the formulation of a common policy on foreign investment and technology transfer, based on a study[35] which found that the only incentive legislation common to all the countries (except the British Virgin Islands) was the CARICOM Common Fiscal Incentives to Industry legislation.[36] Legislation on incentives varied by country, with contradictions between national policies, particularly in the tourist sector, and incentives actually offered to investors. In particular, the study singled out governments' practice of providing duty concessions on food and alcohol to larger hotels, in contradiction of the policy of developing structural links between the agricultural and tourist sectors and encouraging the use of regional products.

Other legislation and regulations which were either in force in OECS countries or were likely to be introduced, with consequences for foreign investment, included the OECS Banking Act, which sought to coordinate currency and financial policies, and legislation on foreign exchange control. They also included double taxation legislation, tax information exchange agreements, and bilateral investment treaties. While individual countries already had bilateral agreements in place, OECS governments increasingly sought to negotiate as a group, even though the eventual agreements were expected to be bilateral.

By the mid-1980s the OECS had moved towards developing a customs union and harmonizing institutional and legal arrangements for customs administration,[37] with draft legislation before member states by 1987.[38] The move towards creating a customs union was given weight by the institutionalization of meetings of customs controllers, as technical support for the management of customs union in the OECS; however, according to Percival Marie of the EAS, union remained a sensitive issue.

The OECS also sought to address problems common to agriculture and tourism on a regional basis, with the development of an agricultural diversification plan for the subregion and a joint marketing programme for tourism. Agricultural diversification within the OECS was driven largely by fears that bananas were unlikely to be competitive in a single European market, which would result in a loss of jobs and revenue. Diversification was not meant to replace the banana industry, but was viewed as a means of increasing income to make up for a likely shortfall from bananas. The agricultural diversification programme developed for the subregion, therefore, was geared towards the export market, as well as towards import substitution to reduce the food import bill, particularly in the tourist sector.[39] It sought to encourage diversification by placing it within a comprehensive framework with fiscal incentives similar to those available in tourism and manufacturing, proposing to revise tax structures to remove impediments to production and export, particularly the export duties imposed on nontraditional export crops. Land was to be made available to farmers by the regularization of titles and the divestment them of state lands. The programme aimed at identifying products and target markets and providing farmers with training and extension services. While seeking to expand the export base of agricultural production, the programme fell squarely within the framework of the traditional agricultural sector, focusing on crop production rather than the development of industrial processes to increase value added by the sector. As a result, its potential to effect meaningful transformation of the sector was limited. Efforts in tourism were also limited. The OECS sought to strengthen its members' presence overseas by appointing a tourism coordinator to the EAS,[40] and seeking support under Lomé III, in 1989, for a tourism programme to market the industry in the United States and Europe, and to attract investment in hotels and other tourism facilities. It did not extend to marketing the subregion as a single tourist destination, presenting a more diversified product.

Efforts at agricultural diversification and tourism were constrained, however, by the absence of nationally or regionally owned shipping lines or airlines, which also presented a significant stumbling block to any serious attempt to integrate the region. This lack had serious implications for attempts to diversify export agriculture, which depended on reliable methods of transport to targeted markets, and for the movement of cargo both within the OECS and between OECS countries and their major regional trading partners. This weakness was felt most acutely in the high cost of inter-island travel. Limited resources prevented the countries from adequately addressing this problem, so they sought to pursue it through CARICOM, since it was also a broader regional problem.[41] They succeeded only in developing a transportation programme among themselves, which was accepted by member states in 1986.[42] The EAS, however, had been working with OECS shippers, through the Council of East Caribbean Manufacturers, to develop a programme for a subregional OECS shipping council.

A great deal of OECS attention was directed at the functioning of the Leeward Islands Air Transport Service (LIAT), which primarily served them, but the ownership of which they shared with other CARICOM countries. They were hindered in their attempts to influence LIAT's operations because it was privately run, and their control of shares was not extensive enough to ensure their influence. They sought to increase their control by purchasing more shares,[43] and to review of LIAT's operations, structure and capacity, and its future role in the OECS and wider CARICOM. The absence of locally or subregionally owned airlines was an important limitation in an area broken up by sea. The importance of the problem was seen in the tendency for individual OECS governments to grant rights to foreign-owned airlines to operate as their national airlines, exacerbating inter-island rivalry; this was evident in the row between St Lucia and St Vincent over the rights of two competing "national airlines", neither of which was locally owned.

OECS cooperation extended to civil aviation with the incorporation of the Directorate for Civil Aviation, which previously had served them on an *ad hoc* basis, as an OECS institution; updating civil aviation laws and incorporating them into national legislation;[44] and establishing an "Aeradio unit" under the Directorate for Civil Aviation, responsible for installing and maintaining telecommunications facilities at airports.[45]

Cooperation also extended to matters relating to the sea, in recognition of its potential as one of the region's most important resources; these efforts led to the establishment of a fisheries unit in St Vincent in March 1987. OECS cooperation in fisheries was three pronged: the first aspect had implications for their shared Exclusive Economic Zone and involved legislation and resource management; the second was designed to enhance the national fisheries sector, primarily through training;[46] and the third concentrated on surveillance and security. The countries harmonized legislation on the delimitation of the Exclusive Economic Zone, the area of jurisdiction of fisheries resources, and the terms and conditions of access to fisheries.[47] They also agreed to adopt a common position on foreign fishing in OECS waters.[48] The Exclusive Economic Zone was of particular concern to the OECS because countries such as Dominica and Montserrat had entered into reciprocal fishing arrangements with France, while Antigua was discussing similar arrangements with France and the European Community, without data on stocks or information on likely advantages or disadvantages.[49] In response to a dearth of statistics by which to effectively manage the industry, the fisheries unit developed a regional fisheries information database.[50] These examples highlighted the need for a common OECS approach, especially on matters of delimiting maritime boundaries. The latter was important in light of Venezuela's dispute with Dominica over the extent of the former's Exclusive Economic Zone.[51]

The OECS, through the EAS, also played an important role in strengthening the data collection systems of member states, developing methods for estimating national income and GDP, thereby facilitating the comparison of estimates of national income across the region, and assisting members in macroeconomic matters.[52] It also assisted governments on tax reform and control, and audit and double-taxation issues.[53] Generally the EAS, through these various innovations, extended its role from a narrow concern with common market affairs to include broader issues of national economic management.[54] Despite these measures, however, in 1989 the basic tax structure of the various islands remained unchanged, with OECS countries operating a varied tax system with income tax as the dominant form of taxation in the Windward Islands (excluding Grenada), and Value Added Tax dominant in the Leewards and Grenada.[55] There appeared to be no serious impetus to adopt a uniform tax structure.

The EAS played an important role in providing expertise to governments either from its staff or through consultants and, along with the OECS secretariat, in securing financial support for projects. The OECS's main donors were the European Community, through the Lomé Convention, and the British government, through agencies such as the British Development Division. Canada and the United States were also important sources of funding through the Canadian International Development Agency and US Agency for International Development, respectively. Other international organizations provided substantial amounts of the funding required for OECS projects. These included the Commonwealth through the Commonwealth Fund for Technical Cooperation, the United Nations Development Programme and UNESCO. The Commonwealth Fund for Technical Cooperation, for instance, provided financial support for the establishment and running of the OECS secretariats, while the United Nations Development Programme provided technical assistance.[56] Other sources of technical assistance were the World Bank and its Inter-Agency Residency Mission, and the UN Economic Centre for Latin America and the Caribbean.

Conclusions

The economic profile of the OECS countries suggests that a broad distinction can be made between the mainly agricultural Windward Islands and the Leeward Islands with their primarily service economies. In the latter, with the exception of St Kitts–Nevis where sugar was still important, the service sector was dominant during the 1980s. There were thus different factors affecting the prosperity of these groups which were likely to influence their support for political union. Moreover, there was a general perception that the islands of the Leeward chain were better off than others among the OECS states. Despite this appearance, however, economic activity in Antigua was financed by a huge trade deficit, leaving it with one of the highest balance of payment deficits in the region. This suggested that the economies of the Windward Islands were no more fragile than those of the Leewards, although the threats to the Windwards were more immediate. Thus while the Leeward Islands, without any impending threat to their service economies, were fairly satisfied with the OECS arrangement, the question facing the Windward Islands by 1987 was whether the OECS could provide the basis for addressing their problems without significant changes to the nature of its relationship and structure. This, as will be suggested below, may have been a major reason why the 1987 initiative came from the Windwards rather than the Leewards.

At the close of the 1980s the international climate in which Caribbean states operated was changing. While they continued to suffer from deteriorating terms of trade, they were faced with increased import barriers in the markets of developed countries. This was coupled with a threatened reduction in the commitment of their traditional donors. Prospects for the 1990s were for reduced, rather than increased, US commitment, particularly in light of the end of the cold war which had reduced the "leverage" which these countries might have been able to exercise previously. The general fragility of the key sectors suggested that these economies had a very insecure and fragile base. While this was true of all islands, it was particularly urgent for the Windwards where the threat to the banana industry was immediate.

The OECS's approach to these challenges was to step up the economic integration process, particularly in terms of harmonizing economic regulations and policies. Its economic programme was geared towards continued diversification of the agricultural base, placing more emphasis on tourism and manufacturing, and diversifying within agriculture to reduce food import bills and lessen the dependence on bananas. These measures, however, fell far short of the kind of economic programme necessary to address the difficulties they faced in manufacturing, which required more creative approaches than simply increasing protection; and in agricultural diversification, which did not speak to a fundamental change in production processes and relations. The OECS's economic programme presented no real options for reducing the high levels of employment that existed, nor did it provide economic alternatives for farmers and agricultural labourers likely to lose their livelihood from a contraction or collapse of the banana industry. This could be addressed to some degree by a closer integration of tourism with agriculture and manufacturing, which could energize local agriculture and contribute to stemming the flow of foreign exchange which tourism expended on food imports.[57]

5 | Foreign Policy, Security and Functional Cooperation

No doubt it will begin with confederation, rather than Federation; a common nationality, a common currency, and common representation abroad. Once established, the links will grow like ivy. Associations should always start on a limited basis, and grow slowly with time.

– Sir Arthur Lewis, *The Agony of the Eight*

Foreign Policy

The major postindependence foreign policy challenge facing OECS countries was securing continued financial assistance for their fragile economies. One of the dissatisfactions with the WISA agreement which figured largely in the desire for independence was the limitation it imposed on their ability to seek aid from countries and multilateral institutions. The importance of foreign capital in development plans meant that it had to be sought externally. From early on, Caribbean countries viewed their proximity to the United States as leverage in accessing financial support. This meant adopting an anticommunist posture, particularly for Eastern Caribbean states, most of which became independent just at the advent of the 1980s;[1] it also meant supporting the United States in international forums. This policy was not particularly successful, as this support was not necessarily rewarded by increased US aid.

Instead, it served to encourage the United States to perceive the region's problems in terms of security, rather than in economic and social terms.[2]

Only Grenada deviated from the regional pattern during the years of the revolution (1979–1983), pursuing what it termed an "anti-imperialist, non-aligned" foreign policy,[3] which was arguably also prompted by economic concerns. This involved widening the traditional base of foreign relations to include countries in the socialist bloc, particularly Cuba. This bore some dividends, evident in the volume of material aid Grenada received from Cuba and others, particularly for the construction of an international airport.[4] It also included continuing and strengthening traditional links with European Community countries and Canada. Grenada's bid to diversify its diplomatic contacts was in response to US hostility to the revolution, which shut the United States off as an avenue for aid.[5]

The economic challenges OECS economies faced did not influence the way in which individual countries conducted their foreign affairs, nor the type of cooperation they pursued. They were influenced by two conflicting trends: on the one hand, they resisted cooperation and continued to act singly, convinced that they could exercise leverage through their voting power in the United Nations; on the other, largely as a result of increasing pressures from the European Community, they were encouraged to cooperate by coordinating their policies and efforts. On becoming independent some governments (Grenada and Antigua, in particular) set up diplomatic offices in major world capitals in an effort to explore the possibilities of an independent foreign policy outside of the restricted WISA arrangement. This desire was particularly strong in Antigua, and was later to be an important factor in their decision not to participate in an OECS political union.

Despite independence, OECS countries continued some joint diplomatic activity in the United States and Europe. There were a number of reasons for this: economic and personnel pressures, the cost of maintaining separate offices in major capitals, and the need to coordinate approaches to Europe, especially in relation to the Lomé Convention. For example, financial pressures, coupled with the need to improve the quality of their diplomatic representation and the need for an OECS lobby in the US Congress, led to some cooperation in their US offices. They were more successful in Europe because the nature of their relationship with the European Community encouraged them to bargain as a group. Additionally, their common interests and problems, particularly in relation to the banana industry, forced on them the need for constant coordination. It was not surprising, therefore, that most cooperation was achieved here. This was limited, however, and fell far short of charter goals. Foreign relations was also likely to be one of the most difficult areas in which to make progress (outside of a political union), because diplomatic representation was still viewed as the defining feature of independence and individuality. Increased cooperation would result only from pressure, and should reflect the nature and intensity of this pressure.

The OECS charter set ambitious goals for member states in the conduct of their foreign relations which included, among other things, joint representation and accreditation to states or international conferences, and coordinating foreign policy (Articles 3 and 11). There was little success in coordinating foreign policy. There was no obvious attempt to adopt a common position on international issues, although the political climate in OECS countries resulted in a convergence of opinion, particularly on issues of importance to the United States. However, there was some attempt to coordinate their foreign relations with Europe, largely in response to the threatened 1992 European single market. In order to enhance the European lobby to protect their bananas after 1992 and reduce costs, the OECS strengthened its mission in London to include a minister counsellor specializing in economic matters, and established a subministerial committee of three senior ministers from Dominica, Antigua and St Kitts–Nevis, to "defend OECS interests" in Europe.[6] The OECS played an important role in the Africa, Caribbean and Pacific (ACP) banana lobby; an OECS minister, Dominica's Charles Maynard, acted as ACP's alternate spokesman on agricultural matters, and ambassadors from OECS countries headed the ACP subcommittee on bananas. OECS prime ministers actively lobbied European capitals for continued protection of bananas on the European market, while members with missions in Brussels made representations to the European Commission on behalf of all member states.

The countries had even less success with joint representation abroad. There were only two such initiatives, an OECS high commission in London and another in Canada, both of which represented only some member states. Antigua, in particular, preferred to run its own offices, while Grenada continued to maintain its own London high commission. Montserrat withdrew from the London mission because none of its nationals was represented on the staff. In the United States, OECS countries maintained separate embassies, located in a jointly owned building in New York.

While cooperation in foreign relations was modest, there were increasing signs that this was likely to be strengthened among the Windward Islands, faced with the banana dilemma. There appeared to be no similar pressures on the Leeward Islands, which continued to act individually in this sphere.

Security, 1979–1990

It is possible to identify two distinct periods defining the security concerns of OECS countries. The first began in 1979 with the Grenada revolution and ended in the mid-1980s, when the second began. Most of the OECS countries began independence forced to accept revolution in their midst. Their preoccupation with security during the first period was closely related to what they perceived as the implications of the revolution for the stability of their newly independent states. The Grenada revolution shook Eastern Caribbean governments and provoked a hostile response from the states in the WISA group, which refused to recognize the new government.[7] In a statement following a WISA council meeting convened in response to the revolution, they expressed concern that "the recent events in Grenada held serious implications for the security of other small states in the region, particularly in view of the stated position by the British Government that it is not responsible for the internal security of the Associated States". At the same time they called for the establishment of a regional security force to "defend their constitutional integrity in the face of armed revolutionaries".[8] Their hostility was clearly generated by perceptions of vulnerability to internal unrest.

The WISA states, some of which were newly independent and others on the verge of becoming independent, found themselves emerging in a context where a precedent had been set for the removal of government by force, and without the safeguard of British protection. They feared that the success of the Grenada revolution would encourage left-wing elements in their own countries to pursue a similar course, ignoring the route to parliamentary democracy. This fear was not entirely groundless since, following the Grenada revolution, there were a number of attempts to overthrow governments in the WISA states, although these did not derive from left-wing elements.[9] It coincided with US security interests in the region which had been defined as:

(1) to promote the continuing development of stable democracies that share US regional interests and concerns, (2) to prevent the Eastern Caribbean States from

moving into an anti-US orbit, (3) to encourage and support the region's security initiatives, and (4) to protect US security interests in the Caribbean sea lanes.[10]

The situation was further aggravated by Grenada's close relations with Cuba, which encouraged WISA governments to locate their internal security concerns within the framework of the East-West conflict and US security interests. These concerns were defined as fear of internal subversion fuelled by external elements – the Soviet Union and Cuba.[11] What were primarily local concerns with staying in power came to be articulated as preserving "democracy" against "communist subversion". By identifying their security interests so closely with the United States, they stood to benefit from increased US attention to their problems.[12] This identification also served to disguise the more concrete fear of their own vulnerability to internal dissent.[13]

The preoccupation with security was evident in its inclusion in the OECS charter, despite the differences with Grenada, and later, in 1982, in the formation of a Regional Security System (RSS) with Barbados, not an OECS member. The charter's security provisions reflected a recognition of the countries' inability to safeguard their security singly, and were the result of a compromise with Grenada's People's Revolutionary Government. The provisions were limited to cooperation on matters of external threats, and required unanimity for the provisions to operate. The charter provided for action "on matters relating to external defence and on arrangements for collective security against external aggression, including mercenary aggression, with or without the support of internal or national elements".[14] In this way, Grenada ensured that there was no threat to its sovereignty from OECS member states. But its decision to cooperate in security at all indicated the perceived vulnerability of all these small countries to external aggression. Thus, the charter reflected Grenada's support for the principle of non-interference in matters internal to member states, which had been earlier expressed in the 1979 Grenada Declaration, signed with sympathetic governments then in power in Dominica and St Lucia. Specifically, the declaration stressed that the governments were "not opposed in principle to the establishment of a regional military force provided it will be limited to the countering of external aggression".[15] Grenada was anxious to maintain full control over its foreign affairs and internal security because of its different political orientation. This delicate balance between Grenada and its neighbours was destroyed when Prime Minister Maurice Bishop and others were killed in October 1983.

Dissatisfied with charter arrangements that did not provide for intervention in cases of internal dissent, OECS states excluding Grenada created, with Barbados, a system with broader powers. The RSS was established under a memorandum of understanding on security,[16] and focused on internal as much as external threats to security, allowing signatories to assist one another in "national emergencies" and in instances of "threat to national security". The latter could arise from internal or external elements. The RSS included the defence forces of Barbados and Antigua and the police forces of the other countries. Barbados was central to the arrangement: it bore 49 per cent of the operating cost and its defence force headquarters served as the coordinating centre.

Grenada, wary of any interference in its internal affairs, refused to participate. In fact it is doubtful whether Grenada's participation would have been welcome, since the memorandum grew out of a desire to prevent a Grenada-style revolution happening in any of the other states. The Antiguan prime minister, Vere Bird, was quoted as saying in support of the RSS that "in this region, we cannot afford another Grenada".[17] Ideologically, therefore, the memorandum could not reconcile Grenada's concerns – which were to resist outside intervention – with that of the other governments, who sought intervention to buttress their regimes.

Although self-preservation was an important issue for WISA states, there were also other security considerations which they felt should be addressed jointly, and which were expressed in the memorandum. These included protection against foreign military intervention and illegal activities such as fishing and drug smuggling, and cooperation in the "prevention of smuggling, search and rescue, immigration control, fishery protection, customs and excise control, maritime policing duties, protection of off-shore installations, pollution control, and other disasters".[18] Nevertheless, the burning preoccupation during this period was with preserving "democracy" and parliamentary rule.[19] The period peaked with the Grenada invasion in 1983, when OECS leaders became convinced that they could not live with the Revolutionary Military Council that had replaced the People's Revolutionary Government after Bishop was killed. Bishop's arrest and death increased their fear that should they accept this new situation, it could serve to normalize revolutionary or violent action as a feature of Eastern Caribbean politics. They also feared that the new Grenadian leaders would pose a threat to their own security; they charged before the United Nations Security Council that the "extensive military build up in Grenada . . . ha[d] created a situation of disproportionate military strength between Grenada and other OECS countries".[20] While there was evidence to suggest that the United States relied on OECS countries to provide the cover for removing the Grenadian regime for its own political ends,[21] there was also sufficient reason to believe that the OECS countries had their own independent reasons for wanting to remove the regime. The Grenada invasion marked another instance where OECS interests and those of the US government coincided. The Grenada invasion marked the OECS states' first significant attempt at cooperation in security, seeking to justify it under the charter.

The greatest development in security cooperation among the OECS oc-curred during the post-invasion period, with unprecedented US involvement. Grenada (after the US invasion) and St Kitts–Nevis (on becoming inde-pendent in 1983) had signed the memorandum, although the OECS treaty itself was not modified. There was an attempt to upgrade the memorandum to treaty status, but this was resisted by Barbados (its new government, led by Erskine Sandiford, was less aggressive and pro-United States than the Tom Adams administration) and St Vincent (whose new prime minister, James Mitchell, was reluctant to sign). The Adams government in Barbados had even sought to use the post-invasion climate to establish a regional defence force geared primarily at neutralizing "local insurrectionists and foreign adventurers".[22] This did not materialize because the US government, the main prospective backer for the force, did not endorse it. It was also rejected by St Vincent and St Lucia on the grounds that it was inappropriate to the region's security needs.[23]

Despite this perceptual shift, the post-invasion period saw for the first time a serious attempt to bolster the security of OECS states, funded largely by the United States. This took the form of further developing the RSS, establishing a Special Services Unit[24] – a rapid deployment force in each island – and providing coast guard facilities.[25] The Special Services Unit comprised a team of policemen in each island trained in military techniques by the United States.[26] In addition, the United States provided military hardware, telecom-munications systems, vehicles and patrol boats to the Eastern Caribbean. The RSS's formation in 1981 coincided with an increased military commitment to the region, as Table 5.1 shows.

The RSS, particularly the Special Services Unit, fuelled suspicion that it was designed to suppress internal dissent. This suspicion was strengthened

6

Political Union Initiative
Rationale and Background

The alternative to our scenario of union is the status quo. In that status quo, we the leaders will soon fade out or go under, one by one. We may even vanish with boredom from the scene. And the same fate, in due process of time, awaits our successors facing the escalating problems.

– James Mitchell, "Thoughts on an East Caribbean Union"

Rationale for an OECS Political Union

A year after he first mooted the idea in June 1986, William Demas firmly set out the case for political union at the inauguration of the St Vincent National Advisory Committee on Eastern Caribbean Political Unity.[1] He promoted union on a variety of fronts: it would make the OECS more effective in international political and economic forums through better quality representation; it could lead to an improvement in public administration, expertise and efficient government; it might also have less measurable benefits, such as an increase in self-respect for the islands. His main emphasis, however, was economic. This had two main aspects. First, these countries, particularly the Windwards, were facing unfavourable economic prospects and economic weakness. Second, the small size of individual islands hampered their ability to address these serious problems, threatening their capacity to deliver what

Table 5.2   Sizes of the Security Forces in the Eastern Caribbean, 1984

Country	Defence	Reserves	Police	SSU	Coast Guard
Antigua	6	0	350	55	19
Barbados	270	250	1,500	50	90
Dominica	0	0	375	80	25
St Kitts	0	0	300	30	0
St Lucia	0	0	425	80	23
St Vincent	0	0	420	65	25

Source: US House of Representatives, Armed Services Committee (1984), cited in Phillip and Young, *Militarization in the Non-Hispanic Caribbean,* 59.

Nanton, "We help one another, we share ideas about party organization, campaigning, and generally how to help one another sustain our democracies in our countries." The CDU was active in Grenadian politics and was accused by the outgoing prime minister, Ben Jones, of intending to disrupt the 1990 elections with violence.[30] The CDU was also active in attempting to heal the rift that existed in 1989 in the ruling New National Party between Prime Minister Herbert Blaize and his minister of communications and works, Keith Mitchell.[31]

Although there was a buildup of military hardware and general military capability in the region in the immediate post-invasion period, this had lessened by the latter half of the 1980s. As early as 1984 there was evidence that governments were worried about economic problems, and increasingly perceived threats to their security as deriving from these. Mitchell, supported by Eugenia Charles and John Compton, was at the forefront in redefining the region's security agenda. OECS leaders attempted to redirect the United States from the cold war paradigm towards accepting economic shocks, such as the precarious position of the banana industry, as the more realistic threat to stability. At a meeting with White House officials in July 1984, Eastern Caribbean leaders identified the economic crisis, and not defence, as the real cause of instability. Compton told the United States that "our problems are not military, they are social and economic".[32] The difficulties facing OECS countries, as Searwar pointed out, lay in the growing disparity in the United States between military and economic power, with the consequence that

Caribbean economic problems were likely to be aggravated by increasing protectionist measures from the United States.[33]

The region was attempting to redefine its security interests in keeping with its concrete realities, as opposed to the more restrictive cold war paradigm that the United States favoured. One can argue, therefore, that although OECS governments were primarily preoccupied with internal stability, and this continued in the period immediately following the Grenada invasion with the strengthening of the US security presence and the formation of the CDU, there was evidence that the emphasis had shifted by the latter half of the 1980s. With the Grenada problem "resolved", the focus broadened to include more immediate threats, such as those posed to fisheries and territorial integrity from drug traffickers. Even more important for the governments of the Windward Islands, the focus shifted to an anxiety over the implications of the threatened collapse of their banana industry.

While security structures put in place in the mid-1980s reflected an anxiety to guarantee the continuity of the political system and limit the activities of the left, there was also evidence of an increasing emphasis on non-ideological issues. This suggested that the system, while devised for internal coercion, may have had more useful functions, ones less influenced by geopolitical issues. The OECS's emphasis on security in the late 1980s was on cooperation in surveillance, directed at illegal foreign fishing in the region, and security, although this was in its infancy.[34] OECS states found it more difficult to police the seas for drug traffickers, particularly in St Vincent and the Grenadines and Grenada, where numerous tiny islands made constant monitoring impossible.[35] None of these countries had a sophisticated coast guard. This was an area that required more OECS action, but needed a substantial injection of modern equipment and financial assistance.[36]

The OECS countries' decision to establish their own security mechanisms both within and outside the organization, rather than seeking to have their security needs addressed within CARICOM, requires some scrutiny. OECS countries emerged as independent states without military forces, in the context of the withdrawal of British responsibility for their defence. They emerged in a decade when the region was prominent in the cold war dynamic; this was reflected in political unrest and change, evident in the Grenada revolution, intense conflict in Jamaica around broadly ideological issues, and Forbes Burnham's socialist republic in Guyana. This instability seemed to spill over into internal politics, with a spate of unrest throughout the region in the late

1970s and early 1980s. CARICOM could not provide a forum for addressing their concerns, given the ideological divergence among the MDCs and Trinidad's policy of neutrality in foreign affairs, reflected in its failure either to oppose or embrace the Grenada revolution or to sanction the US invasion. Furthermore, the MDCs all had their own military forces, so they did not perceive the same pressing need for further mechanisms.

OECS states, despite establishing their own defence arrangement, went outside the organization to develop a separate arrangement with Barbados, which later provided the mechanism for US and Jamaican involvement in the Grenada invasion. This points to a recognition that on their own they did not have the military hardware or clout necessary to effect security as they perceived it. Barbados and the United States stepped in to fill a vacuum left by the abrogation of British responsibility for defence and by CARICOM's failure to provide a forum for addressing these concerns. Given the increased role of ideology in regional politics, security concerns took on an ideological spin, with Tom Adams in Barbados and Edward Seaga in Jamaica forming a counter axis to left-wing regimes in Guyana and Grenada. It is important to note that after the Grenada invasion, and the seeming neutralization of leftist forces in the region, perceptions of OECS security concerns among OECS leaders and the United States shifted, although in different directions. Both shared a common concern with the importance of drug trafficking, but the United States did not share the OECS's conception of security in economic terms. Both, however, lost the cold war lenses through which they had previously perceived the region. In the United States' case, this was reflected in its refusal to upgrade the RSS into a treaty, confident that the "Soviet threat" had been neutralized by the Grenada invasion.[37]

Functional Cooperation

The OECS charter provided for some functional cooperation among member states, and some attempts were made in education, sports and the judiciary, among other things.

The World Bank's assessment of education in the OECS painted a dismal picture of a shortage of places at the secondary level and low enrolment in secondary and tertiary institutions. In addition, the quality of education was low, with a 50 per cent failure rate in the eleven-plus exams and a poor success rate in secondary schools. The World Bank identified a low level of training as a main problem: "most primary teachers are untrained; no more than 40 per cent of secondary school teachers have degrees in their subjects; teacher attrition is high; and equipment and buildings are inadequate".[38] It concluded that many of the changes required could be accomplished at the regional level. The OECS established an advisor for special programmes at the central secretariat to coordinate educational projects in member states, liaise directly with international funding agencies, and administer scholarship programmes. This allowed the OECS to contribute directly towards developing policy in education and training, moving away from the prior ad hoc approach. At the tertiary level, the OECS sought to introduce its own institutions to expand opportunities for students who depended on institutions in the MDCs, thus hoping to reduce costs and increase access. This included establishing industrial arts and business education centres in St Lucia and Antigua, as well as local centres for pre- and first-year university training.[39]

The OECS was involved in a number of activities, including health, sports and the judiciary, which were not specified under the charter, suggesting a significant deepening of the movement. Cooperation in health was minimal, limited to a programme of drug procurement through the Eastern Caribbean Drugs Service,[40] located at OECS headquarters. Bulk buying of drugs under this programme resulted in a 16 to 26 per cent reduction in prices for the top twenty products.[41]

Although the OECS focused primarily on political and economic matters, limited concessions were made in the popular sphere by the organization's involvement in sports, reflected in the establishment in 1984 of a sports desk at the St Lucia secretariat. The OECS's interest in sports suggested a recognition that for the organization to be appreciated it had to increase its visibility among ordinary people, and that sports had the potential, by encouraging popular contact, to contribute to forging a subregional identity. Some of the common problems the unit sought to address were a lack of sponsorship for sporting activities, a dearth of sporting facilities in the various countries, and unavailability of coaches, resulting in poor performance at regional and international events.[42] The sports desk responded by training referees and coaches, and staging competitions in various sports at the subregional level.

The OECS's attempts at increased harmonization invariably required legislative changes in each member country, hence the establishment of a legal unit at the central secretariat in August 1984. Its main responsibilities were for harmonizing the laws of OECS states, preparing legislation for new OECS institutions created, and assisting member countries in legal drafting. J.D.B. Renwick, head of the legal unit, noted that as the secretariat expanded it was increasingly called upon to advise on matters other than legislation.[43] Renwick noted that constraints, such as insufficient and inadequately trained staff and shortages of printing facilities, resulted in countries not being able to take immediate advantage of legislation prepared by the legal unit. Its most important contribution, however, was in preparing legislation to harmonize the laws of member states to give effect to decisions furthering the integration of their economies. The unit drafted legislation on drug use, which formed the basis of all narcotics legislation in OECS countries. In addition, a modern road and traffic act was accepted by St Lucia, Grenada, Dominica and St Vincent.[44] The unit was seeking, with the East Caribbean Central Bank, to develop a new banking act to control banking in the OECS, and was considering introducing common laws on pollution and toxic waste disposal, the environment, company registration and copyright legislation. It was also engaged in working out potentially more controversial arrangements between the RSS,[45] OECS governments and the US government, which would allow the United States unilateral rights of hot pursuit in OECS territorial waters to stop, search and seize ships suspected of carrying narcotics.[46]

The OECS legal unit played an important role in the area of treaty succession, examining all instruments, lists and bilateral treaties applicable to OECS countries at the time of their independence,[47] and advising governments on appropriate action. Such work was important, as most countries did not have a comprehensive listing of all the treaties to which they were party.[48] Renwick intended to develop the unit as a repository of this information.

OECS member countries, except for Grenada, were members of a subregional supreme court. Judges moved freely between the courts of member states. Member states were responsible for paying the supreme court judges through the OECS. Grenada left the OECS court system in 1979, after the headquarters was removed from Grenada as a show of disapproval by the then WISA council of ministers. Grenada later sought to rejoin the subregional court system, but was initially rejected by the other member countries.[49] It was readmitted in 1991, following the completion of the Maurice Bishop murder trials.

OECS Performance, 1981–1987

Successes

The OECS's most important contribution, arguably, was its success in defining the subregion as an area with distinct problems and needs. This was most evident in its relations with CARICOM, in its dealings with third countries, and in its ability to secure technical and financial assistance from external sources. Of equal importance in terms of its success, however, was its ability to make its presence felt within member states. The OECS's contribution was most obvious in CARICOM, where members acted as a significant bloc. As Byron Blake, a CARICOM official, explained, OECS states had the added advantage of two additional secretariats working solely in their interest.[50]

Among the organization's successes were its efforts to keep the markets of the CARICOM MDCs open to the LDCs during periods of economic downturn in MDC countries, when the response was to adopt protectionist measures. OECS countries also made their mark on the EC's regional assistance programme to the CARICOM region, reversing the trend of MDCs receiving the lion's share of European Community commitments.[51] The technical capacity concentrated in the secretariats also meant that they increased their chances of European Community funding by submitting well-prepared proposals covering the subregion.[52]

The common approach was also evident in other instances, such as the development of double-taxation agreements with Canada and common fisheries treaties and arrangements in relation to drug smuggling with the United States.[53] These instances reflected an increasing tendency for OECS countries to adopt a harmonized approach on common issues *vis-à-vis* others outside of the grouping, even though treaties were ultimately bilateral.

Despite successes inside and outside the region in defining its role, the most important test of the OECS's success lay in its ability to make itself felt in the lives of its people. Here the organization had mixed results. That some advances had occurred was seen in the rise of regional organizations identifying with the OECS. These included the establishment of an OECS manufacturers' association, defining the specific interests of its members within the umbrella Caribbean Association of Industry and Commerce, and an OECS athletics association which, although not connected in any way to the OECS sports desk, provided further example of the acceptance of an OECS identity.[54] A subregional identity was also, no doubt, strengthened within the national bureaucracies, particularly in areas where local bureaucrats had to participate in OECS programmes and thus regularly met with counterparts in other islands. Its impact, however, was likely to be felt most in countries where the organization's offices were located.

Location was an important consideration for an organization expected to serve eight different countries separated by water. The OECS began in St Lucia and Antigua with its two secretariats, but its bureaucracy spread to include a fisheries desk in St Vincent and the Grenadines, and the Eastern Caribbean States Export Development Agency office in Dominica. The importance of location came to the fore when the Eastern Caribbean States Export Development Agency was discussed: the advantages of increasing the organization's profile in Dominica were considered more important than the financial savings possible from locating it at the Antigua secretariat. This approach meant that four of eight OECS countries had an institutional presence. Of almost equal importance was balancing the placement of nationals in the OECS bureaucracy; this was highlighted when Montserrat withdrew from the Eastern Caribbean mission in London because none of its nationals was on the staff. Interestingly, rather than criticize Montserrat's action, the other members responded by stressing the importance of the principle of broad representation. Despite this, the OECS came into contact with only limited interest groups in member countries, largely from the business sector. Initiatives such as the fisheries and the agricultural diversification programme, once the latter got off the ground, could serve to broaden the organization's reach.

Apart from limited involvement in sports, there were few avenues providing direct contact between the OECS and the majority of its people. The OECS had yet to make its presence felt in the popular sphere. Cultural activity, although one of the areas envisaged by the treaty for action, had no OECS input, and there appeared to be no imminent plans for this area. So far, the organization exhibited cooperation primarily at the level of the bureaucracy and among the ruling parties. The failure to make its presence felt in the lives of ordinary members of the populations had implications for calls to take the integration process to the level of political integration. The one decision that might have had an impact in this direction was the agreement to remove travel restrictions among member countries, but this was not implemented; there was a lack of follow-up action to give effect to statements, possibly a reflection of weak political will.

Weaknesses

While the OECS made important strides in furthering subregional integration, the movement was dogged by problems which had serious consequences for its development. Weaknesses were manifested in the evidence, all too often, of a lack of commitment to the regional movement and an unwillingness to sacrifice narrow national interests for those of larger regional significance, coupled with an absence of concrete structures to implement OECS decisions nationally. It is probably fair to say that the absence of such mechanisms simply reflected the stage of development of the integration movement, and that the solution depended on the extent to which political commitment to the movement increased. The OECS director, Vaughan Lewis,[55] suggested that the *ad hoc* approach which characterized the implementation process, if allowed to continue, would result in little being achieved. In an effort to strengthen the system, a proposal was made at the June 1989 Heads of Government meeting for the establishment of a system for coordinating and implementing OECS activities and decisions in member states.[56] Lewis suggested that another aspect of the problem was that OECS workers were resented by some civil servants because of their higher pay, a resentment often expressed in tardy implementation of decisions.

OECS leaders themselves sometimes inhibited progress on the very decisions they supported, particularly in relation to the industry allocation programme, where governments sometimes protected local industries in competition with similar enterprises allocated to another territory. Members' commitment was best expressed in the response to financial responsibilities. Governments were reluctant to fund projects they considered important, even as they sought such assistance from donor countries. Where governments had committed themselves financially, with overseas missions and the secretariats, for example, some were constantly in arrears, leading to financial crises at these offices. Part of the problem here was that they had not found satisfactory mechanisms to govern their financial arrangements with the organization. The arrangements for Eastern Caribbean Drug Service funding through a fund set up at the East Caribbean Central Bank provided a successful model, but governments were reluctant to extend this approach to key areas for fear of relinquishing control over financing arrangements. The issue was raised at the 1989 OECS Authority meetings,[57] and was sufficiently important for St Vincent's prime minister, James Mitchell, to comment that members' commitment to the process was reflected by their debt to the organization.[58]

In the unfolding of the integration movement some governments appeared committed to deeper integration. These included Mitchell of St Vincent and Compton of St Lucia. Compton was anxious that the organization should implement measures, such as freedom of movement, by setting a firm target date.[59] He called for steps to be taken towards freedom of travel that should be directed not only towards reducing legal and bureaucratic restrictions, but towards lowering the cost of travel. One way of doing this was to restructure the regional air carrier, LIAT.[60] He argued that such steps should precede political union, so that while formalities were being worked out, people could travel without impediment. He advocated the unification of customs services as "the next logical step" in the process of trade liberalization, and called for the unification of the officer corps of the police forces in order to strengthen regional security. He suggested that a pool of legal officers, to whom the OECS could offer a "regional career", would replenish the judicial services. These developments, he declared, did not depend upon political unification.[61] Mitchell showed his frustration with the slow pace of the movement and some governments' reluctance to pursue political union by charging that there were "a lot of superior attitudes" which needed to be broken down.[62] He scathingly observed that some OECS countries had "a sense of superiority" and felt themselves to be better off than St Vincent, so did not want to support the political union initiative.[63]

Antigua was one of the countries least anxious to extend functional cooperation. It resisted the establishment of a common fisheries zone or a single licensing authority, and suggestions that the fisheries unit should be responsible for assigning observers on foreign fishing vessels. Antigua's reluctance was evident in a number of other areas including the diplomatic arena where, as mentioned, it stood apart from Eastern Caribbean missions in London and Canada; and in an initial reluctance to participate in the drug procurement programme. Despite this, it can still be said that there was widespread support for deepening the integration process.

The OECS was rather successful in securing international financing for many programmes and projects, but this heavy dependence on external assistance was inevitably worrying. It was difficult not to question the concept of independence for countries unable to finance their own development and the integration process. The danger was that if donors withdrew support, the integration movement could find itself in grave difficulty. Additionally, external funding did not always encourage development within the organization on the basis of need. Prospective donors did not always agree with the organization's assessment of areas requiring priority. The solution lay in the OECS using such assistance to develop a permanent technical capability, and in the extent to which activities and structures such as the Eastern Caribbean Drug Service, the Eastern Caribbean Investment Promotion Service, and the Eastern Caribbean States Export Development Agency, and the agriculture, tourism, and fisheries projects, could generate finances that could be ploughed back into the organization's activities.

Conclusions

The OECS played an appreciable role and achieved some success in increasing the strength, and indeed the viability, of its members, particularly in their relationship with external groups. It succeeded in deepening and consolidating integration beyond narrow trade concerns, and initiated the highest level of cooperation achieved to that point among the small Eastern Caribbean states. Despite noteworthy successes in key areas of cooperation, however, the process was beset by weaknesses. The main drawback lay in the tension between the interests of individual countries versus that of the group, an example of the limits of sovereignty. This was manifested in a certain lack of commitment to decisions not necessarily in a particular country's interest, which put a brake on key programmes and initiatives. Another weakness lay in the organization's structure, which had no mechanisms for ensuring compliance by national bureaucracies. Both weaknesses arose from the voluntary character of the organization, evident in the absence of power of enforcement or sanction.

By 1987 the OECS had existed for six years. Its objectives were limited and its success in achieving them was even more limited. There was nothing in the charter to suggest that the OECS was to be a first step towards full political union, yet in 1987 a proposal was made for the creation of a union of all members of the OECS. This raises a question central to this book. Why was this proposal made? Was it due to limitations in the character and objectives of the OECS, or perhaps in partial failure to achieve these objectives? Alternatively, were there new reasons not directly related to the OECS as it then stood? More specifically, were the objectives of the proposed union economic or political, and if the latter, were they primarily concerned with external and internal security? These questions are examined and answers suggested in chapter 6.

6 | *Political Union Initiative*
Rationale and Background

The alternative to our scenario of union is the status quo. In that status quo, we the leaders will soon fade out or go under, one by one. We may even vanish with boredom from the scene. And the same fate, in due process of time, awaits our successors facing the escalating problems.

– James Mitchell, "Thoughts on an East Caribbean Union"

Rationale for an OECS Political Union

A year after he first mooted the idea in June 1986, William Demas firmly set out the case for political union at the inauguration of the St Vincent National Advisory Committee on Eastern Caribbean Political Unity.[1] He promoted union on a variety of fronts: it would make the OECS more effective in international political and economic forums through better quality representation; it could lead to an improvement in public administration, expertise and efficient government; it might also have less measurable benefits, such as an increase in self-respect for the islands. His main emphasis, however, was economic. This had two main aspects. First, these countries, particularly the Windwards, were facing unfavourable economic prospects and economic weakness. Second, the small size of individual islands hampered their ability to address these serious problems, threatening their capacity to deliver what

James Mitchell had called the "economic goods" to their people, and endangering the economic and social stability of their societies. On all these counts a political union was desirable and possibly essential.

This was a broad-based appeal, covering many existing and potential problems. The question therefore must be faced: which of them was primary? Did the initiative result from concern with mainly political problems, such as international relations or internal and external security? How important were idealistic considerations such as the strengthening of an Eastern Caribbean personality? Or was the motive essentially economic? If so, was it the particular economic problems of the Windwards rather than those of the group as a whole that were involved? And how significant in this argument was the fact that the initiative, which was launched by the Windward Islands' leaders, had lost the support of all of the Leeward Islands as early as 1988?

To answer these questions it is helpful to examine in more detail the case made by the proponents of union, which should indicate what combination of these factors was the motivating force behind the union initiative.

Economic Case

Mitchell identified the difficulties confronting OECS countries as the fragility of their economies, the "unfavourable external realities" they faced, and their limited potential for economic recovery in the face of natural disasters or economic shocks. The problem was particularly acute for the Windward Islands, whose extreme dependence on banana production and reliance on a protected UK market and a stable pound discouraged "genuine independence".[2] John Compton put his arguments more graphically, remarking that OECS countries could not exist financially as independent countries nor were they able to fulfil their obligations to the international community, having neither the money nor the expertise to maintain civil services at home and offices overseas, both of which were vital to procuring financial assistance. They owed their existence as independent countries to protected markets or aid, and the fact that "the world [had] been kind". They were "countries of subvention . . . not independent countries".[3] He predicted "difficult times down the road" for OECS countries,[4] warning that they were "threatened" by the attempts of major industrial countries to combat economic difficulties, the result of which was a decline in foreign inflows, "both of capital and foreign aid, and a loss of export markets".[5]

Compton observed that the ability to address these problems individually was severely restricted by the OECS countries' small size. They were too small to make the necessary adjustments to their economies single-handedly, and to attract the kind of attention and financial support they required from the international community. The leaders of the Windward Islands were convinced that union would provide the framework for addressing their pressing economic problems. Compton argued that the policies that St Lucia had to pursue, such as economic diversification, particularly in tourism, could best be attempted at the subregional level since "the trappings of nationhood" – passports, immigration, customs – in each island removed the competitive edge. Likewise, the success of agricultural diversification depended on a subregional approach in order to sustain supplies and market new produce. He argued that St Lucia's economy performed well only because of the common marketing of bananas in the Windward Islands,[6] and that only common action could reduce their economic fragility.[7] Mitchell also believed that the islands' economic problems could not be solved individually[8] because their small size reduced the feasibility of development projects.[9] It also affected their ability to secure loans from financial institutions, many of which found it difficult to disburse the small sums each required.

The conviction of Windward Islands' leaders that union provided an alternative from which to address their problems was based primarily upon an acceptance that the problems mainly derived from small size and the resulting diseconomies of scale. The economies-of-scale argument was popularized in the Caribbean by Demas's work, *The Economics of Development in Small Countries*.[10] Demas argued that small countries suffered from dis-economies of scale which made their production inefficient, a problem which could be alleviated if they were encouraged to form larger units. The economies-of-scale question featured strongly in the arguments seeking to rationalize OECS union. Demas[11] argued that political union would mean pooling markets and resources, which would result in a unified and "truly common" market for goods and services, capital and labour, as well as a chance for exploiting natural resources.[12] In addition, political union would provide a framework for addressing the lack of what he and Alister McIntyre[13] described as a "critical mass" of skilled persons in practically all aspects of the society. It would provide an opportunity for developing, retaining and attracting a skilled labour force, because a larger work environment would provide greater career opportunities and stability. This was particularly important for the civil service and the foreign service.

Union would also facilitate the full integration of the economies and the harmonization of policies, programmes and legislation which, experience seemed to suggest, enhanced their ability to address their problems. More specifically, the union proposal pointed to some dissatisfaction with the OECS's functioning and the conflicts that continued to exist, along with the conviction that the organization was inadequate to tackle the problems of the Windward Islands. Union was therefore supported for its perceived potential for harmonizing national economic policies and development and transforming their relationship from a historically competitive one.[14] Grenada's attorney-general, Danny Williams, perceived union as a means of reducing the traditional dependence on foreign assistance.[15]

Compton and Williams, supported by a number of OECS secretariat technocrats, argued that political union was necessary to facilitate economic integration, the stated aim of the ECCM agreement, and the main basis for the OECS treaty. The absence of mandatory mechanisms to enforce OECS decisions meant that many ECCM objectives remained unimplemented. In addition, it allowed countries to violate regulations governing some of its programmes, particularly the industry allocation scheme. Countries violated regulations not because they were uncommitted to OECS economic integration, but because the competitive character of their economies made it difficult for them to adopt an approach that would bring long-term benefit to the region rather than immediate gains to themselves. In this context, therefore, the OECS's lack of political clout made it difficult to advance the economic integration process. Mitchell starkly predicted that OECS countries would stagnate outside of union, since there were limits to what could be achieved through the existing framework of cooperation. He described functional cooperation as being at a stalemate and predicted that unless the countries formed a union, the treaty itself would collapse.[16]

Foreign Relations

The desire for union was also clearly encouraged by developments in the international community, the experience of operating in the international arena, and the limitations OECS countries faced in conducting their foreign relations. In particular, Windward Islands' leaders identified a tendency for already large, powerful countries to form alliances to increase their clout, which, they believed, further weakened the position of small states. Mitchell, in his Tortola speech, painted a picture of a world where the strong were uniting to increase their importance, contrasted with the insignificance of small states with minuscule numbers of people unable to sustain the interest of the international community:

> At this time in our history, I feel a strong sense of worry about the twentieth century closing and leaving us all stranded. . . . I worry when I see the strong uniting to increase their strength, and I worry about the indecisiveness of the weak and their disunity.
>
> I get a little tired of the patronising sermons on "The Role of Security in Small States", and the like. We have to behave like Grenada or Fiji to get attention. . . .[17]

Mitchell's challenge to OECS states was to decide whether to "make a great leap forward toward unity or . . . continue to crawl, and like a child be only capable of a cry and a whimper".[18] For Mitchell, therefore, the feeling that small size was equated with lack of importance was a significant factor in his acceptance of the need for political union. Demas also argued in similar vein, saying that "West Indians" needed to seek greater "clout", greater room for manoeuvre and increased options, through political union, in view of the "severe geo-political pressures to which we, as a group of very small, economically weak and somewhat disunited countries . . . are being, and will increasingly be subjected".[19]

Windward Islands' leaders were cognizant of the difficulty they faced, because of limited resources, in developing the high-calibre representation which was important in their attempt to make their voices heard in the international arena. Compton noted that the burden of external representation was so heavy that some had to appeal to the Commonwealth for assistance to pay rent for their missions in New York. Neither did they have the human resources necessary to staff these embassies in addition to the local civil service.[20] Political union was thus seen as allowing OECS countries to pool human resources and provide higher-quality representation at international forums, enhancing bargaining power in the international arena by pursuing single policies, action and representation in external trade, diplomacy and financial institutions;[21] to command greater respect and make a bigger impact on "world affairs";[22] and to attract a higher calibre of staff to represent them in the international community, thus enhancing their influence.[23]

Security

Security was obviously an important consideration in the Windward Islands' leaders' support of the union initiative. Most advocates of political union agreed that there were advantages for security, both internal and external. Mitchell, in his "Thoughts on an East Caribbean Union", argued that security would be "enhanced in a single archipelagic state with wider boundaries", of much more importance to the security of the United States, Canada and Latin America – a development which should "improve" their negotiating position in seeking development funds.[24] It was also seen as important in defending their territorial integrity. Demas believed that the establishment of a common defence force and coast guard was important, not just to resist "raids by all sorts of crack-pot and sinister adventurers and mercenaries",[25] but in the fight against drugs.[26]

There was a tendency to see union as encouraging greater internal stability and thus as an important device in preventing the conditions that had given rise to the Grenada revolution. Mitchell argued, "I do not think it is idle speculation to suggest that if we were together in a political union, Grenada would have avoided all its traumas."[27] In like vein, St Lucia's foreign affairs minister, Neville Cenac, argued that "the most important" consideration for union was the guarantee of law and order. He also believed that it would safeguard against a repetition of the Grenada experience.[28] Eugenia Charles felt that internal security would be boosted by a combined police force.[29]

Compton and Mitchell also believed that union would enhance internal stability if it strengthened the economic base of the countries. They therefore made a direct connection between economic success and internal stability. Compton argued that social and political stability, which required economic progress, could come only from political union, as governments could not deliver "the goods" in "little units of 150,000 in a world of giants".[30] Mitchell painted a bleak picture of the future, predicting that the *status quo* could not remain stable and that the internal situation would worsen.[31]

There were indications that the initiative was also influenced by the ideological cohesion existing among the leaders, most of whom were in the CDU. Mitchell, in presenting his vision of union to OECS leaders, pointed to the common "political philosophy" they shared as CDU members, which meant that the time for unity was "therefore fortuitous".[32] Charles asserted that the initiative emerged because they "all [thought] alike" hence, "we were able to bring a lot of things into being in the OECS where we work together, so we thought why not go further".[33]

Other Considerations

Imitation

The European integration process was identified as one of the main catalysts behind the rash of regional integration groupings in the Third World in the 1960s; its effect on the Caribbean integration experience has been well documented.[34] There were indications that the European Community experience had some influence on the current OECS political union initiative. Ben Jones stated that the possibility of forming a union was brought home by the tightening of European integration, as well as the establishment of the United States–Canada free trade area, and what they saw as similar moves in the East and the Middle East. Mitchell also invoked "the rapid pace" of European integration, and "the example of Canada and the US" on the verge of creating a single market, as reasons why OECS countries should form a union.[35] Compton also held up European integration as an example.[36] Charles questioned why tiny OECS countries should want to exist separately while stronger countries were "giving up strength".[37] Thus the so-called imitation effect seems to have operated in the OECS initiative.

The European Community, however, was only one aspect of the international environment that OECS states confronted and which influenced the way in which they operated. Dominica's minister of trade, tourism and industry, Charles Maynard, noted the difficulty "the rest of the world" had in dealing with small countries, arguing that while Europe was not actively seeking to make it difficult for OECS countries to exist separately, it was "the reality of the world that they [could not] deal with these small units". He noted that OECS states had found that in international forums their effectiveness depended on their ability to forge alliances with other Caribbean and Latin American countries.[38] OECS officials, however, were more forthright, reporting that the European Community pressured OECS countries to submit projects for funding under the Lomé Convention that were of a subregional character, as national projects were considered not just a nuisance but more expensive to service. Therefore, while subregional projects such as tourism development, industrial promotion and agricultural diversification developed partly in recognition of common problems, they also reflected external pressure for a common approach. In this sense, therefore, such pressures had the effect of encouraging closer cohesion among OECS states and increasing the organization's prestige. The external environment, particularly the European integration experience, functioned as the "catalyst" Nye had identified in encouraging the desire for the transformation of economic integration movements into a political union. It remains to be seen whether this was sufficiently strong to push the movement toward a union.

Human Rights and Cultural Identity

Demas introduced Arthur Lewis's concern with human rights when he was making his case for a federation of the Windward and Leeward Islands after the collapse of the West Indies Federation.[39] Lewis argued then that union would prevent political abuse that was likely in a small country, especially where one political party dominated,[40] where trade unions were tied to the party, newspapers depended on government advertisement, and the police and civil service were compromised. Demas argued that the case for union on the basis of safeguarding against human rights abuse was valid for all time. Finally, Demas called for union on the basis that "West Indians are basically one people, one nation. All of us know this and feel it in our bones." He argued that it was important to institutionalize and strengthen this West Indian cultural identity in a context where "external forces" were working to diminish it. He observed that people outside the region were never conscious of the existence of the separate West Indian countries, but knew instead of the "West Indies" or the "Caribbean". In other words, the region was already viewed as a nation.

The basis on which political union was supported had not changed from when the issue was discussed in the 1960s and 1970s. Lewis's view that it was "the only framework which will guarantee law and order, good government, financial stability, the recruitment and retention of good technical staff and the ability to attract financial assistance from outside, including the power to borrow, and including also the kind of stability which attracts private investment"[41] was as current to the OECS exercise as it had been when he stated it in the 1960s. The question, however, is which of these factors was most important in providing momentum to the initiative.

The Motivating Force behind the OECS Initiative

This account makes it clear that the factors encouraging the desire among the Windward Islands for political union did not differ much from those that Wheare identified as influencing interest in earlier federations. Windward Islands' leaders hoped to realize economic advantage from both expanding the size of their territory and increasing international clout, and there were arguably some advantages in enhanced security that could be realized. This initiative raises the question of whether the weight these factors had in earlier movements remained consistent in the OECS in 1987. For example, while economic advantage was considered important in the formation of earlier federations, the military advantage which could be derived was often considered the overriding factor influencing the movement's success. Was this also the case in the OECS initiative? More importantly, it raises the issue of whether these factors could be considered, reasonably, as discrete in a discussion of the OECS initiative.

In the OECS initiative the economic case was well made and was the focus for most proponents, while little emphasis was placed on possible security advantages. The economic impetus was obviously the precarious position Windward Islands' economies faced from specific threats to their banana industry after 1992, and a broader apprehension surrounding the loss of financial support to underwrite their general economic development. Issues of European integration and broader transformations in the international arena, therefore, were closely associated with the desire for union. Since less emphasis was placed in the arguments on security implications, these must be investigated with regard to the possible existence of a hidden agenda that might have been influencing the process.

What is immediately clear is that a narrow discussion of Wheare's military threat is of little utility to the OECS experience. A more meaningful discussion is possible if the notion of military threat is integrated into a broader concept of security that speaks to the maintenance of the state or social stability. This is suggested by the broader definitions of security evident in the arguments for and against political union, which include the maintenance of political power against local and external elements through the use of the RSS, and the protection of the state against drug trafficking. It is within this more expansive reading of security that Windward Islands' leaders located their economic difficulties. This inclusion of threats to the state's survival blurs the distinction between economic and military factors evident in analyses of earlier federal movements, and is particularly relevant in the context of failed states, a feature of the post–cold war international scene. Even notions of security which embrace the maintenance of political power in an ideological framework were already becoming outmoded by the time OECS political union was being discussed. There was already a shift in the leaders' preoccupation with the activities of left-wing groups based on a perceived communist threat, that coincided with the marginalization of such groups. After the 1983 invasion of Grenada, the left in the Eastern Caribbean which, outside of Grenada, had never been particularly threatening, was decimated. It was only in prerevolutionary Grenada that the left was viewed as a credible electoral force, and the manner of the revolution's collapse discredited the entire movement, further reducing its already limited electoral support. The disagreements which the revolution's collapse engendered within these movements also weakened them and, in some cases, led to their fragmentation.[42]

The invasion also had other implications that reduced the so-called threat from the left. It served to close the revolutionary option and marginalize Cuba's role in Caribbean politics, particularly in light of the latter's inability to present credible military opposition to US intervention in Grenada.[43] This served to bring home the message that Cuba's influence (and hence that of the Soviet Union) was limited in the US sphere of influence in the Caribbean, and to re-establish US supremacy in Caribbean affairs.[44] Even the formerly pro-Cuba People's National Party (Jamaica), in the run-up to the 1988 elections, was forced to accept that it had to make its peace with the United States in order to gain and hold political power. Again, in Jamaica, the left's marginalization was graphically portrayed in the collapse of the Workers' Party of Jamaica, the region's oldest self-declared communist party, in the late 1980s. More importantly, by 1990, communism's disintegration within Eastern Europe and the Soviet Union had removed the basis for perceiving Caribbean security in ideological terms.

The fact that Windward Islands' governments were no longer seriously threatened by the political left did not mean that a union might not have served other security or ideological purposes. The CDU's formation in 1986 among the region's right-wing parties, and its continued existence, suggest that ideological considerations were still important in regional politics. There were charges that Jamaica's prime minister, Edward Seaga, a close ally of the United States, strongly backed the initiative.[45] Undoubtedly, Windward Islands' governments, who enjoyed a close working relationship and most of whom invited the Grenada invasion, would have seen advantages in a union with their forces at the helm. Naturally, any decision to form a union would have worked to the advantage of the incumbent governments, and they were more likely to win political power in a single state since they were already united. This is not sufficient, however, to suggest that this was the main motivation behind the initiative. It is even more unlikely since most of the individual prime ministers would have had to sacrifice leadership and settle for ministerial positions in any union government.

Security, in the narrower sense of maintaining political power, was definitely an important consideration for OECS states. This, however, was more relevant to their ability to preserve territorial integrity in the face of external threats from mercenaries or drug barons. The Dominican incident, where plots involving local and foreign elements to mount a coup against the government were foiled, suggests that this remained an important consideration. Undoubtedly, a single defence force, facilitated by union, would be a crucial first line of defence in the face of such an attack before international assistance could be sought. However, it is unlikely that in the face of a serious attack OECS countries, union or no union, would be able to mount a credible defence without international assistance.

Nevertheless, while union would not necessarily enhance their defence capability against external aggression, it would undoubtedly allow OECS countries to exercise greater internal control. Thus, as Cenac suggested, it would allow them to guard against a Grenada-type revolution. There would be no question of intervention, as OECS forces would be intervening in a region within a single state and not in a sovereign country. In addition it would facilitate US action, since such action would be responding to the invitation of a legitimate government. Despite this, this is not convincing as an overriding factor propelling the initiative. Moreover, the security advantages to the United States are somewhat unclear, as an OECS political union was not necessary to safeguard US control over the region. By 1987 all OECS governments were cooperating with the United States on security matters, eventually embodied in so-called shiprider treaties which gave the United States unprecedented access to OECS territorial waters in the pursuit of suspected drug traffickers. In addition, Grenada's accession to the RSS provided the legal framework for US intervention in their domestic affairs.

By the mid-1980s, Windward Islands' leaders were clearly preoccupied with the threats to their survival from increased globalization, represented in the Single Europe Act and the move towards larger trade blocs. Their perceived weakness, evident in their interaction in the international arena, coupled with their economic vulnerability, encouraged them to believe that they needed to confront jointly a hostile international environment which threatened their survival. Compton, in an address to mark the sixth anniversary of the OECS in 1987, summed up this view of the world:

> Faced by a growing cohesion from within, which has presented us with some measure of success in combating the threats from without, the political leaders of the OECS conscious of the need to strengthen the organisation for our own survival, have decided to put the question to the people of converting the organisation into a nation.[46]

It was this perceived vulnerability, felt most acutely in the Windwards, that ultimately became the strongest impetus towards union.[47] It also explains why the Windward Islands were not able to maintain the interest of the Leeward Islands, who perceived the difficulties less acutely.

Conclusions

The perspectives of Windward Islands' governments on the threats to the survival of their states suggest that the increased complexities of the environment within which states operate make it difficult to draw neat boundaries between the military and economic factors evident in the analysis of earlier federal movements. An analysis of movements towards political integration must reflect the increased challenges which states confront in an international environment where the forces of globalization restrict their decision making, not only in the economic sphere, but in political and cultural spheres as well. It has to engage with the reality that states can collapse. For the Windward Islands, it is conceivable that collapse could be triggered by the destruction of their current economic base and their inability to find suitable alternatives quickly enough. Since the initiative was mooted, the region has witnessed the virtual collapse of the state in Montserrat, arising from the volcano's destruction of both the economic base and the physical living space of the island. In light of these experiences the possibility of small states disintegrating is not a laughable notion, but one that must be given credibility. Nye's observation that the economic environment within which these states operate was likely to be a crucial factor in their desire to integrate, providing possible catalysts propelling the movement, holds true for the Windward Islands.[48] In addition, the European integration process continues to play a role in prodding the wider Caribbean integration movement.

If we accept that the initiative was driven by the impetus to weather storms challenging their economies, then we need to account for the lapse in activity in 1989. Could it be that the economic threat, even defined in security terms, simply did not have the force which direct military threat had in urging on older federal movements? Or could it be that the initiative's failure to date has been the result of internal factors which overrode the governments' fears of collapse? We now turn to an examination of the reaction of the remaining national governments to the initiative to explain why, after its inception as an OECS initiative, it ended as merely a Windward Islands objective.

7 The Consultation Process
Testing Public Opinion

Men can live at a high emotional level only for limited periods.
    – Sir Arthur Lewis

Why a Consultation Process

The OECS's decision to engage in widespread consultation, leading to a referendum, must be seen as an innovation in the conduct of postwar political unions. Analyses of newer postwar federations – and one might argue even older federations – show a focus on elite rather than popular involvement in the prefederal negotiations. The groups involved in this process tended to be the colonial power and representatives from the educated elite and, in some cases, the newly formed political parties. In the West Indies' case, while debates preceding the federal negotiations had been conducted within the newly formed trade unions and political parties and in some of the newspapers in the various islands, it was limited largely to these elites.[1] The Montego Bay Conference occurred in a period when the franchise was still restricted. Indeed, all postcolonial federations were negotiated in a context of limited franchise and popular involvement.[2] In none of these federations was there widespread popular consultation, since democracy, as it has developed, did not exist. In 1953 when the London Conference was finalizing plans for a West Indian Federation, Mordecai observed that it was novel in producing for the first time "a plan of Federation fashioned entirely by political delegates of governments now controlled by the elected elements – adult suffrage now applied everywhere".[3]

Generally, the literature places no special emphasis on the role of broad popular consultations in analysing the failure of some of these postcolonial federal experiments but, in the Caribbean, it has become conventional wisdom that the Federation collapsed because the "masses" were not consulted. The currency of this view was based on the experience of Jamaica's withdrawal following a referendum on its continued participation in the Federation.[4] This appeared to suggest that no political union experiment within the Caribbean region could be successful without popular participation and support. Moreover, popular support must be assured from the start, since it would be more difficult to secure this once union was in progress and its negative effects were being felt. In this context, therefore, an education campaign pointing to the advantages as well as disadvantages of union was generally seen as necessary before such a union could be attempted. Support in a referendum would be on the basis of concrete appreciation of its likely drawbacks.

More significantly, the OECS political union initiative was being contemplated in a completely different context: that of the political independence of all its member states, except Montserrat. All of these postindependence constitutions contained entrenched clauses that required majority support in a referendum to effect change. How the majority is constituted varied from country to country: St Vincent and Grenada required a two-thirds majority in parliament as well as in a referendum; St Lucia, a three-fourths majority in parliament and a simple majority in a referendum; and Dominica, a three-fourths majority in parliament and a two-thirds majority in a referendum.[5] These considerations obviously played a significant role in the OECS heads' decision to undertake "comprehensive consultation".

The absence of consultation in the federal experience means that the literature provides little guidance on how this process should be conducted. The whole notion of consultation in this sense was novel, and represented an original contribution by OECS states to the federal debate. Parliamentary democracy was well established in the various independent OECS states, but citizens expected to have a concrete role in matters of government that affected them directly, not content to relegate decision making to their representatives. In the small countries of the Commonwealth Caribbean, where politicians were in closer contact with their constituents,[6] people's ability to influence them and to take a more active role in the conduct of government was considerable. In addition, the experience of the Grenada revolution, although ending tragically, introduced the concept of mass participation in government and strengthened the view that ordinary people can and should be involved directly in government business.[7] Revolutionary Grenada, therefore, with its monthly parish council meetings and months of national budget debates, set an important precedent of popular intervention in politics that OECS leaders could not ignore.

Referenda

A referendum[8] seeks to put issues directly to the electorate. Its special characteristic is that voting is done on the basis of individual conviction and not in accordance with party loyalty. A referendum can be raised on the initiative of government, which then decides the timing, subject matter, formulation of questions, proportion of votes needed to make it successful, and whether it is advisory or binding. Or, as with OECS countries, the constitution may require it in certain circumstances. In this case both the government's support and the approval of a certain proportion of the elector-ate are necessary. It can also occur on the initiative of voters, relating either to measures already adopted by government or to those they want government to adopt. The types of referenda that are relevant to this discussion are those that the government initiates and those that the constitution requires. Wind-ward Islands' leaders agreed to hold two referenda. The first was to determine whether there was popular support for a union. The second depended on the successful outcome of the first, and was legally required to secure the required majority for major constitutional changes in each of the participating states.

How the governments intended to respond to the first referendum was implied rather than expressed.[9] The issue of what percentage of a popular vote would be considered sufficient or necessary in the first referendum to pursue union was not made clear. However, this was not urgent, as the referendum itself had not been finalized. The second referendum is not important here, since it hangs on the fate of the first and its parameters are set by individual country constitutions. Butler and Ranney,[10] comparing the conduct of several referenda, note the importance of keeping issues to be tested by referenda separate from party loyalties, thus allowing people and politicians to vote freely and not in accordance with party loyalty.

The Consultation Process

With the exception of Montserrat, OECS governments that had committed themselves to the idea of a political union did attempt in varying degrees to initiate debate. St Lucia was the only exception here, its government preferring to channel debate through an independent committee rather than spearheading the campaign itself. Governments in St Kitts–Nevis and St Vincent attempted to establish broad-based committees although, invariably, these were boycotted by opposition parties and some trade unions. In Grenada, the government formed a parliamentarians' committee which attempted to secure all-party representation. In Dominica, no formal structure was set up, the government preferring to use existing local government structures over which it had control.[11]

St Kitts–Nevis

Four months after the six OECS leaders decided to pursue political union, in September 1987, Prime Minister Simmonds formed a national advisory committee,[12] headed by Dr William Herbert. By 14 June of the following year, it had submitted a report. The opposition groups and trade unions absented themselves from the committee, although a wide range of social and private-sector groups participated. The committee,[13] which held three meetings, was charged with "generating public awareness of, and interest in the issue, and to consider a possible time frame for a referendum". In May 1988 participating organizations submitted position papers that were then summarized and presented to Simmonds. The committee concluded that Kittitians were not ready to entertain a referendum on closer union since "such a referendum will have to be preceded by a period of intensive public education . . . on all the ramifications of political union". It advocated strengthening the OECS, which it described as "a positive force for eventual East Caribbean integration", by intensifying functional integration particularly in "economic integration, harmonisation of laws, health, sport, culture" and dismantling barriers to freedom of movement.[14] Based on this report, Simmonds announced that his people were not interested in pursuing a political union with other OECS territories.

One of the obvious features of the process in St Kitts–Nevis was the absence of opposition parties and trade unions. Opposition parties had rejected the appointment of Herbert,[15] closely identified with the ruling party, to chair the committee and were upset by Simmonds's refusal to remove him.[16] Simmonds responded that it was the government's prerogative to select the committee's chairman.[17] The row between the two main parties over the appointment of the chairman, a relatively small matter in view of the much greater goal of achieving political union, was particularly unfortunate in light of the opposition's acceptance of the need for a national committee and its participation on it.[18] The row not only brought into question the commitment of both groups to the idea of union, but pointed to the relationship that existed between ruling and opposition party. The issue seemed to boil down to the government's view of its role in relation to that of the opposition.[19] The trade unions' failure to participate was also related to this issue, since the St Kitts–Nevis Trades and Labour Union was affiliated with the Labour Party. Lee Moore, former opposition leader and former leader of the Labour Party, was also president of the union.

Another interesting aspect of the St Kitts–Nevis consultation process was the committee's summary of views, which suggested that there was not so much a lack of support for union as insufficient information on which to take such an important decision. Out of this, the groups called for "intensive public education" on the ramifications of political union, throwing into question government's conclusion that people were not interested in pursuing the idea. Government's failure to provide a period of public education on the implications of union raises the question of whether the process, as conducted in St Kitts–Nevis, amounted to meaningful consultation.

The committee's report indicated that the main strategy adopted in the consultation process was for representatives to discuss the implications with their organizations and seek their views. This suggests that, although government was the main organization proposing union, its role was secondary, since the education and information process was left to the committee. This raises questions as to whether committee members supported union and, moreover, whether they were capable of presenting a balanced view of its implications. This suggests that there was a need for a more forthright role for government, which was more likely to be aware of the implications and advantages of union from its experiences within the OECS.

St Lucia

Prime Minister Compton of St Lucia, along with Prime Minister Mitchell of St Vincent, was regarded as one of the main supporters of the political union initiative.[20] Compton stated in the April elections that were his party to secure a two-thirds majority, he would immediately seek to amend the constitution with a view to advancing the process for a political union.[21] He was quoted as saying, "I had political union very much on my mind. Now I guess I have to be in consultation with the opposition to determine if we should really push ahead with arrangements relating to political unity."[22] This seemed to suggest that Compton, had he won a two-thirds victory at the polls, would have regarded this as a mandate to take the country into political union with or without opposition backing. The *Caribbean Contact* article from which this quote is taken claimed that Compton's narrow one-seat victory made him "no longer optimistic" about plans for a political union.[23] In another report,[24] however, Compton toned down the importance of a two-thirds electoral majority, claiming that union had not been an issue in the elections and that the people were not ready for it. Had his party won a two-thirds majority, it would not have been on the political union initiative, but on more "mundane issues like the . . . economy". He denied that the election results had put political union on the "back burner", saying rather that this had placed a greater onus on him to push the idea. He also pledged his commitment to work with the opposition on the political union initiative, saying that it should not be treated as a political issue.

As early as August 1987, Compton was confronting charges that the initiative was faltering, by arguing that although it might not have been "high profiled", plans were in motion to speed up the consultation process. He announced then that he was preparing to bring the issue to the public and that the cabinet was drafting the terms of reference for a consultative body.[25] Despite the lack of government action in initiating debates and promoting the initiative locally, Compton had been consistent in making strong statements in support of a political union of the Windward Islands. Even after Antigua rejected the initiative Compton insisted there was no turning back, declaring "we will go ahead with two".[26] In an address to the OECS in November 1988,[27] he called for "immediate action" on political union, arguing that "the longer we hesitate the more difficult our task becomes as the determination of some of our members appear [*sic*] to flag and other constitutional arrangements appear more attractive".[28] He called on the leaders to fix a "terminal date" for discussions on union and to "let all the other consequential arrangements fall into place" – "As we have done with the freedom of movement of goods, we must set a date for freedom of movement of people among our countries and let our officials work out the details."[29]

Despite these strongly supportive statements, however, Compton failed to launch the consultation process. Instead, this was done in St Lucia by a group largely comprising public service technocrats, as well as a few individuals from outside the government service who supported the idea. According to one of its members (Farrel Charles[30]) this committee, the Independent Committee for OECS Political Unity, sought to be broad based and independent of government and political influence, and to include people who "would investigate dispassionately the pros and cons and the possibilities" of union. It aimed at educating St Lucians about political union through "objective discussion and analysis". Its members were all committed to the idea of an OECS political union.[31] It held meetings in various communities, mounted a media campaign, disseminated reading material on the issue, and met with representatives from various organizations, including trade unions and opposition parties.[32] The committee emphasized its nonpolitical character, on the grounds that the issue should be free from partisan political interests.

The committee included highly placed government bureaucrats who, along with other members, were firmly committed to St Lucia's involvement. This meant that it could not substitute for a more broad-based forum representing different interests and views. Additionally, it was quite legitimate for the committee to exclude government and opposition politicians in order to avoid the intrusion of partisan political concerns in what it viewed as a nonpartisan issue. But the whole involvement of opposition parties in the union debate, or the lack of it, requires closer consideration.

Before the debate was launched in St Lucia, its opposition parties had already joined with others across the subregion to present a common front through SCOPE. Compton raised the issue locally only after the opposition leader, Julian Hunte, had presented SCOPE's position to Compton in his capacity as OECS chairman. Therefore, by the time Compton was ready to seek the support of local opposition groups, the relationship had already been soured by his earlier failure to respond to Hunte's propositions. Hunte simply reiterated the opposition's demands, made earlier, with an added request for local government elections to be held as part of the process of discussion and consultation.[33]

It is plausible that Compton's inability to secure the support of his major opposition party, which he had only narrowly defeated in the general elections, made him hesitant to embark on a campaign for political union. This would explain his failure to set up any structures through which to conduct the "consultation process", which allowed him to circumvent the thorny issues of opposition hostility. Conversely, the opposition could be excused for viewing the independent committee as Compton's attempt to avoid having to deal with them directly.[34] Through this committee, Compton was able to advance arguments in support of political union, while avoiding the political trap of being too closely involved with an idea that might turn out to be politically unpopular.

Dominica

The Dominican government attempted to use the local government structure, assisted by government ministers, as the forum through which to engender debate.[35] Charles spearheaded the debate, speaking to representatives from various groups and to village council chairmen and clerks, who were in turn expected to speak to their villages. Charles said she also introduced the issue when delivering public speeches, and that she met with representatives from some interest groups to ask them to discuss it with their members. Charles defended her approach on the grounds that it was necessary for cabinet members to talk to people, as the people would rather hear from their politicians than from a committee. She believed that a committee or commission would not get very far since people would not be interested. She argued that people were more likely to respond to their political leaders discussing political union, as this provided a forum for raising community issues closer to their hearts.[36] She agreed that the debate in Dominica had been low keyed since 1988, and attributed this to her inability to devote much attention to the issue given the demands of government.

The Dominican process suffered from the absence of support of the major opposition party, headed by opposition leader Mike Douglas.[37] Despite his party's commitment to achieving Caribbean nationhood, enshrined in its constitution, Douglas said his party was reluctant to enter onto a common platform on any issue with the government.[38] Douglas rejected Charles's approach to the consultation process, arguing that it forced opposition parties into either a conflictual or a consensual relationship with the government before elections were due. Were the opposition to join forces with the government, it could jeopardize its chances to win power in a future general election by blurring the distinction between opposition and ruling party. A situation where the government and the opposition shared a common platform was considered unacceptable in a political culture where the role of the opposition was to oppose the government and gain political power. The opposition could very well lose its credibility as an opposition grouping and undermine its chances of becoming the government if too closely identified with the ruling party on such a major political issue. There was no evidence that the Dominican government tried to elicit the support of the then recently formed United Workers' Party. Its leader, Edison James,[39] said he was not consulted at any point.[40] In the context of an uncooperative opposition, it is easy to understand Charles's tactic of avoiding the idea of a committee altogether, and using the political clout of ministers, herself in particular, to raise the issue with her constituents. The opposition appeared content to allow her to follow this route, while adding little to the debate. Charles was therefore unable to secure opposition input into such a politically sensitive issue. The consultation process suffered as a consequence.

There were conflicting accounts of the extent of the government's reach in broaching the issue, although Charles asserted that she met with organizations she "respect[ed]".[41] While it appeared that the government sought support from some quarters of the private sector,[42] there was little evidence among other groups, namely nongovernmental organizations and trade unions, to suggest that these were included. Even some sections of the private sector claimed not to have been approached. Francis Emmanuel, president of the Dominica Employers' Federation,[43] claimed that the government did not raise the issue formally with his organization, although Charles listed the Dominica Employers' Federation as one of the organizations with which she met. Emmanuel's claim raises the question of whether the persons Charles assembled after her return from the Tortola meeting were there in their individual capacities or as representatives of their organizations.

The trade unions, arguably one of the most significant sectors, appear not to have been directly involved. Interviews with representatives of three major unions, the Waterfront and Allied Workers' Union,[44] the National Workers' Union,[45] and the Dominica Trade Union,[46] revealed that they were not numbered among the groups Charles had targeted. Understandably, therefore, the unions were critical of the government's approach. Bernard Nicholas of the Dominica Trade Union complained that his union resented the fact that they were not involved, while Benoit, president of the Waterfront and Allied

Workers' Union, protested that the process had been conducted "too much from the top", "involving academics, diplomats and university graduates", whom people were unlikely to understand, with little participation from the "man on the street". Additionally, the government's failure to consult with unions meant that there were a lot of unanswered questions about the implications of a political union.

Neva Edwards of the National Council of Women also believed that the government needed to widen the reach of its education programme to the zonal and village levels. Some interviewees called for a government position paper to provide the basis for discussion, and most agreed that Dominica was not ready for a referendum. Some felt that any voting in a referendum would be based on partisan political support rather than on an understanding or appreciation of the implications of and need for political union.[47]

While it may have circumvented the thorny issue of opposition participation in the union debate, Charles's approach, *ad hoc* and restricted to what she and her ministers could do, did not have the national reach required. Her approach pointed to the limitations of mounting such a campaign without the input of the opposition parties, in a culture heavily dominated by party politics. Charles's failure to coopt a broader spread of interest groups could be attributed to her reluctance to set up formal structures which would exclude the opposition and infuriate them, leaving her open to criticisms of excluding them.

Grenada

Grenada's prime minister, Herbert Blaize, organized the National Parliamentarians' Committee of selected serving and former parliamentarians,[48] which included a representative from each political party.[49] Representatives from two of the main parties, the Grenada United Labour Party[50] and the National Democratic Congress,[51] declined to participate. The committee was mandated to "educate, inform and advise" Grenadians on political unity, and "to be advised by the people, on political unity". This was to be done through a series of meetings in "every parish and district", and radio and television programmes.[52] However, the committee's chairman, Danny Williams, attorney-general and minister of health, admitted that debate had cooled.

Reports from various interest groups raise questions as to whether the government had launched a consultation process at all. When he was interviewed in July 1989, Williams admitted that the committee had only seven active members and had not been functioning for four months. The Grenadian approach was unique in trying to avoid having to reconcile the various political groupings that existed. At the same time, it sought to adopt what was primarily a political approach by limiting its committee to parliamentarians, past and present. This strategy allowed it to include representatives of the various political groups in the country, including both the Grenada United Labour Party[53] and the Maurice Bishop Patriotic Movement,[54] neither of which was represented in parliament. Such persons were selected to sit on the committee as individuals, rather than as official representatives of their parties.

From all reports, the government declined to approach most interest groups directly. The only group that admitted to being approached was the Grenada Chamber of Industry and Commerce, whose president, Hugh Dolland,[55] said the Grenada Chamber of Industry and Commerce was invited to "two or three" of the meetings of the parliamentarians' committee. Even so, the Grenada Chamber of Industry and Commerce had not met and discussed the implications of the unity proposal in any detailed way. Representatives of the major trade unions said the government had made no attempts either to inform them of its perspectives or to include them in the consultation process. None had adopted individual positions on the issue. Instead, the Trade Union Council, which embraced all the major unions in the country, organized a seminar to solicit their views on the possible impact of union on the trade union movement.[56] The sole union with any contact with the parliamentarians' committee was the Seamen and Waterfront Workers' Union, whose president, Eric Pierre,[57] was also a member of the senate and of the parliamentarians' committee. Despite this, he said that his union had not been approached formally by the government. This experience suggests either that the committee was doing very little, or that its approach was inadequate. It had not even seized the opportunity of having a union leader on the senate to channel its messages to that particular union. Despite the government's failure to involve the private sector more than marginally, and the trade unions at all, these groups organized their own events to discuss the issue.[58] It would appear that little discussion had taken place in Grenada, and the general consensus of the interviewees was that the debate had been low keyed. As DeBourg explained, the Trade Union Council at its forum was "forced to invite the Government to get their views because we never knew what was happening". In the context of little debate in Grenada and the alienation of major interest groups from the initiative, there was also general agreement that Grenada was not ready to hold its first referendum.

An interesting observation from Grenada's experience was the suggestion from several sources that not all members of the government supported the initiative. Williams complained of a lack of support from government members in carrying out the committee's work, which he attributed to a lukewarm response to the idea from some quarters. DeBourg pointed out that at the Trade Union Council seminar on union both Williams and another member of government had said that Grenada was not yet ready for union. Whether this was a correct representation of William's views is secondary, as the message that was transmitted, intentionally or not, was that government support for the idea was tentative, to say the least. The government was also criticized for not providing information on the form and other concrete features of political union. Trade unions, in particular, found it difficult to support the idea of union in principle without knowing the concrete implications.

The Grenada government's approach was probably the most elitist of those adopted, restricting participation to parliamentarians and a few individuals considered prominent in Grenadian society, and excluding crucial interest groups. It is therefore not surprising that there was little debate on the issue. It is unlikely that a committee comprising people who might not be particularly interested in a political union, one way or the other, and who were there in their individual capacities, would have had much success in mounting a "consultation process". Not surprisingly, shortly after they were nominated to the committee and after its first meeting, representatives of the major political parties declined to participate.

The Grenada scenario was peculiar in that Prime Minister Blaize was unpopular and elections were expected at any moment. Moreover, Blaize was unpopular even within his party, with an eventual split occurring in July 1989 that left him with the minority section, forcing him to form a new party, The National Party. Hence, Blaize lacked the political credibility to mount a serious campaign, given his tenuous hold on the country. Additionally, he was viewed somewhat as a maverick both inside the OECS and in Grenada, running the government virtually as a one-man show, alienating his political allies.[59] His decision to choose the parliamentary road suggested contempt for important groups like the trade unions. The positive aspect of the parliamentary approach, however, lay in its potential for involving the parties in both houses, thus bypassing a partisan political approach and providing the basis for the inclusion of the major opposition party right from the start. But any real attempt to consult ordinary Grenadians had to go beyond this.

St Vincent

James Mitchell was acknowledged as the main force propelling the political union initiative. He had the full backing of his party which, in 1987, unanimously adopted a resolution pledging support and congratulating him on his "leadership" of the initiative.[60] Moreover, Mitchell maintained that the New Democratic Party's manifesto had written into it support for the principle of unification.[61] The government tabled a motion in parliament in support of the initiative, which was amended by the opposition and unanimously accepted.[62] The opposition[63] amendment included the principle that union should be "established on a sound foundation and with the maximum consultation with the people".[64] Armed with this support, Mitchell established a National Advisory Committee on a Political Union of the East Caribbean States, with membership open to all interested groups and individuals. After initial complaints from opposition parties about Mitchell's unilateral selection of the chairman and about aspects of the committee's terms of reference, most agreed to participate. Most of the major interest groups – trade union, nongovernmental and private sector – participated, representing some thirty-five organizations.[65] Although the issue initially generated a lot of activity and discussion, this had lessened by January 1989, giving way to election campaigning for the 1989 general elections.[66] This suggests that the initiative was not a major campaign issue for any of the political parties.

St Vincent and the Grenadines were widely considered to have had the most broad-based and participatory consultation process. This, however, was not without resistance from some opposition quarters. St Vincent had three opposition parties, none of which was in parliament after the 1989 elections.[67] These were the St Vincent Labour Party headed by Vincent Beache, and two small left-wing parties, the United People's Movement headed by Adrian Saunders, and the Movement for National Unity headed by Dr Ralph Gonsalves. Despite amendments to the National Advisory Committee's terms of reference, however, only the Movement for National Unity participated. The St Vincent Labour Party stood aloof from the process, opposing the proposal for two referenda. The United People's Movement attended a few meetings but were not active members of the committee. They objected to the National Advisory Committee on the basis that they were being asked to support the government's agenda on political union. They also argued that an invitation to sit on the National Advisory Committee did not constitute real participation, and that they should have been involved from the start, in the establishment, composition and terms of reference of the committee.[68] While all political parties in St Vincent were listed as members of the National Advisory Committee, in reality it was only the Movement for National Unity which attempted to participate in its activities.

The National Advisory Committee was asked to educate and consult Vincentians on "the general principle of political union", to propagate its potential benefits and disadvantages, to request participating organizations to "advance the cause . . . within their own ranks" and report on their progress, and to prepare the people for a referendum "at the earliest possible date on the general principle of political union".[69] The National Advisory Committee hoped to do this by discussing the implications, advantages and disadvantages of union with National Advisory Committee members who would, in turn, initiate discussion within their organizations and provide feedback.

While there appeared to be less acrimony surrounding the National Advisory Committee, and although from all reports it had done a lot of work in trying to raise issues at the popular level, there were problems with its approach. The obvious question that arises from a committee representing different interest groups is how these various perspectives were to be reconciled, if at all, and how the issue was handled by different members. Renison Howell, vicar-general of the Roman Catholic Church in St Vincent,[70] who sat on the National Advisory Committee, claimed that all its members supported union, although not in the same way, with disagreement tending to centre around its form. He observed, however, that the fall in attendance which Venner had noted was due to some people's perception that the National Advisory Committee should have been given more power than it had as an advisory body to government. This suggested that, generally, members who favoured the initiative remained while those who did not left. The latter were not limited to the opposition parties. At least one trade union, the National Workers' Movement, withdrew its participation on similar ground.[71] Whatever the reason for the drop in number of representatives from thirty-four to fourteen,[72] it raises the question of whether the committee approach was best for conducting widespread consultation, and if it should have been the only or main approach. It would certainly suggest that, since the involvement of the opposition parties was crucial to the success of union, it was necessary to find some alternative form that would accommodate them.

Another relevant question that arises is the extent to which committee deliberations filtered to the grass roots, or remained at the level of committee discussion. There were mixed reports on how the relationship between National Advisory Committee members and the general bodies of their organizations functioned. Groups such as the National Youth Council[73] and the St Vincent Union of Teachers[74] seemed to think that their structures allowed for feedback between their members and the committee.[75] On the other hand, others claimed that their representatives on the National Advisory Committee failed to report to them or to organize forums to elicit their views.[76] Support for the committee's efficiency came from the unlikely quarter of United People's Movement leader Adrian Saunders, who asserted that his party was regularly kept informed with minutes from National Advisory Committee meetings, and advised of its decisions.[77] Therefore, it would appear that in St Vincent, despite limited participation by opposition parties and some other groupings on the National Advisory Committee, discussion was fairly widespread when compared with the other countries.

Critique of the Consultation Process

How Necessary Was a First Referendum?

Before assessing the consultation process across the Windward Islands and St Kitts–Nevis, the question of whether the first referendum was necessary or desirable must be addressed. The difficulty with an initial referendum merely to determine the level of interest in a political union was evident in the widespread reservations which people had about voting in a referendum based on general support for the ideal, with no indication of its substance and implications. Trevor Blake of the Rotaract Club of St Kitts described this process as "putting the cart before the horse".[78] The governments' rationale for holding two referenda, according to Eugenia Charles, was to avoid the expense and effort of working out a form and producing the necessary studies to back up their proposals in the absence of support for the idea.[79] They argued that support for the idea did not imply a binding commitment to anything concrete, as the second referendum would address its precise form. This format was particularly unattractive to opposition parties because, as United People's Movement leader Adrian Saunders noted, and contrary to the governments' assertion, the first referendum locked the opposition into supporting an issue without being sure of their ability later on to influence more important decisions concerning form. Certain opposition leaders questioned the need for the first referendum at all, on the basis that there was a historic commitment to unity among Eastern Caribbean people and that a negative vote could set back the process a long time. One could argue whether an opinion poll, much cheaper to conduct, would not have done as well in determining this question, although observers[80] have noted that referenda had the advantage of credibility, as people were more likely to believe them than polls.

Closely linked to this, with implications for the position of opposition parties, was how the decision to conduct the first referendum was taken. Had it been presented as a bill in parliament, as was done in St Vincent when a bill in support of the principle of political union was tabled,[81] this would have ensured the participation of opposition parties. Instead, the heads agreed among themselves to hold referenda and proceeded to seek opposition support, effectively limiting the latter's influence and raising questions of whether the governments seriously intended to involve the opposition in anything that followed.

Yea or Nay?

The other issue that can be raised in respect to the first referendum concerns the question to be put to the electorate. Although the precise wording of the questions had not been worked out, it was expected to be along the lines of a yes-or-no answer to the question of whether the voter supported the idea of an Eastern Caribbean political union.[82] The attitudes of various interest groups to political union[83] showed that while there was widespread support for the principle, opinion was divided on whether the timing was appropriate. A referendum requiring a yes-or-no vote meant that some voters would be forced to say no even though they supported the idea because of reservations, for example, on the timing. If the referendum was lost on this basis, it could create the mistaken impression, probably with irrecoverable consequences, that the majority of people were not interested in union at all. A categorical vote against union, as in the Jamaican referendum, would in effect kill the issue once and for all, with political groups in the future reluctant to raise an issue "officially" recorded as unpopular.[84] The Jamaica experience seemed to suggest that either a referendum on support for union was dangerous and counterproductive, or that the question should reflect gradations between the two extreme positions of yea and nay.

Party Politics and the Referendum

One of the main reasons governments put an issue to a referendum is to make it a national rather than party political question, so their political fate is not dependent on the outcome; were this not a concern, they would make the issue the focus of an election campaign. Interestingly, none of the OECS governments sought to make political union an electoral issue, despite the fact that most were given this opportunity since elections were held in most cases after the initiative was announced.[85] In none of these instances was the initiative a central point in the campaign. In St Vincent, the union debate was shelved until after the elections. Additionally, all opposition parties interviewed said they were not interested in making the initiative an election issue. This suggests either that they did not think it had much chance of success, or that it should be determined outside of an election. It is possible that opposition parties not in support of the initiative were afraid to denounce it lest they be classified as hostile to the idea in a situation where it might be popular, while those in support would not want to strengthen the government's hand in an election.

Once a decision is taken to hold a referendum, its purpose will be defeated if attempts are not made to remove it from a party political framework, and it is therefore critical that the process by which national debates are handled is truly nonpartisan, cutting across party loyalties. St Vincent, however, was the only country where an attempt was made to follow this form, with the other countries balking at the prospect of setting up organizations over which they might not have full control. Even so, the way in which the St Vincent committee was set up, with the terms of reference and members first chosen by the government and political groups simply invited to participate, meant that the process was bound to be less effective than if all political parties had been involved from the start as equal partners. This, no doubt, contributed to their general reluctance to participate on the committee even after some of the requested amendments were made.

The difficulty encountered by the St Vincent government in getting the committee to operate smoothly could be attributed to the failure to separate the supporters from the opponents of union. It might have been better to establish, from the outset, either two opposing camps within the committee or two separate committees. The difficulty of operating one committee whose terms of reference included "propagating the potential benefits of political union" and "advanc[ing] the cause of political union" was that persons who were reluctant to support the idea were being forced into a framework based on its acceptance. An approach with two umbrella organizations, or two subcommittees within an umbrella committee, consistently advocating for and against the proposal, is less confusing. It also allows those with reservations to participate freely. The committee, as set up in St Vincent and to a lesser extent in Grenada, could not claim to be truly nonpartisan when it was based on the principle of support for union. This meant that government ministers and members of the ruling party were not free to adopt positions based on individual conviction, and opposition parties were forced into a situation where they were either embarrassed into supporting the initiative, since they were reluctant to be seen as opposing unity, or did not participate in the debate at all.

The use of committees in the various islands allowed governments to shirk the responsibility of direct involvement in the debate and of bearing the brunt of uncomfortable questions on the implications and form of the proposed union.[86] Some members of St Lucia's independent committee attributed the decline of the debate to the absence of government input. This lack of government involvement in most of the islands leads one to suspect that governments were reluctant to confront the issue directly because they were afraid to stake their political future on it, in case it proved unpopular.

The advantage of two umbrella organizations is that it allows for advocates and detractors to be clearly identifiable, helping to deflect suspicions about government's motives. Fears of a hidden agenda are lessened among opposition politicians when they are able to sit with government and ruling party representatives on a committee opposing union. The same pertains to the people, who see the major parties represented on both committees. The focus then becomes the arguments advocated by each group. In addition, opposition parties who do not want to appear to support the government would feel free to support union as they would have a platform, not closely identified with government, from which to advocate unity. The experience throughout the Windward Islands was that members of the ruling party who opposed the initiative kept their peace and refrained from participating in the debates. In the creation of a nonpartisan atmosphere it would also be important for the anti-union elements within the government and ruling party to feel free to campaign for their position, thereby making the process seem to be nonpartisan.

The weakness of the two-committee approach, however, is that it polarizes the issue unnecessarily between those who support the initiative and those who do not, since those who support it in principle but feel the time is not right might be forced to campaign against it. Also, the formation of two committees in the absence of credible moves by government to genuinely depoliticize the issue does not necessarily guarantee a bipartisan approach, especially if all government and ruling party members are on the pro-union committee.

The challenges of mounting a truly democratic, widely based consultative process, evident in the experience of each island, could have been mitigated by governments making resources available to opposition and other groups to mount their own campaigns. A consistent and definable attempt to target each voter was absent; instead the focus was on interest groups, and a narrow range of groups, at that. This meant that large numbers of unorganized people were excluded. Charles's approach, based on government speeches to constituents, was equally inadequate, as the speeches would target the government's supporters who were most likely to attend such meetings. It was impossible to keep track of the extent to which the same people might be exposed to the message each time, or the numbers of people who, because they did not attend such constituent meetings, were not reached at all. The ability of the campaign in all islands to target each voter was highly questionable given that little written information was disseminated; this would have been the most logical way to reach voters in islands with high literacy rates.

A feature of the campaign in the Eastern Caribbean was the absence of a concrete time frame within which to conclude the debates. Had a specific time frame been set, with a date when referenda were going to be held in each country, it is doubtful that the loss of momentum and interest in the idea, evident in all the countries, would have occurred. The governments' reluctance to decide on a specific date for the first referendum suggested their unwillingness to commit themselves firmly to something that might prove unpopular and result in the loss of political power, as happened in Jamaica after the People's National Party lost the 1961 referendum.

The entire handling of the consultation process, particularly the treatment of the opposition group, SCOPE, leads one to question the governments' sincerity in making the issue truly nonpartisan. Their failure to utilize the plethora of existing subregional and regional organizations, including the OECS secretariats, also shows a series of failed opportunities for broadening the consultation and making it more meaningful.

Conclusions

By 1989 it was clear that none of the governments, with the possible exception of St Vincent, was likely to win a referendum in support of union. In St Kitts–Nevis the consultation process was conducted with little government enthusiasm and clearly produced the desired result. The government did not find popular support for the initiative because it had presented no case in support of union. In the Windward Islands, the governments' general failure to initiate nonpartisan debate meant that voting was likely to reflect party affiliation rather than support for the initiative. This derived from the failure to differentiate among those within both the ruling and opposition parties who supported or resisted the initiative. This contributed to a polarization of the initiative, compounded by the governments' reluctance to allow the consultation process to slip from their control. The main failing of the process, however, lay in the general reluctance of political leaders to go all out and back the initiative, for fear that they would lose their political power if it proved to be unpopular. They contributed to the loss in momentum by failing to establish credible structures through which to promote the initiative. Most importantly, the consultation process foundered because of the character of party politics in the Caribbean, where the government has to rule and the opposition to oppose,[87] and because of the inability of these groups to suspend their traditional hostilities and narrow political interests in pursuit of a broader goal. This tendency for issues to be politicized in the Eastern Caribbean further reduced the possibility of having a referendum where votes were cast on an understanding of the issues raised rather than as a show of party support. Political parties tended to think in terms of the next general election. This short-term approach to politics could well have implications for the readiness of either government or opposition to give up their power base by relinquishing sovereignty in the interest of regional goals.

8 Attitudes to OECS Political Union in the Leewards

Then what I had been told proved true: any federal scheme which you can
sell to Mr Bird, the others will buy.
  – Sir Arthur Lewis, *The Agony of the Eight*

This chapter establishes, primarily from interviews with representatives of
interest groups, the level of interest and support for political union in the
Leeward Islands – namely Antigua and St Kitts–Nevis, both of whose governments rejected closer union. It also examines their fears and reservations. It
focuses on four main groups: political parties (ruling and opposition), trade
unions, the private sector, and an array of social organizations. It examines how
opinions differed across groups in each island, and the extent to which these
coincided with the government's position. Finally, it compares the opinions
and attitudes to union in both islands with a view to establishing any similarities
that might account for their governments' decision not to pursue the initiative.

Antigua

The Ruling Party

The government's official response was to reject the union proposal. Two
possible reasons were suggested for this: that it would be undesirable, even
harmful to Antigua's interests; and that the people did not want it.

The first reason was reflected in Prime Minister Vere Bird's assertion that union would reintroduce a similar situation as had existed when Antigua was under colonial rule; this was supported by Senator Bradley T. Carrot's objection that Antigua's sovereignty would be restricted in a single OECS state. He put this graphically: "We don't want Mitchell to tell us 'you put a toilet here'. That is what the British Government used to do."[1] Closely linked to this perception of the danger of diminished sovereignty was the belief that the Windward Islands were proposing a specific form of union, a unitary state, which would even further reduce Antigua's scope for independent action. This concern was not new. It was the basis upon which Vere Bird had rejected unitary statehood with Trinidad and Tobago, the Windward and Leeward Islands, and Barbados. Bird had argued that "Antigua would be neglected if the local leaders were deprived of the initiative in economic and social matters".[2]

Carrot, describing himself as a "federalist",[3] argued that his government was not against a closer union, but against a "unitary state".[4] He wanted to see a federation "based upon the US style where every state has autonomy". This suggestion, that the Antiguan government was rejecting a specific form of union, a unitary state, was strengthened by the observation of the Roman Catholic archbishop, Orland Lindsay,[5] that Prime Minister Bird supported closer union "but not for what Mr Mitchell is putting forward". Carrot also intimated that employment was a "big factor" in his government's decision not to participate,[6] pointing out that already there were signs of people coming to Antigua to find jobs. While Antigua welcomed this, "up to a point", the implications of union were greater because, once there was freedom of movement, "you would not be able to stop them". He feared that people from "poorer" islands would be attracted to Antigua. Despite these reservations he declared his support for freedom of movement, but cautioned that Antigua had to "safeguard jobs" for its own people. Freedom of movement, therefore, was one of the negative consequences that Antigua could not afford.

The second reason was suggested by Lester Bird's assertion that Prime Minister Vere Bird had rejected the initiative because he felt that the government had to be able to "carry the people" with them. He was therefore responding to popular opinion which did not support Antigua's participation. Lester Bird sought to cast his government's position in a different light, of support for union but with reservations about timing. His words were, although "we are for it, we are with it . . . the timing is not propitious". He pointed to "in built" resistance to political union which reflected "an element of tribalism that existed in the Caribbean".[7] On this basis, therefore, his government believed that the integration process should be "deepened" and "broadened", upon which the need for a union would become clear. This should be facilitated by concrete measures, primarily removing the passport requirement and allowing OECS people to buy land in member countries. This stopped short of removing work permit requirements.

These different accounts of why Antigua did not participate in the initiative might reflect a difference in attitude between the older and younger generations in the ruling Antigua Labour Party, represented by Prime Minister Bird and Carrot, on the one hand, and Lester Bird on the other. Lester Bird appeared to be more sympathetic towards the initiative. For instance, he had supported an education programme, drawing on persons from the OECS secretariats, as a basis on which to ground Antigua's involvement. He also regretted that, while he had headed the move for WISA to be formalized into the OECS, Antigua felt it had to withdraw from a political union.[8] The participation of Antiguan representatives in the early union meetings would suggest that there was some interest in government circles in the initiative. If this suggestion of differences in attitudes towards the integration process is borne out, it may well have implications for Antigua's future participation.

The question remains, therefore, whether Lester Bird was right in his judgement that Antiguans were not willing to support a union in 1987, and if not, why this was so.

Opposition Parties

The official parliamentary opposition, the United National Democratic Party,[9] and the small left-wing Antigua Caribbean Liberation Movement, both supported an OECS political union, not as an end in itself, but as part of a wider Caribbean political movement.[10] They differed, however, on their preparedness to support the proposed initiative. Tim Hector,[11] leader of the Antigua Caribbean Liberation Movement, although pessimistic about the possibilities of an imminent OECS political union, supported it nevertheless, while United National Democratic Party deputy leader Baldwin Spencer was prepared to support it as an "eventuality". He argued that there was too much "haste" in pursuing the idea and that there was more scope for developing economic and functional aspects of the relationship before a union became necessary. While Spencer was more interested in political integration of the broader CARICOM region, he did not rule out the likelihood of a smaller OECS political union, conceding that this might have greater possibilities for success than the wider grouping.[12] In effect, therefore, the United National Democratic Party's position was not radically different from the government's. Both parties raised the possibility of extraregional influences propelling the initiative, but rejected this as a basis for dismissing it. Hector was particularly concerned that the unitary form Mitchell favoured would enhance US control over the area, as they would have to deal with only one government. Moreover, it was "virtually going to deny any sort of internal power to any of the states".[13]

One could conclude, therefore, that while opposition parties were not particularly hostile in principle to Antigua being part of an OECS state, the opposition United National Democratic Party was not prepared to support the proposed initiative, and the Antigua Caribbean Liberation Movement, like the government, had misgivings about a unitary state. Both parties, nevertheless, were convinced that such a union was desirable, given the difficulties Commonwealth Caribbean countries faced in surviving economically as individual units.

Trade Unions

The major trade union groupings were closely affiliated to the political parties. For instance, Baldwin Spencer was the assistant general secretary of the Antigua Workers Union, while Bradley Carrot was advisor to the Antigua Trades and Labour Union, in which he had been involved for over fifty years.[14] Their positions, therefore, tended to coincide with those of their affiliated parties. The Antigua Workers Union,[15] according to Spencer, supported the call for political union but did not agree with the "haste and the approach" adopted.[16] At the same time, however, he asserted that the Antigua Workers Union had adopted the position of the Caribbean Congress of Labour (CCL) in support of the initiative, but called for more trade-union participation. Carrot claimed that the Antigua Trades and Labour Union was also concerned about the concept of a unitary state, although he did not believe that Antiguan workers were "sufficiently knowledgeable as to what to expect from a closer union".[17] Both Spencer and Carrot, therefore, supported political union in principle, although both expressed reservations about the proposed initiative.

Carrot thought union was desirable in light of the uncertainty that a single European market in 1992 would create. As he put it, "we do not know what is going to happen to us". He supported a federation on the basis that "we feel we are one nation". This support was tempered by his perception of the "insularity" (more prevalent in other OECS countries) which needed to be broken down.

Private Sector

There was no real indication of the level of support for political union among Antigua's private sector. Peter Harker, chairman of the Council of East Caribbean Manufacturers and president of the Antigua–Barbuda Manufacturers' Association, described himself as "a regionalist by nature".[18] However, he was unable to speak about the attitudes of fellow businessmen since, according to him, union was not an issue in Antigua. Harker revealed, however, that businessmen had sought the removal of trade barriers and of labour restrictions within the OECS. They wanted to see more efforts by the OECS to break down barriers at the popular level through developing cultural ties and strengthening other non-economic areas of cooperation, before talk of union. Harker supported the idea of an OECS political union, although he agreed with his colleagues that this should come after the free movement of people, skills and capital. He supported the free movement of labour on the ground that Antigua's labour shortage was likely to make its industries uncompetitive. However, he acknowledged the existence of fears as to the implications of such a policy, in light of which he believed the government's decision to reject the initiative was practical. Because he believed the government was responding to what was feasible, rather than acting on a strong objection to unity, he did not preclude Antigua's later participation.

Harker supported unity on the basis that the OECS countries were too small and union would give them a more effective voice internationally. The benefits would therefore derive more from the international than the national sphere. While political union would not necessarily solve problems facing the Antiguan business sector it was nevertheless economically expedient, particularly if the interests of the region, rather than individual states, were considered. Harker also believed that Antiguans were not ready for a union, and was pessimistic about the possibility of union in his lifetime because of the "petty jealousy" and "insularity" he believed to exist. While he disagreed with the

Windward Islands' pursuit of a union without Antigua, he thought it might be the basis for the start of a broader union.

General Interest in Political Union

Because the Antiguan government made no attempt to solicit popular views, there was no information as to the level of interest. Assessment of popular sentiment, therefore, was based on interviewees' comments. Orland Lindsay, Anglican archbishop of the West Indies and bishop of the Eastern Caribbean and Aruba, based in Antigua, said that the various churches in Antigua supported the initiative. He himself supported union on the basis that it was necessary to solve common OECS problems and enhance their political clout at the international level. Despite this, he cautioned Antigua to be "aware of what they were going into". He did think, however, that it would be "unfortunate" if the country did not also participate in a political union of Eastern Caribbean states, in the event that this came about.[19]

Lester Bird[20] asserted that from his "grounding and sounding" in Antigua "there was strong nationalist feeling about the retention of one's sovereignty", inferring that Antiguans were not ready to relinquish sovereignty. This view was supported generally by the people interviewed. Lindsay,[21] from his interaction with his congregation, detected no "real interest on the part of the average individual" in political union, while Hector[22] stated categorically that there was "no interest at the base in any kind of union". Hector was more optimistic, however, in observing that there was no hostility either. Spencer[23] echoed this hopeful note, believing that the "average Antiguan and Caribbean person is an integrationist" and that the problem lay with the politicians. Generally, however, most felt that Antiguans' lack of interest was rooted in the absence of an education programme on the implications of union. There was general support for the view that some attempts should have been made to make Antiguans aware of the issues involved, and to allow them to decide. Lester Bird had favoured such a process in Antigua and, according to him, had asked Prime Minister Bird "to allow the consultation process to take place".[24] Spencer even believed that if an education programme were properly "channelled", Antiguans would respond in time.

Lester Bird identified, as a popular concern, the belief that Antiguans would lose their jobs to a "flood" of people from the other islands.[25] Lindsay supported this, stating that people were wary that Antigua's economic position would be undermined in a political union.[26] Bird hastened to establish that this was not his government's position. His own view was that Antigua needed to increase its population substantially, and that this increase should come from within the OECS, "where there is a greater understanding and compatibility among our people".[27] Hector charged, however, that Prime Minister Bird had gone on record saying that OECS unity would result in "the poorer territories" coming to Antigua.[28] He also charged that a government minister, speaking privately, had stated that "if we went into unity then Ms Charles and others would tell them to close down casinos which are here". Hector argued that the government had no interest in "any kind of economic integration in the Caribbean", being orientated towards the United States. He was sceptical that the ruling party, which had won its fourth consecutive election, would be interested in participating in an OECS political union.

It would appear, then, that the government was correctly assessing popular perceptions about unity. At the same time, however, its rejection of the initiative might equally have reflected its own reservations, especially in terms of the erosion of sovereignty. The general view that popular perception could have been swayed by an education campaign suggests that had the government mounted such a campaign, it might have been able to influence popular opinion.

St Kitts–Nevis

The Ruling Party

After a half-hearted attempt to solicit popular opinion, Prime Minister Kennedy Simmonds withdrew from the initiative. He justified his decision by concluding that from the report of his National Advisory Committee on OECS Closer Union,[29] St Kitts–Nevis was not ready to entertain a referendum on OECS political union. It would appear that St Kitts–Nevis was an open-and-shut-case. The government found no popular support, so declined to pursue the issue. Moreover, Simmonds stated that the decision to withdraw was also influenced by his own perception of what the people wanted.[30] He inferred that they were not ready to make the adjustments a union necessitated, noting that it would involve "give and take" and an acceptance of making sacrifices for the greater whole.

There is evidence, however, that there were other factors at play, suggesting that the government's own misgivings might have influenced its approach to the consultation process. The first possible factor was the relationship that existed between St Kitts and its federation partner, Nevis, which made Simmonds reluctant to pursue the initiative wholeheartedly. William Herbert, chairman of the National Advisory Committee and founder of the ruling People's Action Movement party, suggested that this relationship made the country more sensitive to the implications of a political union. Although St Kitts and Nevis became independent as a federation in 1983, Nevis had a strong secessionist movement and, although the government was a coalition of the People's Action Movement and the Nevis Reformation Party, the latter was still committed to secession. Its leader, Simeon Daniel, was said to have named 26 October 199031 as the date for Nevis's secession.[32] Herbert explained:

> One of the fundamental issues which is quite clear to us is if you had to go into the question of an East Caribbean union, what would happen? Would Nevis go in as an individual part of the union, or would they go in with St Kitts? This is a very problematic issue because you have to re-adjust the structure – everything we have worked so hard to create.[33]

There were two other factors that influenced the government's decision: the view that the country did not need union and the perception of a different agenda between the Leewards and the Windwards. The first was suggested by the government's official position on union, which was that while Caribbean integration was an ultimate goal, a narrower OECS political union was not a matter of urgency, given St Kitts–Nevis's relatively better economic performance over other Caribbean countries. Political union, they believed, would "flow naturally" out of greater cooperation, which could continue outside of union. The relationship between St Kitts–Nevis's economic performance and its response to the initiative was made even more explicit by Herbert, who argued that, unlike the Windward Islands which were facing problems with their banana industry, St Kitts–Nevis had no such problems. He queried: "Why create a case [for political union] when you don't need to create a case? We don't have a fundamental problem here. We don't have an issue right now."[34] He expressed "sympathy" for Mitchell's motivation in seeking a political union:

> if you live in a banana economy or in an area where you are vulnerable to the vicissitudes of nature, you do tend to look at things differently and say tomorrow

anything could happen to any of us. We have to have a balance. We have to have more strength. I think that is basically it.

Both Simmonds and Herbert dismissed the economic value of a union, arguing that a union of five hundred thousand people could not solve problems associated with small size. Herbert believed that its effects were likely to be negative since it would mean the loss of each country's individual vote in international forums which, in his perception, provided important leverage in attracting funds. For Herbert, an OECS political union was a "no-no". The idea was attractive emotionally but not economically.[35]

Finally, there was evidence to suggest that in the government's mind there was a divide between the Leeward and the Windward Islands which did not make union between the two groups desirable. This came out clearly in Herbert's statements. Like Antiguan ruling party officials, he believed that the Windward Islands already had a planned agenda for union that did not take account of the interests of the Leewards. Their approach to the initiative gave rise to allegations, from various quarters, of a *fait accompli*, intimating that the structure, form and time for the referendum had already been decided upon. This "panic[ked] a lot of people in the north Caribbean", in particular, Antigua.[36] However, even before the initiative was formally announced Herbert, from his deliberations with Mitchell, Demas and Shridath Ramphal (former Commonwealth secretary-general) had detected differences:[37] "I realised they had a very committed point of view when we up here did not have a committed point of view. They know where they want to go. Up here we do not know as yet. . . ."[38] He therefore believed that from early in the day the Windward and Leeward groupings had different perceptions on, and commitment to, the need for political union.

The Leeward Islands were also set apart from the Windwards because of what Herbert described as "the distance from the rest of the islands", which, he said, was "very fundamental up here because St Kitts–Nevis is out on a limb". The Windward Islands, on the other hand, were "almost one geographical area". The underlying differentiation between the Leeward and Windward Islands, evident in Herbert's description of the "south" and "north", was reflected in his views on how the Leewards would respond to a union of the Windward Islands: "there would be a tremendous pressure up here for Antigua, St Kitts, Montserrat, to form some kind of link up . . . almost like a defence mechanism".[39]

In summary, there were clearly other important factors influencing the St Kitts–Nevis government's decision not to participate in the initiative beyond soliciting the response of interest groups. Rather than suggesting a lack of interest in the initiative, the interviews with Herbert and Simmonds reveal a well-developed perspective on union and its likely effects on the country; one which emphasizes difference over commonality. Nor is it possible to dismiss Herbert's view as maverick and not necessarily representative. As the founder of the People's Action Movement, his views were important. To determine whether the government's position found broad support, we now examine the views of opposition parties and the various interest groups that participated on the National Advisory Committee on OECS Closer Union.

Opposition Parties

The opposition St Kitts–Nevis Labour Party supported the principle of union, but expressed reservations about the proposed initiative. Denzil Douglas,[40] leader of the opposition and of the St Kitts–Nevis Labour Party, said that his party was concerned that the governments appeared to be forcing the initiative on the people. This concern had two elements: that the initiative was occurring at the convenience of the political parties in power, and that it was externally motivated. According to Douglas, suspicion of the governments' motives was raised because the initiative was announced by Compton, who succeeded Simmonds to the chair of the OECS, which seemed to suggest that the initiative had been discussed while Simmonds was OECS chair. The party felt that, as prime minister, it was Simmonds's duty to provide his people with details, and they interpreted his failure to do this as signifying that the initiative was a response to impending elections throughout the subregion, and was therefore something the governments were using to try to maintain themselves in power. Further, Douglas's party believed that the initiative either originated with the United States, or was a response "to an agenda pressured from outside".

Despite these reservations and the fact that political union had been taken off the St Kitts–Nevis agenda, Douglas asserted that, were his party to win power, political union would be put back on the agenda if it were still being discussed by other OECS governments. In addition, in the event of a national election in St Kitts–Nevis, the opposition was prepared to make political union an issue. If, at the end of a campaign, the people supported the initiative, the party was prepared to proceed with a political union with the other OECS countries. The party's 1988 manifesto declared its "positive interest" in the initiative but "strongly" believed that the people should be consulted and given a "proper opportunity" to participate in the creation of any union.[41]

This measured approach was in sharp contrast to the tone taken by former party chairman and head of the affiliated St Kitts–Nevis Trades and Labour Union, Lee Moore,[42] in rejecting the initiative. He argued that the political climate in the OECS countries, which curtailed freedom of speech and denied opposition access to state-owned media, was not right for union. He feared that rather than enhance freedom, the initiative would restrict it. He declared: "the truth is we cannot accept the good faith of those putting forward the proposal for closer political union".

Private Sector

There appeared to be little support for a political union among the business sector. Ricky Skeritt,[43] president of the St Kitts–Nevis Chamber of Industry and Commerce, supported such a union but admitted that the business community opposed it. George Warren, secretary of the St Kitts–Nevis Manufacturers' Association, stated that the association had found "little or no enthusiasm" for the initiative.[44] The St Kitts–Nevis Jaycees[45] declared that it was not "in favour of the 'rush' " towards a unitary state without careful examination of the benefits for St Kitts–Nevis and for the OECS as a whole. Instead, the sector was more interested in strengthened functional cooperation.

The Chamber of Industry and Commerce's position reflected general thinking in the sector, which supported more initiatives geared towards bringing OECS people together, and allowing for the free movement of people, goods and capital – measures which were all possible without political union.[46] The Manufacturers' Association echoed this view, suggesting that "all the islands should show full economic and social unity before closer political union takes place".[47] The sector also had a number of reservations about possible consequences, which were largely the result of their perception that the likely form was unitary. In particular, they were worried that it would increase the cost of government, retard the development of individual states, and make the government less accessible. Skeritt[48] noted that they were satisfied with the national government's performance and, while not happy with some aspects of it, were not prepared to replace it with a regional government. The Jaycees, in particular, were worried that union might result in the reinstatement of personal income tax. They were also concerned about the "actual operation" of freedom of movement, particularly its application to "persons deemed undesirable because of political beliefs and actions".[49] Despite these reservations, Skeritt felt that the business community had not closed the door on a possible OECS political union. This was evident in their hesitance to put out a public statement on the issue, as they did not want to be "straight jacketed [*sic*]".[50] He could not detect any "real solid philosophical basis" on which they opposed union but felt the opposition was due, rather, to their perception of themselves as St Kitts–Nevis businessmen, rather than as OECS businessmen. Here he differentiated between manufacturers and other businessmen: manufacturers tended to see themselves as OECS businessmen because they understood the need for larger markets, so were more interested in aligning themselves with the regional movement, while distributors were more interested in protecting the local market from outside competition. Unfortunately, the brevity of the report on the views of manufacturers[51] did not provide information to support this observation, nor do the interviews with manufacturers support it.

The interviewees identified three factors that influenced the business community's response: the timing, the suddenness of the idea, and a distrust of the sincerity of the political leaders. Skeritt observed that St Kitts–Nevis "has been almost feverishly . . . preoccupied with its own internal reorganisation at the political and business level". The timing of the initiative, therefore, was "slightly out of phase" with this inward focus. In light of the relative ignorance about the integration process, the union proposal was unexpected. This was compounded by a lack of familiarity with political leaders from other islands, which encouraged opposition.[52] Both Skeritt[53] and the Jaycees[54] identified a lack of confidence in OECS leaders' commitment to union, Skeritt attributing this to their lack of political will to follow through on the initiative. This encouraged a perception of them as "jokers". Like Herbert, Skeritt differentiated between the "northern" Leeward Islands and the "south", noting that Antigua, St Kitts–Nevis and Montserrat were still preoccupied with economic goals and were thus more likely to view issues in terms of "bread and butter". In addition, he detected a slightly different "cultural alignment" between the two groups, with the Leewards more strongly linked with the Virgin Islands and St Maarten. They tended to look "north" rather than "south" because there were too many "outside influences", deriving from their more open, tourist-dominated economies.

In summary, therefore, the St Kitts–Nevis private sector did not support the country's participation in a political union, but neither was there developed hostility. In fact, there appeared to be support from certain quarters, which left Skeritt hopeful that a successful "sales job" for union could be done on the private sector. He himself supported an OECS political union on the basis that it made economic sense, especially in the running of the bureaucracy.

Social Groups

Women

A wide range of social groups participated on the National Advisory Committee. These included women's and youth organizations as well as a number of service groups. The three women's organizations represented, the Inter-Ministerial Council of the Ministry of Women's Affairs, the Business and Professional Women's Club, and the St Kitts Chapter of the National Secretaries Association, all preferred continued cooperation under the OECS treaty to political union. Only the Business and Professional Women's Club viewed union as "the ultimate goal" of the integration process,[55] with the Inter-Ministerial Council settling for "closer co-operation".[56] The Secretaries Association was deeply hostile to the initiative. Their rejection of it echoed Prime Minister Bird's position: "Having fought hard for, and gained, our independence, the Association's members have no wish to return to a form of 'colonialism', as would be the case under an OECS unitary state."[57] The secretaries provided the most extreme example of the tension between national and regional interests. On the assumption that they enjoyed a superior standard of living and education, they feared that union would lower their quality of life. More importantly, though, they feared they might well lose their national "identity". They were also worried that union would have negative consequences for labour, concerned that a central OECS administration would deplete the skills available nationally. They were already concerned that the East Caribbean Central Bank, based in St Kitts, employed non-Kittitians, and were "extremely apprehensive" about freedom of movement. These fears, as expressed, bordered on xenophobia.[58] To them, therefore, political union offered no obvious advantages but threatened to deprive St Kitts–Nevis of the little that it had. Contrary to this xenophobic trend, the other women's organizations supported freedom of movement within the region, although the Inter-Ministerial Council wanted work permit requirements to remain.

Youth

Like the women's organizations, the three youth organizations rejected the initiative on the grounds that there was room for increased functional cooperation. They viewed union as a longer-term goal, following a long period of education and consultation. These groups were the umbrella group of youth organizations – the St Kitts Youth Council and the Nevis Youth Council – and the Young Pamites, the youth arm of the ruling People's Action Movement party. The youth arm of the opposition Labour Party was not represented on the advisory committee. All three groups were convinced of the need for increased popular awareness about the OECS before union was broached. In particular, the St Kitts Youth Council and the Young Pamites supported the free movement of people within the OECS, although they differed on the free movement of labour. The Youth Council wanted work permit requirements abolished, while the Young Pamites wanted them retained, but with the relevant regulations standardized. Both believed that measures facilitating popular interaction among the islands were essential to a union. The St Kitts Youth Council felt that continued functionalism was necessary to demonstrate that governments could cooperate. They pointed to the withdrawal of some countries from the OECS high commissions in Britain and Canada, describing this as a negative "backdrop from which to forge political union".

It was clear that the hesitance of these groups to support the proposed initiative was related to deep-seated reservations as to its consequences, particularly for the country's sovereignty. The St Kitts Youth Council and the Young Pamites were concerned that union would mean a loss of voting rights in international organizations and loss of control over foreign affairs. In addition, the St Kitts Youth Council was worried that union, especially in a unitary form, would limit people's ability to influence political leaders. Most of the reservations voiced, however, came from the Nevis Youth Council, concerned about Nevis's position in a union, particularly as regards its relationship with St Kitts. This arose because of statements from the island's representative, Simeon Daniel, that Nevis would enter an OECS political union as an individual state. The Youth Council therefore wanted clarification on whether Nevis could in fact opt out of its federation with St Kitts to join an OECS union, and on what its relationship with St Kitts would be thereafter. They were concerned about the implications of Nevis's relatively small size in a union, particularly if proportional representation were to be adopted. This, they feared, would reduce its ability to attract financial aid and limit its political clout and bargaining powers *vis-à-vis* the other states. They were also worried about the effect of the free movement of people, given Nevis's size and "high rate of unemployment". They were concerned that pressures on employment and land, arising from an influx of OECS nationals, could result in "serious social problems" and the loss of Nevis's identity. The Youth Council shared the more general concern of whether union would allow each island to keep its system of taxation, or would lead to the introduction of a common system.

Service Groups

The other groups which presented reports to the National Advisory Committee – the Rotaract Club of St Kitts, the Lions Club, the St Kitts Christian Council and the Nevis Cooperative Credit Union Limited – all rejected the initiative in favour of continued functional cooperation. The Rotaract Club cautioned that since political union held "long term economic and social implications" it should not be rushed; the club was "unconvinced" that all possibilities for cooperation under the OECS treaty had been exhausted. The St Kitts Lions Club[59] advised the states to "use caution and hasten slowly", advocating the phased introduction of political union. The Christian Council[60] supported "unequivocally" the idea of closer union and wished to see it "vigorously pursued", but described "the idea of a political unitary state" as immature. The Nevis Cooperative Credit Union[61] wanted a "trial run" before a union was formalized, in light of the experience of "many attempts and . . . failures". The primary basis on which these groups rejected the initiative was a lack of information on specific details such as its likely form and implications. The Rotaract Club[62] conceded that there might be a case for political union, but argued that it had not been made.

Conclusions

Evidence from St Kitts–Nevis and Antigua shows that while public opinion generally accorded with that of the governments, there was no developed hostility to the principle of an OECS political union. The governments were correct in saying that there was no real or active interest in political union but, as many interviewees noted, this was based, in Antigua, on the absence of any attempt to inform the public of the implications. The same applied to St Kitts–Nevis, where only a rudimentary attempt at public education was made. The evidence suggests, therefore, that the low level of interest among the general population was above all related to the absence of any attempt to make the idea of an OECS political union attractive.

The genesis of the initiative also explains the response in St Kitts–Nevis and Antigua. The initiative came from the Windward Islands, proposed by Mitchell and supported by Compton and Blaize. Mitchell's coherent, well-thought-out statement, in which he presented not only the idea but also details of a form and system of government, discouraged the Leewards. It suggested that the Windwards not only had their own agenda for union, but had already agreed on a form, a unitary state. This presented a difficulty for St Kitts, with its problematic federation with Nevis, and for Antigua, with its strong desire for autonomy. This perception was evident in Herbert's comment that the "south" was not keen on the federal concept, and that Mitchell wanted "unitary statehood or nothing".[63] This suspicion was reinforced by Mitchell's proposed time frame, with which the Leewards were unhappy. Moreover, Compton raised the issue in his general election campaign even before it was formally mooted at the level of the OECS, and certainly before Antigua had made its own position clear. Further, Bird, not being a member of the CDU, did not share the same cosy relationship which existed among the other prime ministers. Mitchell's emphasis on their common CDU membership must have made Bird wary. In addition, the initiative took many by surprise, as there was no public buildup to it.

The second factor that shaped the Leewards' response was the Windward Islands' inability to convince them that they had much to gain from the union. While union appeared to offer a platform for addressing the urgent economic problems confronting the Windward Islands, there were no such crucial difficulties facing the Leewards. They were satisfied that their economic concerns could be addressed by the OECS mechanism as it stood. Furthermore, union was likely to have more negative consequences for the Leewards, reducing rather than enhancing their stature. Herbert put this sharply when he stated: "I don't see that you are going to take people and tell them that their national anthem and their flag that they look forward to – that they are getting for the first time after all these years of colonialism – you must just throw aside and start all over."[64]

Reservations tended to be common to both countries. The idea that a political union would necessarily benefit the participating countries was rejected in ruling-party circles, based on the conviction that a loss of voting power in the international system would reduce the political leverage necessary to secure economic gains. They also feared that union would lead to the neglect of the economic interests of Antigua and St Kitts–Nevis, as their ability to negotiate for resources as a single state would be curtailed and benefits would have to be shared among seven. This preoccupation with the consequences of political union in the international arena reflected the importance of international relations and the international community to these open econo- mies of the Leeward Islands. This reluctance to give up newly won sovereignty arises from the conviction that only an independent state could secure the needs of the population. The reluctance to relinquish sovereignty was under- standable, as Antigua had become independent only in 1981, and St Kitts– Nevis even more recently, in 1983. Since then, both had found it easy to exist as states, despite their small size, as was reflected in their relative economic prosperity. In addition, the politicians were reluctant to relinquish their new-found political power. For both the people and the politicians, the symbols of independence – a new flag, an anthem – were potent after the colonial experience.

This new-found power and national pride was also closely related to the fear that the states would be neglected if they were no longer independent countries. It contributed to a deep suspicion that the interests of each island would be neglected by an OECS state.[65] This sentiment was nowhere clearer than in the relationship between St Kitts and Nevis. Nevis was convinced that it was not benefiting from its political association with St Kitts, hence its interest in entering union as a state in its own right, with equal powers. This unique problem set St Kitts–Nevis apart, not merely from Antigua, but from other OECS countries. Consequently, it had an important bearing on the country's relationship with the OECS. The strong secessionist sentiments that existed in Nevis made the government vulnerable. The government's position was even more tenuous, since it was based on a coalition with the Nevis Reformation Party, which was openly committed to secession.

Finally, the Leewards were unconvinced that they shared sufficient cultural values with the Windwards to make union attractive. The identification of the basis for a separate relationship among the Leeward Islands was therefore an important factor influencing their attitudes. This view, which was expressed strongly by leading government figures in both countries, was that there might be a sounder basis for a Leeward Islands' grouping than a broader OECS state. It was based on the perception of distinct historical identity and political affiliation forged during the colonial period.[66] Carrot, for example, noted the cultural similarity among the Windward Islands, particularly in the French-based creole that was spoken. He thus concluded that the basis on which the British colonial power had divided the subregion into Windward and Leeward groups remained valid, and would determine how they decided to cooperate in the future.[67] Generally, this view saw a deep division between the "northern" Leewards and the "southern" Windwards, based on cultural differences and economic structure. In particular, the Leeward Islands shared more economic and cultural ties with their "northern neighbours" – Jamaica, the Bahamas, and the British and United States Virgin Islands. This suggested that although they were in the OECS, the Leeward Islands might feel a stronger cultural and economic pull towards more northerly Caribbean islands. The concept of a "north" Caribbean destiny was made explicit by Vere Bird's call for some form of union of the Leeward Islands.[68]

Despite the rejection of the initiative by Antigua and St Kitts–Nevis, however, there remained enough interest in an OECS union to suggest that the issue was not dead. People were generally willing to accept that an OECS political union remained a desirable goal for which to strive, even when they were unclear as to the concrete benefits it could offer. One of the most significant revelations arising from the interviews was the interest in both countries in more popular programmes geared towards bringing OECS people together, thus reducing insularity. It was clear that people in both islands were keen to know more about their OECS neighbours, as reflected in the widespread support for the removal of travel restrictions within the OECS and, in some cases, even for the abolition of work permit requirements. Such people-oriented activities were generally viewed as prerequisites for an OECS political union. This desire for closer contact at the popular level heralds well for the subregional integration process, even if political union is not realized.

The Windward Islands Respond to Political Union

The virtual absence of effective machinery for implementing regional decisions has become a major impediment to the progress of the integration
movement. It has generated a degree of scepticism, if not of inertia, among
important sectors in the Region. This is damaging to the credibility and
effectiveness of the regional process.

    – Time for Action: The Report of the West Indian Commission

This chapter focuses on the attitudes of leaders of important interest groups
whose opinions were likely to affect the outcome of the more limited Windward Islands' initiative. It identifies factors likely to inhibit the initiative's
progress, and establishes the extent to which there was support for the
initiative, and among which groups.

Grenada[1]

The Ruling Parties

In 1989, when these interviews were conducted, Herbert Blaize, leader of the
New National Party, was prime minister; the New National Party was
represented by the deputy prime minister and minister of foreign affairs, Ben
Jones;[2] and the National Democratic Congress, then in opposition, was
represented by its deputy leader, George Brizan. After Blaize's death and the

subsequent elections in 1990,[3] the National Democratic Congress and the National Party (a faction of the New National Party),[4] led by Ben Jones, formed the new government. This meant that Jones, the member of government interviewed in 1989, and Brizan, the leader of the opposition, were now both in the new government. Brizan was made finance and planning minister in the new government.

Blaize, despite agreeing to pursue the initiative, was not as vocal in his support as other leaders. This prompted Ben Jones to assert that while his government "[did] not talk very much" about political union, they were "just as much committed to OECS unity as any of the others".[5] Even so, the government's lukewarm response suggested less enthusiasm for the idea. Williams, who chaired the parliamentarians' committee set up to initiate debate, complained of a lack of support from many government colleagues and charged that in Grenada, as in other Windward Islands, there was political division on the issue. Politicians who did not support the initiative did not feel free to come out openly against it, as they were reluctant to go on record as opposing it.[6]

While in opposition, the National Democratic Congress[7] rejected the initiative on the basis that union was an "evolutionary" rather than an immediate prospect. It suggested that governments focus on functional cooperation and fully implementing the OECS treaty as the foundation upon which union could be built. This would facilitate union by strengthening popular confidence in the process. Brizan suggested that the National Democratic Congress's cautious position was influenced by the many failed attempts at union. He warned against a "rush" into establishing a single state[8] but left his party's options open by saying that it would reconsider its position once in power. The National Democratic Congress did just that. On forming the government, it agreed to pursue the initiative with the other governments.

Opposition Parties

Mitchell's wing of the New National Party became the parliamentary opposition after the 1990 election. The split occurred a year after the interviews and there was no indication of what Mitchell's position was on the initiative at the time of the interview. The opposition parties represented, therefore, were the rural-based Grenada United Labour Party[9] and the small left-wing Maurice Bishop Patriotic Movement.

It was clear that Eric Gairy, leader of the Grenada United Labour Party, did not support the initiative. Although he declared that his party had no position on the issue, he suggested that it did not want to "rush into" a union since the OECS was "not doing badly" at present. Gairy's disinterest was influenced by a perception that Grenada was able to exercise leverage, presumably with the United States, as a result of its "strategic geographic location" in the "traffic lane" of oil tankers,[10] and its "traumatic experience . . . with the communists".[11] He called for "more integration in practical terms", such as the removal of work permits and barriers to immigration. Gairy did not see much value in a union of the four Windward Islands, arguing that what was necessary was a closer political affiliation of CARICOM countries, beginning with "immigration, employment, and other things of common interest". He regarded the OECS itself as divisive in terms of the broader regional movement.

The Maurice Bishop Patriotic Movement,[12] formed after Maurice Bishop's death, supported the initiative, but this was conditional upon popular participation and the absence of outside involvement. Einstein Louison,[13] deputy leader of the Maurice Bishop Patriotic Movement, believed that union should be preceded by freedom of movement to allow the people of the various islands to "get to know each other". The Maurice Bishop Patriotic Movement supported political union because it believed that "only a united OECS state could . . . match [the] demands of today's world", which did not facilitate the development of small states. Union would allow OECS states to make better use of resources and strengthen their negotiating position, and would also serve to bring the people closer together and remind them that they shared the "same culture". Louison supported the Windward Islands' decision to pursue union without the Leewards as a first step towards a "united Caribbean". While he wanted an eventual union of the entire Caribbean, including the non-English-speaking countries, he did not object to a more modest grouping in the short term which would serve to satisfy people's need for an "overall identity". Although he believed the governments were pursuing union because of "stumbling blocks" they had encountered in the international community, he nevertheless noted what he described as a coalescence of right-wing parties in power, to whom union presented an opportunity to maintain political power. He was wary that the close alliance between ruling parties and the US government would result in a union that would serve US interests. He also speculated that the leaders might have been attracted to union as a means of preventing the recurrence of a Grenada-type revolution in the region. The danger lay, he felt, in ruling parties interpreting support for union as a "mandate for them . . . to stifle or liquidate left forces".

Trade Unions

In Grenada the umbrella Trade Union Council[14] discussed the initiative, concluding that union was desirable but that the initiative was being rushed. It advocated increased functional cooperation, with trade union involvement, to enhance people's appreciation of how the OECS functioned and how union would affect their lives.[15] All the unions interviewed – the Commercial and Industrial Workers' Union,[16] the Technical and Allied Workers' Union, the Seamen and Waterfront Workers' Union, and the Bank and General Workers' Union – had attended the Trade Union Council seminar which adopted a position on union. All interviewees agreed that more time should be allowed for the initiative and that it should include more popular participation. Anslem DeBourg, Commercial and Industrial Workers' Union and Trade Union Council president, argued that this was particularly important because there was an absence of popular involvement in the OECS. Bank and General Workers' Union president Derek Allard, also a member of the Trade Union Council executive, suggested 1992 as a target date for completing remaining areas of functional cooperation. Eric Pierre of the Seamen and Waterfront Workers' Union, also a member of the senate and the parliamentarians' committee, supported political union but felt that the education process had not gone far enough, and that the initiative was being rushed "a bit".[17] He also agreed with the opposition that more structures should be put in place before political union. Despite this, he was prepared to support it. The first vice-president of the Technical and Allied Workers' Union, Matthew Stephens,[18] said the union executive supported the idea, but felt that the government should have involved trade union and other organizations in the debate. He was the only leader who believed the time was right.

DeBourg[19] noted that although the Trade Union Council supported a political union, its members, sceptical of the political leaders' commitment, had concluded that the kind of union spoken of was a long way off. DeBourg believed that OECS politicians were more inclined to support union when elections were distant but were less enthusiastic when they were nearer.[20] Allard accused politicians of "gunning" for the OECS presidency and seeking a place in history, while Pierre suspected that they might be motivated by the "kudos" they would receive from achieving a union while in office. Both Allard and DeBourg believed that there were "contradictions" among the leaders in terms of their support for union. This led the Trade Union Council to question whether the incumbents were capable of "pulling off" a political union, particularly in light of the boxing plant conflict which raged between St Lucia and Dominica.[21] This, he believed, reflected a tendency for them to first seek their own interests – a view which Allard echoed. DeBourg saw increased functional cooperation as necessary to eliminate their "selfish nationalist" attitudes.

The Trade Union Council was reluctant to support the initiative because some members feared that it might weaken the trade union movement and be used in the service of US security interests, although not all trade unions shared this concern. DeBourg warned that freedom of movement and capital, which would follow from a political union, could have a "serious negative impact" on trade unions, making them less attractive to workers. This danger would be reduced if trade unions were allowed an "equal chance" to discuss the implications and to ensure that their rights and benefits would be protected by legislation. Allard claimed that workers were wary of the possibilities of "a flood of people" coming to Grenada or "a flow of Grenadians" moving out of the country towards areas where industries were allocated. Despite these reservations, both supported the free movement of labour, Allard suggesting that this be introduced before union.

Pierre[22] was not worried that union would weaken the movement, because dock workers were skilled, so were thus less likely to lose jobs to workers from other states in the union. Further, they were protected because his trade union operated a "closed shop". He maintained that there was no opposition to political union, believing that workers would support it because of the trade union movement's historical support, and the Caribbean labour movement's experience of cooperation and unity. DeBourg, like Louison of the Maurice Bishop Patriotic Movement, was suspicious that the United States would seek to control a unified subregion. His scepticism was strengthened by the Windward Islands' decision to pursue union without the Leewards – "even with two countries"[23] – which gave the impression that union was possible only at that time.

Trade union leaders tended to perceive the advantages of union as occurring in the spheres of economics and administration: avoiding duplication in administration, which was large in the small OECS countries, reducing costs, and providing a wider pool of workers.[24] Both Allard and Stephens argued that union might bring economic improvement by making available a greater level of expertise, and providing wider scope for trade, which should increase job opportunities. Nearly all had a vision of a broader pan-Caribbean movement that included the non-English-speaking countries. DeBourg argued that the entire Caribbean was "historically and geographically" the "same people with the same roots". Allard supported a wider regional state beyond the OECS countries, although he was aware that this could not happen immediately as there were many barriers to overcome. Pierre also felt that such a union was a long-term goal. They all therefore supported an OECS union as the beginning of what would expand to include the Commonwealth Caribbean, and eventually the non-English-speaking Caribbean. Pierre supported a union of the Windward Islands as a first step, with the hope that the Leeward Islands would enter. There was little interest in the actual form union should take, although Pierre preferred a unitary government to avoid the Federation's experience with a weak central government.

Private Sector

Certain sections of the private sector supported the initiative, although no official position was adopted. These included leaders of the Grenada Chamber of Industry and Commerce – President Hugh Dolland[25] and Executive Director Adrian Redhead[26] – and Auslyn Williams,[27] president of the Grenada Manufacturers' Association. All believed that their members accepted the need for union. Dolland believed that members were convinced by developments in Europe[28] and between the United States and Canada,[29] which gave the political union movement some urgency, that "it was the right direction for us to move [in]". Redhead identified an interest in increased functional cooperation, particularly in the economic sphere, from which union would develop. Redhead and Dolland agreed that the private sector was seeking mechanisms to safeguard OECS decisions, thus introducing stability to the arrangement. Williams was convinced that union would settle current problems surrounding the OECS industry allocation scheme, which the Grenada Manufacturers' Association wanted to see implemented, as well as other inter-island conflicts on economic matters. Further evidence of private sector support was provided by a newspaper article on a symposium on union, sponsored by the Grenada Chamber of Industry and Commerce, which reported that George DeBourg (another Grenada Chamber of Industry and Commerce representative), Royston Hopkin of the Grenada Hotel Association, Norris James of the commodity boards and R.O. Palmer of the Grenada Employers' Federation "all supported the idea of union, saying it would bring benefits to their various organisations".[30]

Dolland justified his support for political union on the basis that OECS countries were too small to make economic gains on their own. Union would thus create bigger markets for agriculture and manufactured goods, enhancing their competitiveness, and create more jobs, with "multiplying effects" for other areas of the private sector. It would also strengthen their bargaining power and make better use of their human resources. Union would also bring benefits for education and the judiciary.

Despite supporting union, interviewees were worried about the viability of a smaller Windward Islands' grouping. They supported it, as did Pierre, as the first step in a longer term goal which would include the Leewards.[31] Williams believed that the time was right for an OECS union.

Reservations

Because there was no education campaign and little debate on the initiative, there was little evidence of popular sentiment. Interviews indicated that there was no overt hostility, except from some sections of the trade union movement, suspicious that it was a means of keeping incumbents in power and strengthening US influence. Above all, they were worried that they would lose influence among workers, as well as the gains they had won from employers – a fear engendered by government's failure to involve them in the consultation process. The other interviewees, while not hostile, did share some of this scepticism. This arose from competition between OECS countries, evidenced in the many references to the conflict over banana boxing plants and "national" airlines. Anthony Boatswain, a member of the Grenada Manufacturers' Association, cited such conflicts as "an example of the [leaders'] hypocrisy when it comes to talk about a political union".[32]

Interviewees believed there was popular interest in union but that more details and discussions were required. A newspaper article lent support to this, declaring that the proposal found "widespread support in Grenada".[33] Only Gairy argued that there was little interest in union. Neither did there appear to be any deep-seated reservations about its possible impact, although some were identified. These included concern that land would be "lost" to people from other states and that development would flow in one direction. Williams, of the Grenada Manufacturers' Association, was worried that Grenada was being "left out" of the benefits of integration, pointing out that the country hosted no OECS institution. An interesting feature of the interviews was the absence of consensus on a specific form for union, evident in support for both a strong federal government and a unitary state.

Dominica

Opposition Parties

Neither of Dominica's two opposition parties – the Dominica Labour Party, led by Michael Douglas, who was opposition leader at the time; and the newly formed (at that time) United Workers' Party,[34] led by Edison James, which became the formal opposition after the 1990 general elections – supported the union initiative. Douglas,[35] while declaring his party's commitment to "the achievement of OECS nationhood", refused to join Eugenia Charles on a common platform in support of union. James[36] dismissed union as unnecessary, given the success of functional cooperation. Both parties, however, said they would be willing to consider the initiative once in power. James was prepared to consider it before deciding whether or not to change his position, whereas Douglas was committed to pursuing it. James was wary of political union because of the region's history of failed experiences. His reluctance was further strengthened by the Leewards' decision not to participate.

The Dominica Labour Party's refusal to support the initiative was not the result of lack of interest in union. On the contrary, as Douglas was careful to point out, the Dominica Labour Party was the only party in Dominica to include the "struggle for the achievement of Caribbean nationhood" as a goal in its constitution.[37] Rather, its decision was based on a deep suspicion that the initiative was merely a ruse to keep incumbents in power and marginalize opposition parties. This distrust was fuelled by Douglas's interpretation of a "confidential" paper[38] from Mitchell to the other leaders that suggested that their membership in the CDU gave them the opportunity to write a common OECS constitution.[39] He particularly distrusted the motives of Charles's ruling Dominica Freedom Party because of the poor relationship that existed between the parties.[40] James, likewise, was suspicious that the initiative was a strategy designed to keep incumbents in office. He stated:

> It appeared as though the Heads had their own little club which they wanted to maintain. When this is taken against the reluctance to put out a proposal on the union and the form it will take, the advantages it is expected would be derived, you wonder whether it is not simply a reflection of the desire of people who have developed a good relationship, to stay together.

Douglas was also suspicious that the initiative was being propelled by "forces from outside of the region", namely the United States, United Kingdom and Canada, who would find it "more convenient . . . in terms of aid" to deal with a single country. Moreover, the United States' interest in political union was influenced by security concerns and the desire to secure its "frontiers". Nevertheless, he conceded that such extraregional influence was not necessarily negative since it was "coincidental with the best interests of the Caribbean people". Douglas explained that he was reluctant to support the initiative because there was no guarantee that it would address problems, particularly that of high unemployment. Instead, it might mean simply the addition of more bureaucracy with few attendant benefits. He wanted assurances that political union would result in "a real nation in substance" rather than "just . . . another flag [being] raised". Despite these reservations, Douglas rejected the argument that continued and deeper functional cooperation was adequate to address the islands' problems, since the success of functional cooperation was limited by the absence of measures to bind leaders to their commitments. Douglas, in rejecting the initiative, explained that his party's position was "tactical", but "without doing damage to the principle".[41] James did not see any particular advantage from union, arguing that because of the country's small size, union, especially without the Leewards, could not make a difference to its economic fortune.

The Dominica Labour Party's support for the principle of union was premised on a view that political integration, including the non-English-speaking Caribbean, was a necessary prerequisite for the "total liberation, freedom and development of the Caribbean people", and to create economies of scale. Douglas admitted, however, that this was not likely to be a short- or even medium-term objective; therefore, like many others, he saw an OECS union as "an essential first step" towards this greater goal. Because of the many differences that still existed among OECS states, Douglas supported a loose form of federation as having the most potential for success, despite the likelihood of this enlarging the bureaucracy.

Trade Unions

Trade unionists were generally sceptical of and expressed reservations about the initiative. Louis Benoit[42] and Heric Augustus,[43] leaders of the largest union, the Waterfront and Allied Workers' Union,[44] and Rawlings Jemmott[45] of the National Workers' Union[46] were against it, preferring a broader union of the Commonwealth Caribbean. Jemmott, in particular, viewed the initiative as a means of "dividing the wider Caribbean".[47] Despite their reservations, Benoit and Jemmott did not reject the proposed union out of hand. Bernard Nicholas, the leader of the oldest union – the Dominica Trade Union,[48] whose members came largely from the agricultural sector – expressed some support. He said his union favoured deepening and strengthening "existing functional cooperation", and therefore viewed union as a deepening of what already existed. He supported it because he believed that OECS countries could not survive "the rigours of 1992".[49] He felt that an OECS union should be easy because the countries already had much in common. Despite this expressed support for union, however, Nicholas also had reservations.[50]

Generally, reservations derived from distrust of OECS political leaders. Jemmott, in particular, questioned their commitment in light of the evidence of inter-island competition,[51] and of the difficulties which OECS nationals faced in securing work permits in Dominica, or which certain groups encountered in attempting to enter the country.[52] These barriers, he noted, were erected not by OECS people but by their governments. He argued that unless such restrictions were removed OECS union was not possible. Benoit was equally sceptical about the leaders' commitment, saying he did not trust them.[53] Nicholas accused them of "in one way or another, subvert[ing] the rights of their nationals", and of victimizing workers, particularly those who did not support the ruling party. Furthermore, he was suspicious of their involvement in the CDU, claiming that it was a means of "keeping out what they call left wing elements".

Trade unionists were also concerned about the security implications of a union. Jemmott[54] was suspicious that it would facilitate American militarization, and was deeply hostile to the prospect of US involvement. He feared that a common security force would function "to protect the US from drugs [and] kill our own people with American guns", and charged that security forces in the OECS[55] were trained to "kill their own people". OECS countries' concern with security, he believed, was "just a smoke screen to secure the US dollar". He was suspicious of US interest in regional security,[56] declaring that their aim was "to crack down on marijuana . . . so as to bring in their crack into the region". Jemmott was also suspicious that union would make it easier to devalue the Eastern Caribbean currency.[57] While declining to say that the United States was encouraging OECS countries to unite politically, Benoit felt that both US and UK governments would prefer a "Charles government" which would prove easier to control than the opposition parties.

Both Augustus and Benoit were worried that union might hold negative consequences for Dominican workers, limiting their scope for independent action. Benoit feared that Dominican workers taking industrial action could either be replaced by workers from another state, or repressed by police forces from outside Dominica. He called for increased inter-island travel, facilitated by cheaper airfares and hotel rates, as a means of increasing awareness of the OECS among port workers whom, he believed, did not even know what the OECS was. Nicholas believed that workers supported union but acknowledged that there were reservations, which he attributed to the failure of the Federation.

Generally, trade unionists seemed unsure of what concrete benefits political union offered. Benoit accepted that it might enhance employment opportunities, but worried that it would lead to increased taxation and reduce trade union strength, while Jemmott was wary that it would be used to diminish benefits.[58] Augustus was more optimistic that union could strengthen the movement, but most trade unionists feared that union would result in jobs being lost. Nicholas's own reservations related more to the need for "checks and balances" in a new state to curb the power of the leader and to ensure autonomy for individual countries. He called for the removal of restrictions prohibiting the free movement of OECS people and inhibiting entrepreneurs from operating freely throughout the OECS; he believed such a change would result in a wider market and increased job security.

Private Sector

There appeared to be some private-sector support for the initiative, although the sector had adopted no formal position. Francis Emmanuel,[59] president of the Employers' Federation, and Ninian Marie,[60] chairman of the manufacturing subcommittee of the Dominica Association of Industry and Commerce, both supported the idea and believed there was broad support for it. Emmanuel argued that it was desirable from the standpoint of widening the market and permitting the free movement of labour. Marie believed that union would benefit the manufacturing sector, particularly by increasing the level of skills available and widening the arena for private-sector operation, specifically in terms of the opportunity it provided them to buy land in member states. Marie, convinced that OECS countries were too small to exist separately, also supported union on the basis that it would enhance their effectiveness, enabling them to "command a lot more respect". Emmanuel supported union in the hope that it might help to diffuse "the political partisan-type island politics" that existed,[61] and increase efficiency since the countries were too small to sustain existing bureaucratic structures. While supporting a political union of the OECS, however, Emmanuel preferred to see a broader Caribbean union.

Social Groups

Two representatives of nongovernmental organizations were interviewed: Neva Edwards, president of the National Council of Women[62] and managing director of the Roman Catholic Church's social centre, and Joey Peltier, a member of the Small Projects Assistance Team.[63] These groups all participated in or held workshops discussing union. Edwards[64] said that while women generally supported the initiative, believing it to be the only alternative for OECS countries, they cautioned against union being "rushed into" without widespread discussion. Edwards herself shared these misgivings, arguing that the process should be gradual to avoid the fate of the West Indies Federation. She felt that the process should be based on increasing cooperation, leaving "little left to be done" in the end to form a union. Although Edwards was not sure that a union of the Windward Islands was viable, and wanted increased efforts to involve the Leewards, nevertheless she did not want the reluctance of the Leewards to hinder a Windward Islands' union.

Peltier supported the initiative and believed that there was general support for it, although not without reservations.[65] He believed that it was influenced by, among other things, pressure from "conservative industrial democracies, particularly the US, Germany, and Britain", "fed up" with dealing with several small countries. From the US perspective, in particular, union would strengthen conservative governments, thus ensuring "a CDU government in power", while Windward Islands' leaders were seeking to ensure their own political survival. Peltier suggested that internal security concerns, arising from Bishop's killing which would have reinforced feelings of vulnerability, might also have influenced the call for a political union. The RSS and political union were means of repelling "pressures" from mercenaries or "the left". Edwards, on the other hand, rejected the idea that the leaders could have been motivated by security concerns or outside pressure.

Reservations

There appeared to be broad support, despite deep reservations, for Dominica's participation in a union. Most interviewees agreed that in a referendum, despite the limited education programme, Dominicans would vote in support of political union, although they disagreed on the reasons for this. Nicholas, of the Dominica Trade Union, felt that governments would formulate their questions in such a way as to get the desired result, while Jemmott, of the National Workers' Union, believed that workers, having voted for a political party, would support whatever it did. Douglas believed that the vote would be divided along party lines and would therefore amount to a vote of confidence in the government. He admitted, though, that the idea held a certain emotional excitement for young people who, with the introduction of free movement, would be able to leave Dominica and seek jobs elsewhere.[66] Benoit of the Waterfront and Allied Workers' Union was highly sceptical about union's consequences for workers, but was prepared to support it in a referendum.

Despite the absence of pronounced hostility, Dominicans had deep reservations about the proposed union. There was widespread concern, related to the failure of the West Indies Federation, that the initiative might be "rushed" before its full implications were understood. They believed that if the initiative were properly thought out and its implications fully known, a union would have a greater chance of survival. This caution about the pace of union, however, reflected less a reluctance to enter a union than a manifestation of how little people knew of the likely consequences. As Ninian Marie put it, the "man in the street" was uncertain about the benefits of union.[67] There were echoes of the Federation in the concerns about freedom of movement which

Marie[68] and Attorney-General Brian Alleyne[69] identified, and in the anxiety that Dominicans would lose jobs to other OECS nationals. It is worth noting, however, that interviewees did not identify this as a major concern.

A more serious reservation, particularly among farmers, was that Dominican land would be bought by other OECS nationals.[70] There was also a general concern that Dominica's problems would be less important in a political union and its people would be neglected. Both Charles and Edwards detected a concern among Dominicans that they would not have their ministers and prime minister at "their beck and call", as well as a reluctance to give up national symbols, such as passports, and a fear of losing national identity. Peltier[71] noted that Dominicans were concerned about whether a union would enhance or diminish their rights. He also identified some scepticism about the governments' commitment, arising from intergovernment wrangling and their treatment of OECS nationals.

St Lucia

Opposition Parties

The position of the St Lucia Labour Party on union appeared contradictory: at first, the party adamantly refused to support the initiative, but in 1989 its position had shifted to support for a union by 1993. Initially, when the initiative was mooted, St Lucia Labour Party leader Julian Hunte rejected it as not being a priority because there were "too many problems to be resolved at home first",[72] despite his party's strong commitment to close cooperation "with OECS and CARICOM" member countries.[73] He acknowledged that one could identify a "general consensus . . . in any Caribbean territory" on the need for "some form of unity", but said that the question surrounded how "we go about it and . . . the conditions precedent".[74] He reiterated this position a year later,[75] but this time presented his party's reticence as fear that an ill-timed initiative would set back chances for a union.[76] His party therefore supported union, preceded by deepened functional cooperation, without a set time frame, but would "have nothing to do with" the present initiative.[77] Peter Josie, deputy leader of the St Lucia Labour Party, was more unyielding, though less ambiguous. He emphatically stated that his party, for as long as he remained a member, would "have no dealings whatsoever, with a political federation of the OECS".[78] St Lucians, he argued, had not "even exhausted [their] own independence". This statement went beyond suggesting reservations about the initiative, to an apparent rejection of the principle of union itself.[79]

Moreover, Hunte rejected the justifications for union advanced by its supporters,[80] arguing that savings from combined foreign representation – already an objective of the OECS treaty – could occur outside of union, while union could result in increased spending and additional bureaucracy. He dismissed the argument that union would make it less difficult for OECS countries to secure loans from international bodies, arguing that, while it might enable them to attract larger loans, it might also result in a larger debt burden. Hunte challenged the government to produce a "white paper" on union, detailing how it would address popular reservations such as safeguarding jobs and land, and what would happen to people, such as policemen, who were displaced when services were combined.

A later statement by Hunte in July 1989[81] seemed to suggest that the St Lucia Labour Party's position on political union, especially whether or not a time frame could be put on union, had been greatly modified. He reiterated the St Lucia Labour Party's commitment to the establishment of a single Caribbean nation and condemned the "indecent haste and secrecy" as well as the absence of "specific proposals" on the form of union. He presented his own proposal for a "realistic timetable for unification", which would allow for union without "entrenching the position of any current heads of government". The St Lucia Labour Party proposal called for the fulfilment of the "spirit and letter of the OECS Treaty", which required harmonizing legislation in member countries on a long list of issues including freedom of movement and citizenship, before any "formal integration of our several people". The St Lucia Labour Party also called for the establishment of a "non-partisan Integration Commission" in each country by 1 August 1989, and set a target date of 1 January 1993 for the "political unification" of the OECS.

This detailed and specific time frame for political union as early as 1993, while the party had rejected the current initiative, suggested that the St Lucia Labour Party was hostile less to the idea of union itself than to those initiating it.[82] The St Lucia Labour Party's position that the OECS treaty should be fulfilled before political union was even considered suggested a long-term process, whereas the target date of 1993 suggested union in the short term. Even while saying that work should begin on the areas of functional cooperation outlined, the proposal did not require work in this area to be completed before a union was considered. Instead, it provided a plan for union alongside which progress would be made on fully implementing the treaty.

The seeming contradiction in the St Lucia Labour Party's position on union was probably related to its suspicions of an external motivation and its hostility towards the ruling parties. Hunte described the initiative as "a scheme hatched somewhere in North America", as reflected in the "undue haste" with which it was being pursued.[83] He made a connection between the "external" influence and the CDU involvement of many of the governing parties.[84] The coincidence of right-wing governments grouped in the CDU gave these external forces the opportunity to forge a union, thus making their job easier by creating one government, rather than several, with which to deal.[85] The St Lucia Labour Party saw the initiative as a means of maintaining the present pro-United States ideological thrust of the region. It was designed "to catch the opposition completely off guard and to perpetuate the right wing conservative system currently enjoyed by the region from Jamaica, all the way down, because they are all like-minded, as Mitchell said".[86] By supporting political union, therefore, the leaders were simply looking after their own partisan interests. The observation of Ralph Gonsalves, leader of the left-wing Movement for National Unity in St Vincent, was probably more to the point. He suggested that opposition parties were revising the timetable for political union to suit their own political agenda.[87] In Hunte's case, he had a strong chance, judging from his showing in the 1986 elections, to win the subsequent general elections which were due before 1993. Moreover, in his initial response to the initiative, he had demanded that general elections be treated as part of the process of education and consultation.

The left-wing Progressive Labour Party unequivocally supported the union initiative, viewing it as an initial step towards wider Caribbean integration, including the non-English-speaking Caribbean.[88] Its leader, George Odlum, even advised people to "say yes" in a referendum on the principle of a union.[89] Nevertheless, Odlum expressed the now typical suspicion that the ruling parties were interested in marginalizing the opposition, which would be achieved "by ... CDU manipulation" of the election process, in order to secure the geopolitical interests of the United States in Caribbean politics. Odlum believed that the Americans were initially behind the idea of an OECS political union. This, he said, was suggested by Mitchell's account of how the initiative started: "Mitchell denies that vehemently but even the way he gives his account – meeting them and the meeting of the IMF and the World Bank, and at a breakfast meeting, he mentions this – he saw the need for the islands to come together and mentions that to them."[90]

Odlum believed that there was a legitimate case for OECS union, which turned upon the implications of the 1992 Single Europe Act and other international factors, the inability to achieve competitiveness due to the small size of national markets, but above all, the cultural strengthening of the region.[91] Odlum wanted to see a "strong central government", although he was prepared to concede that OECS countries might not be ready for this.

Trade Unions

It is difficult from the two interviews with union representatives to make conclusive comments about the movement's position on political union. The unions represented were the Seamen and Waterfront and General Workers' Trade Union and the Civil Service Association. The Seamen and Waterfront and General Workers' Trade Union and the St Lucia Workers Union, at a conference held by the CCL, supported the initiative.[92] Despite this pledge of support, the issue did not seem to particularly concern the Seamen and Waterfront and General Workers' Trade Union. According to its president, Hilford Deterville,[93] the union was unlikely to "contradict the position held by the CCL on matters like these", but was also unlikely to make an individual statement since the issue did not have a direct impact on the union. Deterville himself appeared to support the principle,[94] although he believed that the more pertinent issue was the type of structure envisaged by leaders. He appeared sceptical of the initiative's chances of success, saying that it was raised because politicians had "their games to play".[95] Civil Service Association president David Demacque[96] said that the initiative had been discussed in an "informal manner" within the executive and with other unions. These unions, such as the St Lucia Workers Union and the Teachers Union, represented workers in other branches of the civil service. The Civil Service Association, however, had not taken a position on whether to support the initiative, because of the lack of details and their consequent uncertainty about its implications.

Both Demacque and Deterville identified reservations about the initiative. The Civil Service Association suspected that union would negatively affect its workers since it might result in a trimming of the bureaucracy,[97] concluding that "while union may have its advantages, it might probably dig the graves for our own members, and it is for this reason we have not taken a clear cut position on the issue". Demacque did point out, though, that the union's concerns might not necessarily have been shared by its workers. Support for union, he believed, would be closely linked to political support. He acknowledged that, despite problems facing the service, a large percentage of civil servants supported the government. While Deterville did not believe that OECS people would object to union, he believed that they would have reservations about the consequences of other nationals coming to their islands. Such reservations, he felt, had been "fuelled by some politician", because people generally did not have a problem "talking to OECS people".

Both Deterville and Demacque were sceptical about the government's motivation for and commitment to seeking union. Deterville observed that Compton "probably feels that he is too big a fish to be swimming in that little pond and that is a political way of saying it",[98] while Demacque believed that Compton's support had more to do with his ego than the conviction of union's advantages for the "advancement of grass roots people". Deterville believed that local "technocrats" might have played a key role in propelling the initiative, and observed that they had more "zeal" for it than did the politicians. Likewise, Demacque was not convinced that the government was seriously committed to the initiative. He pointed to the absence of an information campaign and pronouncements in support of union from government ministers and parliamentarians, which he interpreted as a lack of clarity about how a union would function. Demacque, like many others, was suspicious that the United States might be behind the initiative, as a single government would guarantee them tighter control over OECS countries. The governments, he believed, would go along with this because of their political orientation. Furthermore, union would strengthen the RSS, since it would make it impossible for any island to withdraw. While he supported the free movement of labour, Deterville was not sure what benefits workers would derive from a political union.

Despite the union's reservations, Demacque himself supported "integration in its total form" as the answer to many of the region's problems. He believed that it was meaningful to strive for OECS political union since it would increase their resource base, but that a union with the larger territories was necessary to bring greater advantages.

Private Sector

Interviews with representatives from the private sector suggested that, as in Grenada, they had not discussed the union proposal formally, and so had no official position. Interviewees representing the St Lucian business community were Craig Barnard, president of the St Lucia Hoteliers Association, and A.F. Valmont and Farrel Charles, two retailers and distributors. The response was mixed, although most supported the initiative. Barnard[99] supported it, despite the absence of the Leewards, and believed that hoteliers would welcome it. Only Valmont was more reserved in his support, describing it as a "good thing", but calling for further "economic unification".[100] Charles[101] was an ardent supporter of the initiative and was a member of the St Lucia Independent Committee for OECS Political Unity. Geoffrey Devaux, president of the Chamber of Commerce, also supported the initiative,[102] but disapproved of a referendum on support for the principle, insisting that it was "procrastination" since "we all want unity". Instead, the question which OECS countries should be asking was what form that unity should take.

Barnard supported union on the basis that it would strengthen the Windward Islands since they would be cooperating in more areas. It would allow hoteliers to broaden their field of operation into the other territories, spread risks more evenly and ultimately strengthen the St Lucia Hoteliers Association. It would thus address the problem of small internal markets which inhibited the sector, particularly in marketing, where the efforts of individual countries were minimal.

Charles was active in promoting the initiative among St Lucians. Like Barnard, he argued that OECS countries could not continue to exist separately and be viable, particularly in light of the formation of larger economic groupings such as the European Community. He argued that union was also necessary to meet the aspirations of OECS nationals, since no island could satisfy these "by encasing them in a couple of square miles". Charles also argued for union on the ground of political stability, saying that small states were liable to have dictators or "people who could cause the instability we see in Grenada and attempts in other islands". A larger unit would "dilute" the effects of irresponsible political behaviour in any one island. He pointed to the advantages already achieved from regional endeavour, such as the strong Eastern Caribbean dollar. Valmont supported free movement of people on the ground that it would increase the labour supply available to the private sector.

The interviewees, except for Valmont, had no reservations about the initiative or about the motivations of the political leaders. Valmont, however, questioned their sincerity, noting that they still viewed their islands as "separate entities", as reflected in inter-island disputes. This gave the impression that "when one [political leader] wanted to do something he [was] not going to be mindful of the others and how it [was] going to affect the whole". He questioned: "Supposing [*sic*] Miss Charles decided that she is going to do something for Dominica and the others don't agree, what can you do to stop her doing it[?] Are you going to put the SSU [Special Services Unit][103] on her?"

Charles said that the Independent Committee was hoping for a broader union, beginning with the OECS countries, followed by Barbados and then the wider Caribbean community. He "ultimately" wanted to see a union extending to embrace the non-English-speaking Caribbean countries, although he admitted that this would be difficult because of the plurality of political systems which existed. Valmont preferred a unitary state in the event of a political union.

Other Groups

St Lucia Banana Growers' Association

Banana growers, most likely to be immediately affected from the fallout of a single European market, had not discussed political union, nor had the government used the St Lucia Banana Growers' Association to raise the issue. Gregory Downs,[104] president of the St Lucia Banana Growers' Association,[105] the umbrella organization representing farmers, thought that the position of banana growers on political union would vary. He could not say whether farmers made a link between the political union initiative and the problems the industry would face after 1992, as he himself did not see any concrete benefit to banana growers from the proposed union. He pointed out that the Windward Islands Banana Association[106] was already bringing the benefits which could be derived from the islands working together. A political union with the Leewards would not contribute to the interest of banana growers, in his opinion, since the Leewards "did not know anything about bananas".

Despite not perceiving any concrete benefits, Downs nevertheless supported an OECS union because, according to him, "it makes the voting process more exciting. Somebody, say from Antigua, would have to come down here and convince us so the guys down here won't just sit around and say . . . vote for me because I am from Castries".[107] It would appear that, certainly at the management level, there was no conscious connection made between the gloom hanging over the industry and the political union initiative. As Downs's observation suggested, a regional approach already underpinned the industry, so the benefits of a formal political union remained unclear.

National Youth Council

The umbrella youth organization, the National Youth Council,[108] did not adopt a formal position on the initiative, although it was discussed at the district level. These discussions sought clarity on issues and aired young people's perspectives on union. There was some hostility within the National Youth Council towards the government, which affected their openness to the initiative; this was aggravated by Compton's failure to speak to them on the issue, which they interpreted as reflecting government's neglect of youth. It is not surprising, therefore, that much of the discussion reflected anxiety as to the consequences of union, although Mario Michel, president of the National Youth Council, pointed out that there was no consensus either for or against union. He was supported in this by a report on a forum held by the Progressive Labour Party's youth arm; the report noted that from the discussions it "was clear that the young people had no firm position on OECS unity, since more information was needed on the matter".[109] Generally, they were unclear as to how they would benefit, especially in the realm of employment, their primary concern: would union present greater opportunities for employment, or exacerbate existing problems with an influx of people from other islands? They were also suspicious about the initiative's timing and the motivations of those proposing it. Michel suggested that these concerns were common throughout the OECS.

Michel was convinced that young people would be unwilling to vote in a referendum in light of these reservations without details of what was "in store" for them. He believed that, in light of the animosity which existed between the opposition and the government, a referendum would be a test of political strength, but that if those behind the initiative would clarify their own concepts and meet with other mass organizations, a referendum could get "a pretty resounding affirmative answer". Michel described himself as an "unapologetic regionalist [who] would support almost anything that seeks to bring together the countries of the Caribbean".

St Vincent

Opposition Parties

All opposition parties in St Vincent supported the principle of a political union, but had reservations about the conduct, specifically the time frame, of the proposed initiative, resulting in varying degrees of hostility. The opposition St Vincent Labour Party[110] and the small left-wing United People's Movement[111] worried that the initiative was rushed, and believed that it should be pursued more slowly.[112] United People's Movement leader Adrian Saunders argued that because union had serious implications for the sovereignty of newly independent OECS countries, it required a longer time period with more specific proposals on how it should work. It should therefore be a gradual process, beginning with an attempt to fully implement all areas of the OECS treaty before "altering political and constitutional structures", as "achieving these goals would touch people" and increase their willingness to support a union. The St Vincent Labour Party was particularly hostile, rejecting the initiative on the grounds that it sought to entrench the incumbents and their ideological bent. It did not reflect a "genuine desire to unite the people", nor did it allow for their "fullest participation".[113] The left-wing Movement for National Unity, led by Ralph Gonsalves, was the only party that supported the initiative without rejecting the time frame, although Gonsalves[114] warned that the party did not support "Mitchell's agenda". Gonsalves objected to the "process" by which union was being advanced, on the basis that it excluded any real participation, and to Mitchell's proposed constitution and "economic security programme", which he interpreted as an attempt at regionalizing the IMF programme of structural adjustment.

Both Saunders and Gonsalves were suspicious of the motivations behind the initiative, linking it to the "security agenda" of the ruling parties.[115] Saunders believed that they perceived union as presenting "a more reliable guarantee against the communists and . . . against subversion", while Gonsalves felt that they saw union as a device for preserving US hegemony over the OECS "security apparatus", and as a "mechanism through which they can make the sub-region safe for democracy, US-style, and prevent something like Grenada happening". Saunders's United People's Movement was also critical of the OECS and what it viewed as its aloofness from its nationals, suggesting that it might be "degenerating into a regional right-wing party coalition".[116]

Both the St Vincent Labour Party and the Movement for National Unity supported a wider Caribbean union, but were prepared to accept an OECS union as a first step. Gonsalves supported a narrower Windward Islands' union in the absence of the Leewards. A Caribbean union, he believed, offered the most "viable form of socio-economic development" for the region given the small size, particularly of OECS countries, and the financial difficulties of supporting separate administrations. It would reduce these costs, create greater economies of scale and a larger market, enhance the quality of international representation, and increase the spread of territorial waters, giving them a significance beyond size and population. Gonsalves, noting the imminent creation of a single market in Europe and a free-trade arrangement between Canada, the United States and Mexico, argued that the countries' development problems required them to move beyond functional cooperation to a "central authority".[117] He warned of "economic turmoil" if OECS countries did not become economically viable.

Trade Unions

In St Vincent three union representatives were interviewed: Colin Williams of the Commercial and Technical and Allied Workers' Union,[118] Fitzroy Jones of the St Vincent Union of Teachers[119] – two of the largest unions – and Noel Jackson of the National Workers' Movement – considered the most active union.[120] All three accepted the need for an OECS union, but only the Commercial, Technical and Allied Workers' Union and St Vincent Union of Teachers supported the proposed initiative, with the National Workers' Movement refusing to support "any political union under the present administration", despite Jackson's observation that OECS countries were "doomed without a union". He viewed the initiative as an instrument of "convenience" rather than a genuine attempt to bring together the peoples of the region; he advocated instead "economic, cultural and social" integration.[121] His antipathy stemmed from conflictual relations between the government and his union. He accused the government of pursuing "anti-worker" policies, so was not convinced that union would benefit workers.[122] Both Williams[123] and Jones[124] pointed to their unions' historical support for Caribbean union, Jones noting that it was a goal enshrined in the constitution of the St Vincent Union of Teachers. The St Vincent Union of Teachers, therefore, supported a union of the Windward or Leeward Islands, although it wanted to see this eventually extend beyond OECS countries. Jackson[125] supported a broader union involving Barbados, Jamaica and Guyana. He recognized that there was "a tremendous need for economic integration", but felt that the process should involve more concrete dialogue and trade-union participation. Williams, however, was critical that despite his union's expressed support, a political union was not viewed as a priority by the Commercial, Technical and Allied Workers' Union or as something that it should actively pursue, although a representative did sit on the National Advisory Committee. The St Vincent Union of Teachers also sat on the National Advisory Committee, but the National Workers' Movement refused to participate.

The trade unionists believed that there was support for the initiative among workers, but that a vote in a referendum would depend on the extent to which the initiative was marketed by the governments, as well as the support it had from political parties. Jones, in particular, believed that people would vote as if on a political issue. However, despite this perception of support for union, they noted some reservations towards the proposal, particularly concerning migration, which workers feared would result in a "flood" of other OECS nationals into the country. The trade unionists had their own reservations. Williams disagreed with Mitchell's attitude that there was no room for people with reservations about supporting the initiative,[126] which suggested that if union were not formed then, it would never happen again. Although Williams supported a political union, he could not say how he would vote in a referendum. Jones criticized the consultation process, noting that there needed to be more community-based discussions. All were suspicious of the governments' motivations in pursuing the initiative. Jones and Jackson, in particular, worried that it coincided with US security concerns with avoiding a repetition of the Grenada revolution.[127] Jackson suspected that its purpose was to keep incumbents in power.

Jackson and Jones (and, according to Jones, the St Vincent Union of Teachers and a number of other unions) accepted that the region's economic problems, particularly the impending banana crisis, justified political union. Although Jones did not believe that union would necessarily eliminate these problems, he predicted that they would worsen outside of a union. Despite this, he advanced the criticism that the main motives for the initiative appeared to be economic, rather than stemming from any real concern for the people. Trade unionists further supported union as a means of strengthening the labour movement in the face of "pressures" from government and the private sector, arising from governments' implementation of IMF programmes which affected workers negatively. Jones said that the St Vincent Union of Teachers viewed union as the only means for removing travel restrictions within the OECS – a problem commonly experienced by its teachers.

Private Sector

The St Vincent Chamber of Industry and Commerce publicly supported the initiative in a resolution endorsing it and pledging to cooperate with the National Advisory Committee and "those other private sector organisations associated with it". The chamber was satisfied that "net benefits" would accrue to participating states, particularly in regard to trade, industry and commerce.[128] The chamber's acting manager, Noel Venner,[129] also secretary of the National Advisory Committee, said that although members expressed support there were reservations, especially about the form it would take.

Social Groups

The initiative received mixed responses from social groups in St Vincent. The representatives of three such groups were interviewed: the St Vincent National Youth Council,[130] the umbrella organization of youth groups in St Vincent; the Committee for the Development of Women; and the Roman Catholic Church. The Roman Catholic Church, as well as the broad-based National Council of Women,[131] of which the Committee for the Development of Women was an affiliate, both supported the initiative, but the youth council and the Committee for the Development of Women reserved their support. Interestingly, the umbrella groups which brought these various organizations together at the regional level generally supported the initiative, but their affiliates in St Vincent adopted a more cautious approach. For instance, a meeting of regional youth groups supported the proposal in principle,[132] but at the local level, the St Vincent youth council did not support the initiative, because, according to Geoffrey Samuels,[133] the administrative coordinator, members were unclear about the "kind of unification" governments had in mind. Likewise, although the umbrella National Council of Women (which also sat on the National Advisory Committee) supported the initiative, the Committee for the Development of Women, according to coordinator Nelcia Robinson,[134] was reluctant to adopt this position, preferring a strengthening of OECS structures first. Again, while the broad regional groupings of mainstream churches supported the initiative, the local St Vincent church wanted more concrete action. According to Father Renison Howell,[135] vicar-general of the Roman Catholic Church of St Vincent and the Grenadines, both the Antilles Episcopal Conference[136] (which coordinated the Catholic church in the region) and the Caribbean Conference of Churches supported the initiative. However, the local Christian Council, which grouped various religious denominations in St Vincent and which Howell chaired, had not taken a position on the initiative.[137] Howell pointed out that there were some independent churches who thought it was "a good thing". He said the Catholic church felt strongly that it had to lead the way on the initiative, although it had not decided what kind of union was best.

The youth council's reluctance to support the initiative was directly linked to reservations surrounding its implications, particularly for employment, and its effects on Vincentians more generally.[138] The reluctance of the Committee for the Development of Women was also related to reservations that union would "further diminish" women's position in the decision-making process. As Robinson commented, "we could end up being squeezed out".[139] More-over, they were dissatisfied with the education process, which had not reached a majority of people. Howell identified a general concern that Vincentians stood to lose jobs and be exposed to more criminal behaviour, especially with the introduction of a customs union which would facilitate drug trafficking. On a positive note, Howell noted the popular expectation that salaries in St Vincent, among the lowest in the OECS, would be increased to the level of other countries.

Interviewees identified a number of bases upon which union was sup-ported, the primary being economic. Howell and Samuel believed that popular support was influenced by the perception that union would improve funding prospects for members, create a larger market and reduce the costs of foreign representation. Howell, while also justifying union on economic grounds, was convinced that economic factors, rather than prospects for working and sharing with other Caribbean people, were the main reason that Windward

Islands' leaders were promoting the initiative. This suggests that he that believed cultural and political factors, rather than economic concerns, were more credible bases upon which to advocate union. He noted that the Antilles Episcopal Conference supported union because of the shared culture of Caribbean people.

Howell, however, was not optimistic about the initiative's chances of survival, arguing that people were becoming increasingly insular. Such insularity, he believed, could be broken down by strengthening cultural and historical links, beginning with the removal of passport requirements for travel. However, he was sceptical that this would happen. Howell himself supported political integration, "even as a youngster", and believed that Mitchell was genuinely interested in seeing the Caribbean advance as a whole, although he admitted that it would be a feather in Mitchell's cap to be recorded in history as the founder of the united nation.

All interviewees thought that in a referendum on union, Vincentians would vote in accordance with political affiliation rather than interest in union.

Conclusions: Comparing Windward Islands' Responses

Interviews throughout the Windward Islands suggested that the perception that the consultation process was not properly conducted was an important factor influencing popular response. Nor did interviewees believe that proper consultation was likely within the proposed time frame. While mostly in support of union, they were unable to commit themselves fully to the initiative because of a lack of concrete information, specifically on how union would affect them. Despite this, however, there was broad-based support for and acceptance of the need for a political union of OECS countries. Such a union was accepted, either as being necessary to address the islands' problems or as having potentially positive effects, even when there were fears about possible negative consequences. Willingness to support the proposed union initiative, however, varied somewhat among the countries, with sentiments ranging from indifference to support. There appeared to be greatest enthusiasm in St Vincent, even among those hostile to the government. Popular opinion in Grenada was more reserved, reflected in a preference for continued functional cooperation and fears that the initiative was being rushed. Even so, none of the interviewees identified active hostility towards the initiative. In Dominica, interviewees believed that despite the limited education programme, the initiative would find support in a referendum. This perception of support was remarkable, as Dominicans had expressed deep reservations about the implications of union.

Concerns surrounding union were uniform throughout the Windward Islands, although some, especially those pertaining to access to land, were more strongly voiced in Dominica than elsewhere. One of the most common concerns was that the free movement of people would result in a loss of jobs to other nationals. There was a general fear that union might push the islands farther from the centre of collective decision making, reflected in Dominica and St Vincent in concerns that prime ministers or ministers of government would not be accessible and, in Grenada, in the concern that development might be neglected. There was a common lack of clarity as to what the consequences or implications of union would be, hence the call in all islands for detailed proposals on its form. People viewed the form chosen, and the surrounding institutional mechanisms, as important in indicating the likely consequences, so they were unhappy about separating the principle from the form. It is worth noting that one of the most widely expressed views was that a primary obstacle to a political union was a lack of will on the governments' part. This perception of a lack of political will retarding the regional movement was not unique. Boxill, in an opinion survey among elites in St Lucia and Jamaica in the first half of 1988, found that "lack of political will" was the most common reason given for CARICOM's perceived failure.[140]

There was a consistent pattern, throughout the Windwards, regarding those groups who were most vocal against the initiative. The most outspoken critics were invariably among opposition parties and trade unions. It is important to note, though, that although these groups viewed union as a tool through which government could curtail their powers, they were careful to direct opposition at the governments rather than at the initiative itself. On the other hand, it was difficult to identify groups that strongly supported the initiative, although there was general support. The most consistent support came from the private sector, which appeared more convinced of the benefits.

To conclude, the fairly muted response to the initiative was a consequence of the governments' failure to conduct the consultation process and make a case for union, and thus to excite the popular imagination. There was sufficient general interest to suggest that they might have got a more positive response if they had been bolder in proposing the initiative. This, however, does not present the full picture. The general hostility towards the initiative among political parties and trade unions – two of the most influential social groups – must have had some impact on the governments' approach to the initiative. To determine the role of these and other interest groups, we need to examine the part they played in the course of the initiative.

10 *Why the OECS Political Union Initiative Failed*

Ultimately West Indians will come together again in political association, but only after the present generation of leaders is dead.
– Sir Arthur Lewis, *The Agony of the Eight*

By 1988, the political union initiative appeared to have run out of steam. Towards the end of 1987, when governments attempted to launch the consultation process, the acrimony this generated, especially among political parties, fed popular interest for a while. Governments in all Windward Islands except St Vincent, in response to opposition hostility, backed off from fully promoting the initiative. The initiative suffered from the absence of a common approach to the consultation process and the failure to set specific target dates for referendum. Yet, despite the reluctance of three out of four Windward Islands' governments to fully initiate widespread consultation, given the implications this had for their hold on national power, the governments did not reassess their approach until a year later when the initiative was already being viewed as having failed.

The chapter addresses the issue of why the initiative had such limited results in the Windward Islands. It establishes interrelated patterns of response among the Windwards, in an effort to determine whether there was any relationship between the attitudes of interest groups and a cooling of the governments' fervour for union. It discusses government attempts to revive the process between 1990 and 1992, and suggests why this, also, ultimately failed. It also investigates how perceptions of the initiative differed between the Windward and Leeward Islands, and what accounted for this.

Comparing Interest Groups across the Region

This section seeks to draw broad comparisons between the attitudes of interest groups across the islands, to determine whether there were any identifiable patterns in their responses. It also introduces a number of interest groups which were not examined in the country discussions, since it was felt that it would be more meaningful to treat them as a regional grouping in their own right. Important among these were bureaucrats from the national civil services and the OECS itself, and intellectuals who were vocal on the issue. In addition, there were important organizations, such as the churches and the University of the West Indies, which had contributed to the development and sustenance of an ideology of regionalism and the goal of political union. Because such organizations were concerned with issues that affected the region as a whole, and so functioned across national boundaries, they consciously worked in a way that served to promote a regional identity. Even trade unions, which also worked closely together in their regional groupings, contributed to the consolidation of a broader identity.

Opposition Parties

The most consistent rejection of the initiative came from opposition parties, most of which accepted the goal of a united Caribbean. Their response was largely a reflection of antipathy towards the ruling parties, arising from their confrontational relationship with government. This hostility between opposition and ruling party is a recognized feature of Caribbean political life, which invariably surfaces whenever there is any talk of constitutional change. For instance, when these islands were negotiating with the British government for political independence, ruling parties were bitterly resisted by opposition parties that were equally committed to independence. This was the case in every WISA state.[1] It also led to the abandonment of the 1972 attempt to forge a union between the WISA states and Guyana. University of the West Indies social scientist and integration advocate Patrick Emmanuel observed that opposition leaders had rejected the 1971 proposal for a union of WISA states (excluding Antigua) and Guyana, on very much the same grounds as the opposition parties were doing.[2] Rosina Wiltshire[3] has also documented this feature of "oppositionist" politics in the Caribbean and its effect in restricting the development of the integration movement. This relationship goes back to the history of the formation of these parties, where their similar ideological affiliations encouraged shifting alliances on the basis of expediency. In the absence of significant ideological and policy differences, personality became the focus of party politics. Wiltshire dates this to the development of representative government where, because Britain still exercised political and economic control, local politicians were involved in the form rather than the substance of politics. This facilitated a perception of politics as a "game of manipulation".[4]

In the context of the 1987 initiative, opposition parties were made even more defensive by the fact that ruling parties had their own ideological grouping in the CDU and were thus operating from a common platform. Ironically, although most of these parties were formed in response to the same influences, namely region-wide movements for better conditions and greater electoral rights, there were few formal structures connecting them. While the governments came into contact at regional forums, at the level of the party such contacts were minimal. The CDU, therefore, was the first successful attempt at formalizing a relationship among parties of similar orientation.[5] SCOPE was therefore an attempt by opposition parties, both inside and outside of parliament, to present a common front to ruling parties organized within the CDU.

The nature of this relationship was one of the main reasons why governments practically abandoned the consultation process. Although Mitchell had noted that, like the CDU, opposition parties needed to form their own grouping,[6] the governments must have been surprised by the ability of opposition parties of different shades to find common ground so quickly in response to the initiative. Moreover, from SCOPE's initial demands it was clear that the initiative could increase their profile and access to power to which they were not normally entitled. For example, SCOPE had demanded more access to the electronic media, which tended to be controlled by government, and the ability to travel without restrictions to member countries to speak on the initiative.[7] This frightened governments, who were afraid of the implications of enhancing the electoral prospects of opposition parties. This was evident in St Lucia's refusal to allow Roosevelt "Rosie" Douglas, a Dominican politician, to enter St Lucia to attend a SCOPE function on the initiative.[8] The governments had hoped to secure a national consensus with opposition parties, reflected in opposition support, but with the latter firmly occupying the position of junior partner. It was more difficult to control the initiative if opposition parties were united in their position. This scared governments, aware of their own precarious hold on power. Thus, even while agreeing to relinquish power in favour of a single state, ruling parties still sought to maintain their grip on national power.

There was thus an obvious relationship between the governments' willingness to formally mount the consultation process and electoral strength. It was no mistake that the process went farthest in St Vincent, where Mitchell's electoral position was strongest.[9] This meant that if, as predicted, voting was likely to coincide with party loyalty, Mitchell did not need opposition support either to win the first referendum or secure the necessary two-thirds vote to change the constitution. He therefore found it easier than the other governments to make overtures to secure opposition participation. Even though he was unable to win over the opposition St Vincent Labour Party, his attempts to meet their demands for amendments to his National Advisory Committee gave him credibility. In both St Lucia and Dominica, where governments failed to secure opposition backing, the ruling parties were in a weak electoral position. In Dominica, Charles's tenuous hold on power was evident in the 1990 general elections, in which she regained control of the government by only twenty-eight votes. In St Lucia, Hunte's strength was evident from early on, when his party's showing forced Compton to hold two general elections in the hope of gaining a convincing victory. Neither Charles nor Compton, therefore, could hope to win a two-thirds majority in any referendum that did not have opposition support, hence their reluctance to forge ahead with the initiative. Grenada's position was similar. The Blaize government, by then quite unpopular, was weakened by a haemorrhage of elected members to the opposition.[10] In addition, whereas statements by Prime Minister Charles and Prime Minister Compton reflected some commitment to the initiative, there were fewer pronouncements from Blaize. This encouraged the popular perception that Grenada was not interested in union, and that the initiative had been whittled down to three countries: Dominica, St Lucia and St Vincent.

Despite the appearance of coherence among opposition parties within SCOPE, there were differences in their responses to union, evident in a broad division between the more conservative parliamentary parties and left-wing parties outside of parliament. All left-wing "non-parliamentary" parties, except for St Vincent's United People's Movement, were prepared to support union, in contrast to formal opposition parties which were decidedly more hostile, fearful of being marginalized.[11] This difference requires explanation, especially in light of the fact that ruling parties, supported by the United States and feeling their ideological strength, sought, after the Grenada invasion, to marginalize left-wing parties. This difference between the two groups was not only suggested by the interviews, but there was evidence that it was recognized within SCOPE itself. Odlum revealed that there was an attempt, when SCOPE was formed, to differentiate between "parliamentary" and "non-parliamentary" opposition parties.[12]

There are a number of factors that can explain the difference in response between these two groups. The most obvious was the fact that most left-wing parties had not yet experienced electoral power, and many were unlikely to do so in the foreseeable future. Consequently, so-called non-parliamentary groups had less to lose from a union. For official opposition parties, especially Hunte's St Lucia Labour Party and Douglas's Dominica Labour Party, who were only narrowly defeated at the polls, achieving power was a feasible goal. Political union would, consequently, serve to increase the strength of ruling parties at the regional level, beyond that which they enjoyed at home.

Unlike parliamentary opposition parties which stood to lose from regional elections, left-wing parties believed that they stood to gain, so they had little to fear from supporting what was viewed as a long-standing West Indian goal. They already had little hope of winning national elections, and saw regionalism as providing a "fillip" to their ambitions.[13] They would be identified with adopting a principled stance on the issue, which would generate some goodwill towards them, and the ensuing popular activity preceding union would increase their prospects for electoral support. Odlum[14] stated this explicitly, noting that parties such as his stood to gain since they were skilled at taking issues to people through informal channels, such as door-to-door visits and mass meetings. At the same time, this would provide them with an opportunity to present their own agenda for the type of union they sought. Another factor which accounted for this difference was the opportunity which union would provide for left-wing groups to merge and broaden their influence as a regional party. Their chances for electoral support would be enhanced if, as Mitchell had proposed, a system of proportional representation was introduced.[15] Under such a system, parliamentary opposition parties, seeking to oust a CDU party, might find themselves forced to form alliances with these groups.

As for "parliamentary" parties, their response brought their commitment to the principle of political union into question, as none attempted to propose a serious alternative agenda for a union. This, and their apparent willingness to see the initiative cool rather than injecting it with their own fervour, brought into question the depth of support for a union even in principle. One could argue, therefore, that had these groups really been interested in union, they would have seized the opportunity the initiative provided to make their own mark by presenting proposals on what was required to achieve such a union. Such a response did not require collaboration with ruling parties. This failure to present their own vision raises the suspicion that their position was essentially opportunist, rejecting the initiative because they were not in power.

These differences in response between formal parliamentary and left-wing opposition parties could have been exploited by the ruling parties, but for their anticommunist paranoia – a holdover from the Grenada revolution.[16] By failing to join forces with the left-wing parties (fearful that this would give them legitimacy), they lost an opportunity to isolate those parliamentary opposition parties most hostile to the initiative. The ruling parties' failure to win the support of parliamentary groups, and the latter's willingness to reject the initiative in response to narrow political interests, was probably the most significant factor in the limited success of the union movement up to 1989.

Trade Unions[17]

Trade unions tended to be deeply hostile towards the initiative, but, unlike many of the formal opposition parties, more were willing to support it despite their objections. The similarity in their response to that of the opposition parties can be partly explained by the fact that trade union officials were, in many instances, political figures or allied to political parties.[18] Despite this connection, however, the trade union movement represented a distinct constituency. Because of the nature of trade unions, they had control over a significant constituency across a wide range of occupations, making them a force to be reckoned with. This potential power could not be taken lightly. The governments generally preferred not to target this group, treating it as hostile. This, in turn, fed the hostility. Their relationship with governments already tended to be acrimonious because, like opposition parties, their contact was primarily confrontational. This was aggravated by the fact that government was the largest employer of labour, and they were forced to negotiate with government for better conditions for their workers. The situation was further aggravated when the trade union was affiliated to the opposition party. Moreover, trade unions within the Windward Islands were already beginning to feel the effects of IMF-imposed structural adjustment programmes or public reform exercises, which inevitably resulted in job losses.[19] Windward Islands' trade unions were also highly politicized, as their responses, particularly to possible US involvement, showed. This was a consequence of the way in which the trade union movement had developed in the Caribbean, out of protest in the 1930s for improved social conditions, their role as precursors to the political parties, and their close identification with the regional integration movement.

The trade unions' response reflected a schism between the goals and ideals of the broad movement and their functioning at the local level, evident in the divergence between the official position of the CCL, to which most were affiliated, and the local response of unions. The CCL's position reflected the traditional commitment to the union ideal,[20] so its response was positive, whereas the national response reflected the relationship with government at the local level, and the deep distrust that this bred. The CCL's position[21] on the initiative closely mirrored its historical position, supporting union "in principle" but calling for trade union involvement in the process. It therefore requested that trade unions be "accorded full recognition in all discussions and formulation of plans towards the objective of a political union" so as to ensure that they were an "integral part" of the process leading up to the union. The CCL showed its concern that rights which the movement had won should not be affected by union, by requesting the entrenchment of rights, such as collective bargaining, in any constitution of the political union. The CCL called for a meeting of all major regional organizations recognized by the OECS and CARICOM, including the Heads of Government and SCOPE, and representatives from the East Caribbean Central Bank and OECS secretariats. In 1989, two years after the initiative was made public, the CCL restated its position, saying that its support for OECS unity remained "strong and unwavering", but urging meaningful popular involvement.[22]

That national unions were responding to local considerations was suggested by the absence of any obvious pattern in their position, some supporting the initiative and others calling for increased functional cooperation. The only valid basis for comparison was at the national level, which showed more consistency among responses. In Dominica two out of three unions were hostile towards the initiative; in Grenada three out of four supported functional cooperation; in St Vincent two out of three supported the initiative unconditionally; and in St Lucia two out of three also supported the initiative. Despite this variance in their willingness to support the initiative, however, these groups were uniformly suspicious and shared the same common reservations.

In conclusion, except for St Vincent, governments did not involve local trade union groups because of their inability to control them. The trade unions' relationship with government, therefore, affected the governments' willingness to push the initiative, which, in turn compounded the problem by fostering trade union suspicion and hostility.

Private Sector

The private sector was the only group which was supportive throughout and which generally tended to be taken into governments' confidence, a factor likely to have affected their response. The sector's support, particularly that of manufacturers, was not surprising. The private sector was the group most closely identified with the regional integration movement, within both CARICOM and the OECS. The regional private sector, particularly the manufacturing sector, was instrumental in negotiations preceding the West Indies Federation and in determining the shape of CARICOM.[23] The entire Caribbean integration experience, which equated development with the creation of an industrial base, privileged the manufacturing sector. Its focus was on developing a manufacturing sector and encouraging foreign private investment, hence a preoccupation with trade and the protection of industries. This was no different for the OECS, where the private sector enjoyed a close working relationship not only with government, but with the organization itself. Throughout the 1980s OECS governments sought to strengthen ties with the private sector, providing specific avenues for the sector to influence the integration process. For instance, the EAS, along with OECS ministers of trade and industry, met with the manufacturers' lobby group, the Council of East Caribbean Manufacturers, twice a year.[24] Additionally, in November 1990, an umbrella group of OECS private sector interests was established to represent the OECS private sector at CARICOM, even though the Caribbean Association of Industry and Commerce, to which these groups were affiliated, already had representation at CARICOM.[25] This meant that even before the initiative developed, the OECS had been working closely with these groups who were thus able to see, in more practical terms, what benefits could accrue from a closer relationship. The initiative, therefore, would hardly have caught them by surprise. Despite Skeritt's observation that Kittitian manufacturers were more likely than retailers to support union (see chapter 8), or Archie Singham's observation in 1968 that the Caribbean economic and business elite were likely to resist integration[26] because separate existence guaranteed their control, a survey of private sector interviews in the Windwards reveals uniform support among all groups represented. It is possible that a larger sample might have revealed some differentiation.

The private sector's close working relationship with both the OECS and CARICOM, therefore, had made it well aware of potential benefits from political union. Of all the major interest groups discussed, the private sector was the most organized *vis-à-vis* the regional integration process, the advantage of a close working relationship with the OECS ensuring that their interests would be guaranteed in any political union. In fact, private sector interests in a political union were so well articulated and propagated that they appeared consistently in the rationale for union given by practically every interviewee, even those wary of union. It was thus the dominant ideology motivating the movement. The most common of these arguments were the need to create larger economies of scale and to break down barriers to trade, as well as the free movement of labour and capital. Furthermore, the private sector was the only group which seemed to have a clear idea of how its interests would be secured under a political union, in contrast, for example, to trade unions which appeared unclear as to how workers would benefit. This contributed to the emphasis on the economic aspects of regionalism. In this context OECS political union, or even wider CARICOM political integration, was likely to be seen in terms of the framework this provided for enhancing economic performance. The governments, already enjoying congenial relations with this group and recognizing their interest in regional integration, concentrated efforts on winning their support. They were well aware, as Wiltshire noted, that the attitude of the "local business elite" was crucial in the success of any development in the integration movement.[27]

Social Groups

The Church

Generally, the more established churches in the Eastern Caribbean supported the political union initiative, although they were concerned that it should be preceded by a properly mounted consultation process. Their position was publicized in statements by groups as well as individuals. The most broad-based regional church grouping, the ecumenical Caribbean Conference of Churches,[28] officially supported the initiative but cautioned against setting a timetable for union.[29] The Roman Catholic Church, the predominant church in the Windward Islands, publicly supported the initiative with a statement[30] from five of their bishops from Eastern Caribbean countries.[31] They called for the "full implementation" of the OECS treaty as an immediate step, to allow for the "natural evolution" of union. The bishops said that they "could not remain indifferent to the major political event" of the proposed initiative. They commended the political leaders for their "initiative in striving to achieve greater political integration" and the "thinkers, writers and artists for keeping alive the vision of Caribbean unity", saying that "never before has there been such a degree of consensus on this matter in our area".[32] This support, however, was conditional upon widespread consultation, a process in which church leaders generally agreed the church had a role to play. As Allan Kirton, chairman of the Caribbean Conference of Churches, observed, the church had "the most broad-based, well-organised, and readily mobilised informa-tion, consultation, and education network".[33] Support for the initiative was not without reservation. The bishops, for example, wanted to see a "human rights clause" included in the constitution of any political grouping,[34] while Kirton had "grave misgivings" about the "motivating force":

> And when one hears that "security" concerns are high on the agenda and that the prospect of facilitating foreign aid may thus be enhanced, one begins to wonder, once again, whose agenda is being used to push the region together. Do the ruling considerations necessarily arise out of the heart, soul, mind and gut of the Caribbean experience, and do they have in view a destiny with which the majority can identify?[35]

This support for the initiative was not surprising, since the church in the Caribbean regarded itself as a regional rather than national institution. This was manifested in the way in which the Roman Catholic and Anglican ministries were organized, with persons being responsible for more than one country. For example, Archbishop Lindsay was bishop of the "North Eastern Caribbean", which included Antigua and Aruba. In addition, church officials were moved around the Caribbean, which gave them experience of different countries. The church was also concerned with issues that transcended national boundaries, thus encouraging a regional perspective. Dr Phillip Potter, former general secretary of the World Council of Churches and a member of the Methodist Church, listed among the church's duties ensuring fundamental human rights, emphasizing solidarity with the poor, and assisting in the search for a Caribbean identity.[36] The Caribbean Conference of Churches shared this view of the church's role in safeguarding or developing a Caribbean identity, identifying "a growing erosion of Caribbean identity" through the cultural penetration of the electronic media.[37] Potter believed that the churches had "hardly begun to play the creative public role their faith demands". He urged them to "read the signs of the times and throw all their weight into whatever enables our people to unite for human dignity, justice, and mutual well-being as an authentic part of the whole human family".[38] Despite the churches' obvious predisposition towards union, the governments failed to enter a partnership with them which would have furthered the cause. This served to encourage suspicion of the governments' motivations, even from these quarters.

Youth and Women

The initiative appeared to have had no direct message for women and youth groups. The impression gleaned from interviews is that women were either noncommittal or apathetic towards the initiative. They appeared to have no concrete indication of its possible effect on their lives, a consequence of the absence of any attempt to target them specifically, or to identify their possible interest in a union. Despite this, they appeared willing to go along with the initiative.

Youth were also not targeted as a separate group; this failure had negative consequences. Their interests were specific and clearly identifiable: unemployment (a major issue in countries of generally high unemployment), training, and the possibility of being able to seek opportunities in other islands were important concerns. As Linden Lewis noted in a study on Barbadian youth, Caribbean youth "live in times in which they feel the impact of austerity measures and cash flow problems associated with economic crises of the societies in which they live".[39] The governments were short-sighted in not treating this group, which constituted a high proportion of their populations, as important. In St Vincent, for example, as much as 57 per cent of the population was under twenty years old.[40] Windward Islands' governments failed to appreciate that the very uncertainties which fuelled their interest in a political union also fed uncertainty and insecurity among young people concerning their future. This explains why Vincentian youths were generally fearful of the repercussions of union, particularly freedom of movement and the implications this might have for increasing unemployment. Interestingly, Angela Patrick noted that a regional grouping embracing OECS national youth councils had agreed to support the initiative.[41] Their reluctance to support the initiative, therefore, was in part a response to the governments' contempt in refusing, in some cases, to speak at their functions, or to target them specifically. Their response reflected more the failure of the consultation process to target them as a specific interest group, and to address their concerns, than any deep-seated hostility towards the initiative.

The governments also failed to target women as a specific interest group. Women would also have had concerns about how their lives were likely to be affected by changes in the international environment, especially in the banana industry upon which a significant number relied, either directly or indirectly, for their survival. Generally women play a central role in the economic life of the Caribbean, with the West Indian Commission estimating that two-fifths of households depended on them for survival.[42] Both youth and women, the latter comprising at least half of OECS populations, were significant constituencies to win over if any union proposal were to succeed.

The Bureaucracy

National Bureaucrats

As Haas and Schmitter observed,[43] the bureaucracy was an important group influencing integration movements. This group could either sabotage or assist in advancing the movement. In looking at the national bureaucracy it is important to note that there were likely to be different elements with varying interests in union. There were those who stood to gain from the broader regional scope it should provide, and those likely to be hostile since they stood to lose their jobs in a scaled-down national bureaucracy.

Interviews with representatives from the national bureaucracy were biased towards the upper echelons, close to the prime ministers, where support for union was strong. Persons interviewed from this stratum were Dwight Venner, director of trade, and Earl Huntley, permanent secretary in the Ministry of Foreign Affairs in St Lucia; Randolph Cato, permanent secretary in the Ministry of Finance in St Vincent; Brian Alleyne, attorney-general of Dominica, and Alick Lazare, financial advisor to the Dominican government. While some of these bureaucrats supported the initiative, many were not involved in the debates surrounding it. On the other hand, most interviewees from this group had actively advocated union by writing articles and speaking at forums debating the issue. Huntley[44] and Venner, for example, were leading advocates of union through their membership in St Lucia's Independent Committee for OECS Unity, actively canvassing support among representatives of important interest groups and in public forums. In addition, both had written in support of their ideas.

It is important to note that there was little evidence of dissidence among senior civil servants. The more vocal tended to support the initiative, basing this on an appreciation of the difficulties these countries faced. It is unlikely, however, that those who opposed union would have expressed dissent openly, as such dissent would not have been looked upon kindly. Further, it is unlikely that a civil servant would publicly oppose an initiative that his prime minister publicly supported. Earlier discussions on the functioning of the national bureaucracy *vis-à-vis* the OECS indicated that there were bureaucratic barriers to implementing decisions taken at the regional level. This would suggest that certain important sections of the national bureaucracy were unconvinced of the importance of OECS integration. Nevertheless, the years of functional and economic cooperation had given rise to groups whose interests were furthered by integration. These were to be found not only in the regional bureaucracy, but in the upper echelons of the national bureaucracy.

In conclusion, the role of the national bureaucracy in the OECS initiative was limited to the involvement of a few key figures in the upper echelons of the civil service, who tended to be close to their prime ministers. At the lower levels of the civil service, which would be represented by civil service associations in each country, there was likely to be a lack of clarity as to the consequences of union. Because of the under-representation of this group in the trade union sample, however, it is difficult to make specific statements on their attitudes, although the response from the St Lucia Civil Service Association suggested some insecurity surrounding the initiative, especially in the context of restructuring exercises underway in other Windward Islands and discussions around the large size of the public sector. It was also likely that at this level of the civil service, the general concerns which most of the trade unions expressed would have been shared.

Regional Bureaucrats

An interesting feature of the representatives of the regional and national bureaucracies was the similarity of the basis upon which they supported an OECS or Windward Islands' union. There was a definite preoccupation with the economics of the issue. Venner put the case bluntly when he argued that "the sheer arithmetic of the case [was] compelling".[45] There was a tendency to see political union in terms of its implications for the economic fortunes of the countries, based on the need to create economies of scale to overcome difficulties presented by small size;[46] pooling skills to increase bargaining power in the international arena;[47] and improving prospects for human rights and democracy,[48] among other things. There was also a general consensus that the loose arrangements that characterized functional integration should give way to political union because the OECS had exhausted the possibilities for cooperation. Lewis, Venner and Marie, in particular, argued that there was a limit to which functional integration, especially in the economic sphere, could progress in the absence of a centralized political structure. Venner argued that it was inevitable, as one climbed the ladder of economic coopera-tion, for political sovereignty to be seen in terms of the good of the whole.[49] Lewis and Marie argued that OECS programmes of cooperation had become too complex to be handled efficiently by existing machinery. Lewis believed that this required a more centralized approach for mechanisms and decisions to be effective.[50] Marie argued that political union had become necessary for the efficient functioning of the industry allocation programme and the reso-lution of conflicts that arose.[51] This approach treated political union as simply a by-product of functional cooperation: another bureaucratic structure. It was a convenience for achieving a more efficient management structure for the states and for providing a more secure framework for economic activities. It ignored other, less tangible justifications for union, such as cultural affinity and identity, mentioned by other advocates, and offered little attraction for groups which did not stand to benefit directly from union premised upon economic grounds. This explained, to some extent, why the entire initiative was being promoted on the basis of economic expedience, rather than on any deeper goal.

At the same time, this group had the potential to provide concrete support to governments promoting the initiative. However, their involvement was limited to the production of several booklets providing background information on the OECS and the broader integration movement and, in some cases, to members speaking at public functions discussing the initiative. Governments' failure to draw on the regional bureaucracy and the OECS secretariats, in particular, to support the initiative, helped to keep it a national issue and made it more susceptible to considerations of national politics. A possible explanation for this failure may lie in the Leewards' rejection of the initiative, which may have made such use of the OECS bureaucracy by the Windwards problematic.

The University of the West Indies, particularly its campuses in Trinidad and Barbados, could have played a significant role in the initiative by addressing questions raised around such issues as costs, form and popular participation, through studies or by fostering debate. Unfortunately, the prospect of a union of the OECS/Windward Islands did not generate the degree of enthusiasm that earlier efforts, particularly the establishment of CARICOM, had. The institution's involvement occurred on a narrow plane, confined to the action of interested individuals[52] or the use of its national extramural centres to house discussions. The university's lack of interest reflected the diminished influence of OECS countries following the decision to allow each campus autonomy, and the general disadvantage which noncampus territories faced in bringing their problems to the attention of the academic community. It is inconceivable that an issue of comparable significance to Barbados, Trinidad or Jamaica would have had the same response. Vaughan Lewis, commenting on the possibilities for Caribbean political integration, noted that the "thinking and writing on the possibilities for integration" in the post-Federation period had shifted from the academics to the technocrats and those involved in the policy process.[53]

Summary

It is clear that while there was a great degree of openness towards the initiative generally, this went hand in hand with suspicions about governments' moti-

vations and reservations about possible negative consequences. Such suspicions were strongest among groups whose support was key to the initiative's
success – trade unions and parliamentary opposition parties – but were also
mirrored in the broader population. Governments' ability to wholeheartedly
promote the initiative was thus compromised, which, in turn, exacerbated
these reservations. Windward Islands' governments failed to mobilize support
from groups with a regional focus. This was probably a reflection of the
national focus of the consultation process. Equally important, groups with a
regional focus, and avowedly committed to political integration of the Caribbean, did not use the initiative as an opportunity for advancing the cause. This
was probably attributable to the fact that regional groups are comprised of
national groups, which were primarily concerned with national issues. There
was a discernible trend of regional groups professing support for the initiative
while their national members either openly rejected it or expressed deep
reservations. Another possible interpretation might lie in the comment that in
the region the vision of a Caribbean union had been ossified into an ideal.

In conclusion, the response of various interest groups suggested some
relationship between their perception of threats or expectation of benefits
arising from union. This would explain why the private sector was generally
supportive and why most trade unions and youth organizations were reserved,
despite their support for the concept. Without clear economic benefits, either
offered or threatened, other interest groups were less motivated one way or
the other, most accepting the initiative on the basis of a common cultural
identity. The governments, apart from a broad appeal to national development, were unable to make a credible case for how union would benefit interest
groups other than the private sector. Moreover, the economic threat was not
strong enough to convince those sectors inclined to be hostile that union was
the only way to stave off economic collapse. While the international situation
presaged a rough time ahead, OECS countries had weathered crises far better
than other much larger countries, and this weakened the argument that their
small size reduced their viability. Rather, the support they had received from
the United States and Europe, facilitated by the very factor of their small size,
helped them to maintain an acceptable standard of living for their people.
Consequently, the benefits of a union, precisely because it involved a leap into
the unknown, appeared ephemeral and marginal.

Despite the forebodings of the leaders of the Windward Islands that
international currents were moving against OECS countries, curtailing their

room to manoeuvre, their people remained unconvinced that the tide would so change as to remove the traditional pillars of their support. This is unlikely to change until the consequences of such changes are manifest in increased hardships, such as observers predict could result from a collapse of the banana industry. Despite the interest of Windward Islands' leaders, therefore, it was unlikely that in the absence of economic disaster, such a union would materialize. Whether this scenario develops is directly related to the character of the relationship the countries develop with Europe after the commodity protocols run out; their ability to find avenues for greater economic opportunities within the FTAA, and their success in generating some sensitivity to the peculiarities of their economies on the international plane, manifested in concrete measures to further their economic development. If the union movement in the Caribbean continues to be promoted as an economic venture, then the likelihood of these islands forming a union remains directly related to their ability to survive comfortably as individual units.

Regionalizing Consultation: Regional Constituent Assemblies

The main reasons for the initiative floundering up to 1989 among the Windward Islands were the governments' failure to adopt a regional rather national approach to the consultation process, enlisting the support of regional institutions; their inability to secure the support of important constituencies such as opposition parties; the limited reach of the consultation structures established; and the absence of legitimacy of the consultation process itself. In response to the lull in the initiative, the Windward Islands' Heads of Government (Grenada was represented by Nicholas Brathwaite who had replaced Blaize as prime minister) met in Palm Island, St Vincent, on 31 August 1990, and issued the "Palm Island Statement" which relaunched the consultation process. This raises the essential question of how successful the revised process was in addressing the main weaknesses identified in the earlier attempts.

The main innovation of the Palm Island Statement was the decision to establish a RCA comprising "parliamentarians, political parties and special interest groups to discuss and make recommendations on the necessity for political union and on appropriate institutional arrangements for bringing it into effect".[54] This represented an attempt to shift the initiative from the national plane, where it had become bogged down by the dynamics of local politics, to the regional level. The RCA, which would number forty people, ten from each island, would meet four times between 1990 and 1991, once in each of the Windward Islands. The OECS secretariat was to provide a supportive role, seeking funding for its operations and providing the necessary documentation.[55] Two weeks later, the Heads announced a formal timetable for RCA meetings and the decision to hold a first referendum "on the principle of political union" under a common referendum act, by early June 1991.[56] This would be preceded by the circulation of the final report of the RCA, in the form of a white paper for popular discussion, which would then be presented to parliament in each state for approval.[57] In the event that the referendum found approval, a constitutional motion would be passed in each state to convene a constitutional conference and approve a draft constitution on the recommendation of the RCA. A bill for the draft constitution would then be presented before parliament in each country for approval. This would be followed by the preparation of a "regional economic development pro-gramme", for which funding would be sought.[58]

Another important feature of the RCA was the attempt to include opposi-tion parties early in the process, as reflected in the suggested composition of the RCA: five members from political parties – opposition and government – and the other five from the private sector, trade unions, church, youth groups and the farming community.[59] A meeting in St Vincent on 26 October between the governments and SCOPE to discuss SCOPE's participation failed to arrive at a consensus on the "nature and function" of the RCA. After a subsequent meeting on 24 November, the heads agreed to postpone the RCA's first sitting, scheduled for 26 November, to the following January to accommodate SCOPE's request for the RCA to be established by a parlia-mentary bill which would include its terms of reference. A draft bill, to be prepared by OECS and SCOPE secretariats, would then be discussed and approved at the first RCA meeting. The bill was to include an intergovern-mental agreement establishing the RCA, as well as an annex to the agreement which set out its terms of reference, duties and power, the latter to be approved at the first RCA meeting. Despite general agreement on the annex, there were some outstanding points which SCOPE wanted addressed: an increase in the number of RCA members over the ten per country proposed by governments; an extension of the timetable for RCA consultation; and an adjustment to the schedule of RCA meetings, to allow for more meetings than the four proposed.[60] Contrary to SCOPE's expectation that outstanding issues would be resolved before the RCA's first sitting, the governments referred these to the RCA for resolution. They did, however, respond to SCOPE's request for broadening RCA membership, with the decision to include a women's representative. This, however, was not sufficient to secure SCOPE's participation. SCOPE refused to participate on the RCA, but attended the first sitting to present its reasons. Ralph Gonsalves presented SCOPE's position, which reaffirmed its members' "commitment to the principle of political union" and acceptance of the RCA as a mechanism for consultation, but argued that the governments had failed "to respect and accommodate the concerns of SCOPE, which . . . are designed to strengthen and deepen the process of consultation".[61] So from the start, the governments failed to secure opposition support. Not all opposition parties were happy with SCOPE's decision, however. Odlum, in a general allusion to their position, characterized it as exhibiting "a lack of principle and opportunism".[62]

The Heads also sought to put the initiative on a more formal footing, by establishing the RCA through a parliamentary bill and establishing a timetable for meetings. RCA deliberations were to follow parliamentary rules and procedures. The RCA was given specific functions which went beyond establishing interest in union to include consideration of the "economic and social viability of the union, the economic cost, . . . external relations and administrative implications of union", its form, and "structure of government and elements of a constitution . . . including the administrative and electoral mechanisms".[63] This addressed concerns expressed earlier about the lack of any consideration of the substance of union.

Finally, the Heads sought to include specific interest groups in the process, although they were in danger of repeating the earlier exclusion of women. They also sought to address the problem of representation of unorganized sections of the population by broadcasting RCA debates across the region and holding open sessions for public participation. This strategy was not successful, as an analysis of RCA deliberations shows very little participation in the public sessions. Such a strategy might have been more successful if based on village- or parish-wide discussions either preceding or following RCA debates, summarized and included in RCA reports.

The final report of the RCA, which found widespread support for a Windward Islands' political union based on a federal model, was tabled before the parliaments of three Windward Islands, where it won majority support. According to Huntley, in Grenada it was supported by all parties in parliament; in St Vincent it received full support from a parliament which had no official opposition; and in Dominica it won a parliamentary majority although the United Workers' Party voted against it. The report was never tabled before the parliament in St Lucia. It was submitted just before the general elections in 1992 which returned Compton's party to power. Although Vaughan Lewis, former OECS secretary-general and ardent advocate of OECS union, took over as prime minister from Compton for a year, he never tabled the report. The new government of Kenny Anthony, which took power from Lewis in 1997, did not table the report either. In fact, Anthony declared that OECS political union was not on the "horizon".[64]

Despite these attempts to correct the failings of the earlier handling of the initiative, the outcome was pretty much the same. It failed to secure the support of opposition parties and to elicit popular participation, and it did not go beyond the initial stages of parliamentary support for the principle of union, with St Lucia's failure to table a bill in support of the initiative. The RCA process was successful, however, in putting on record support for political union among a wide cross-section of interest groups, and in settling the question of which form was considered most desirable. It also registered support for freedom of movement within the Windward Islands and documented the widely held perception that the main failing of the integration process lay in an absence of political will. The first RCA report noted,

> None of the delegates argued against political union. Some did, however, express doubts as to whether it could achieve what it was hoped it would achieve. . . . The most persistent cause for these doubts was the deep distrust with which all politicians were viewed. . . . Delegates expressed the view that the politicians were far removed from "the people" and concerned solely with the maintenance of a system from which they benefited at the expense of "the people". Even the expressed desire to surrender high office to achieve union was viewed with suspicion or at worse [*sic*] disbelief.[65]

Comparing Attitudes in the Windward and Leeward Islands

One of the important differences in the responses of interest groups in the Windwards and Leewards was on the need for a union. Most interviewees who supported a union of the Windward Islands were convinced that it would improve their islands' prospects for development; this did not hold for the Leewards, where popular perception was that union would detract from what had already been achieved. The second main observation was the preference in the Windwards for a broader union including the Leewards, which contrasted with the Leewards' conviction of a common destiny for the Leewards alone. These two factors accounted in large measure for the difference in response of the two groups of islands.

In the Windwards there was little evidence to suggest that a differentiation was made between people of the Windward and Leeward groupings. In the Leewards, on the other hand, the acceptance of a basis for closer cooperation among the Leewards, as opposed to the Windwards, coupled with the desire for more contacts with the Windwards as a prerequisite for union, spoke to a perceived distance between the two groups.

This goes some way towards explaining why people in the Leewards preferred an acceleration in functional integration, including the removal of travel restrictions among OECS countries, to talk of a union. It is worth noting that, even then, the people of St Kitts–Nevis and Antigua supported the goal of a political union of the OECS. Grenada came closest, among the Windwards, to approximating the Leewards' preference for increased functional cooperation. Despite this, however, important groups were willing either to support the initiative or to consider it.[66]

In both the Windward and Leeward groupings, the initiative's announcement evoked suspicion. In the Leewards this took the form of a conviction that Windward Islands' leaders had already agreed on a form which they meant to force on the other islands. This arose from Mitchell's proposal of a unitary state in his first presentation to the Heads. There was no real justification for this suspicion as, although St Vincent and Dominica preferred a unitary state, Compton wanted a federation and Grenada appeared not to have considered the matter. Because their governments decided not to support the initiative, suspicions in the Leewards were therefore directed at the Windward Islands, and took the form of concern that benefits and characteristics of the Leewards would be lost in union with the Windwards. In the Windwards, on the other hand, the suspicions of political parties and unions were primarily directed at the governments and their motivations for supporting the issue. Additionally, in the Leewards suspicions tended to mirror the government's reservations about participating in a union, primarily the implications for the country's development prospects of the loss of international status. This coincided with the belief, particularly in Antigua and St Kitts–Nevis, that the country's strength lay in its ability to exert influence in the international community through its voting rights.[67] To the contrary, the tendency among the Windward Islands was to believe that union would strengthen their bargaining power which, because of their size, was minimal.

Popular reservations were similar between the two groups. Both feared neglect by a distant central authority, although this was more strongly expressed in Antigua, St Kitts–Nevis and Dominica; and that land and jobs would be lost to people from other OECS territories. Interestingly, despite the negative effects expected from political union, people throughout the OECS tended to support free movement, even without union.

A cursory comparison of the attitudes of both groupings suggests that the Antigua and St Kitts–Nevis governments' decision not to pursue the initiative played a major role in the opinions expressed. Given the widespread support that existed for the principle of union, it is not inconceivable to imagine that, had they embraced the initiative, a more positive response might have been possible. Additionally, in most OECS countries there were important interest groups (namely opposition parties) which, like the Antigua and St Kitts–Nevis governments, subordinated political union to increased functional cooperation. The difference between the two groups was that Windward Islands' governments were prepared to participate in the initiative. Interestingly, the Windward Islands' perceptions that voting would closely mirror political affiliation appeared to hold as much for the Leewards, given the close mirroring of governments' responses by the people.

This does not mean that there were not perceived differences between the two groupings which may have affected attitudes. The Leewards' perception of themselves as a more cohesive group, arising from physical closeness and historical links, was important. Economic interdependence among the Leewards, central to which was the informal movement of labour and people, would have contributed to this. Montserrat was closely tied to Antigua and St Kitts–Nevis, and links with the British Virgin Islands were stronger in these countries than in the Windwards. Moreover, differences in the economic fortunes of the two groupings would have been a major factor influencing the response of the Antigua and St Kitts–Nevis governments. Mitchell inferred this when he charged that there were "a lot of superior attitudes" in the other islands which needed to be broken down, and scathingly observed that some OECS countries who had "a sense of superiority" and felt themselves to be better off than St Vincent did not want to support the initiative.[68]

The basis for a distinct Windward Islands' position was obvious in the structural similarity of the countries and the economic challenges they faced. Undoubtedly, the conviction of Windward Islands' leaders that their countries faced certain doom outside of a political union was heavily influenced by the banana industry's uncertain future and its centrality to their economies. The economies of the Leeward Islands, on the other hand, were not directly threatened by European integration, so there was no urgent need to join forces with other OECS countries. This explains why the Leewards feared relinquishing sovereignty and the effects this would have on their relatively favourable economic performance. It also explains why all Windward Islands, even Grenada, supported the initiative. It is also possible to attribute Grenada's lukewarm response to its more diversified agricultural export industry and the decreased importance of bananas, which made it less vulnerable to a collapse of the banana industry. Nevertheless, the industry's destruction spelt political chaos and instability for all Windward Islands. The economic differences between these two groupings, compounded by a perception of cultural differences in the Leewards, was the crux of the difference in attitudes, particularly among the governments.

Conclusions

The economic foundation driving the OECS integration experience lies at the heart of the initiative's failure to galvanize the OECS. Ironically, successes achieved at the functional level had encouraged the view, particularly within the Leewards, that political union was not essential for cooperation to move beyond existing limits. The primacy of the economic motive underpinning the initiative also explains why the Windwards were not able to carry the Leewards. The Windward/Leeward split was the direct result of differing perceptions of this threat. The Leewards, basking in the relative security of service economies, did not feel the same urgency which the possible collapse of the banana industry forced on the leaders of the Windwards. Nor were they dissatisfied with the results of the integration process. While they shared the Windwards' concern with deepening the process and increasing popular contact through the unrestricted movement of people, they did not accept that they needed to sacrifice sovereignty for this to happen. And while there was general consensus in the Windwards that they would fare better in a union, the Leewards were convinced of the opposite. There were also other factors which encouraged the Leewards to reject the initiative. The most significant appeared to be the perception of a cultural difference between the two groups of islands. While this difference was slight, in the absence of any compelling advantages for the Leewards its importance was exaggerated. Closely related to this was the perceived geographical difference between the two groups of islands, which were separated by the French Caribbean islands. In the final analysis, it is difficult to say whether a mere information campaign designed to promote union would, by itself, have overcome this perception of difference.

Because increased economic and functional integration requires more political compliance, it remains possible that at some point, in the not-too-distant future, the movement might run out of steam in the face of political resistance, forcing a decision one way or the other. It is clear that this point had not yet arrived at the time under discussion, and that the general attitude, particularly in the Leewards, was that it was a long way off. Neofunctionalists' optimism about economic integration's potency in catapulting the movement towards political union has not yet been established in the case of the OECS.

An OECS–Barbados Confederation?

The RCA's failure to proceed beyond the consultation process raises the question, whither OECS political union? The movement appeared to receive new life when Barbados's prime minister, Owen Arthur, announced in 1998 that Barbados was interested in becoming a part of the OECS and in establishing a confederation with the OECS.[69] The confederation would be based on areas of common interest, such as the RSS and the fight against drugs, and would circumvent thorny issues of relinquishing the trappings of formal sovereignty which Leeward Islanders, in particular, found unpalatable.

Arthur's interest in an eventual union with OECS countries suggests that political union among CARICOM's small states is not a dead issue. The motivations for such a union are likely to extend beyond narrow economic goals, but will likely derive from their perceived vulnerability brought on by concerns for economic survival. It is important to note that, so far, the response to feelings of insecurity has been to focus inward and, in the case of the Windward Islands, and now Barbados, to seek to consolidate political units. In other words, they have not sought to explore alternative arrangements which would compromise their formal political sovereignty *vis-à-vis* the United States or the European Union. In fact, the appeal by Dominica's prime minister, Rosie Douglas, to the European Union for a special relationship with Dominica, was met with outrage among political leaders.

Owen Arthur's interest in pursuing deeper ties with the OECS puts the question of leadership high on the agenda of OECS political union. Both the elite interviews conducted for this study and the RCA findings suggest widespread disillusionment with the available leadership, its sincerity in pursuing union, and its ability to carry it through. In both the Windwards and Leewards leadership was crucial in influencing the outcome of the initiative. In the Leewards, Antigua's reluctance strongly affected the willingness of the other countries to participate. In turn, Antigua's decision was a consequence of Vere Bird's place in Antigua's political life.[70] Bird, often referred to as the old man of Caribbean politics, had dominated Antiguan political life since the formation of indigenous political parties. While he was at certain times a strong advocate of Caribbean integration, he was also, at others, instrumental in the collapse of attempts at union among the smaller Eastern Caribbean states. In particular, his rejection of the attempted "Little Eight" federation with Barbados and the WISA states, simply because it meant that Antigua would lose control over its post office, encouraged the perception that Bird was reluctant to have his influence over Antiguan life reduced.

The leadership which prime ministers of the Windward Islands provided had a significant effect. Wheare noted that the desire to unite was not of itself sufficient to prevail over countervailing forces. A great deal depended on the leadership or statesmanship available. "This factor of leadership, of skill in negotiation and propaganda, can make all the difference between stagnation and an active desire for union."[71] The Windward Islands' leaders' common membership in the CDU, and their similar conservative ideological stance, generated the kind of solidarity which encouraged the belief that they could work together. This was an important factor accounting for the proposal of the initiative at that particular time. On the other hand, the initiative stalled because, in the final analysis, they were not sufficiently strong politically to force it through. Mitchell was its clear leader and consistently promoted it. The other leaders had neither the courage nor the political strength to do this.

They were compromised by their weak political power at home and their reluctance to sacrifice their national leadership in the event that the initiative should prove unpopular.

Arthur's grounds for supporting political union are instructive, in that, while he recognizes economic concerns, he shifts the focus towards other more ephemeral, though no less legitimate, goals of nationhood. This is summarized in his statement that

> notwithstanding the nuances in our individual experiences in nation-building and development, we are essentially one Caribbean people, one Caribbean family moulded by the experience and the essential vitality of a distinctive Caribbean way of life. . . . This is still the most powerful basis for Caribbean integration at all levels, and the source of our inspiration that we have nothing to fear in seeking to move the causes and mechanisms of Caribbean integration beyond the structures that have evolved over the past quarter of a century.[72]

Commenting on Barbados's bid to join the OECS some time ago, and the form that this was likely to take, I made the following observation:

> It (political integration) is likely to develop in the direction of a confederation of states, along the lines proposed by Owen Arthur, which involves pooling resources in specific areas, but retaining separate statehood. Then again, this may change if Barbados or maybe Trinidad were to express interest in a union with this group of countries on a dignified basis. But why would they do this? This is likely to occur only in the rare context of enlightened leadership which sees a particular role for small Windward Islands states and perceives union as a way of achieving it. Owen Arthur's proposal for a Barbados/OECS confederation suggests that such enlightened leadership may well be in the offing.[73]

11 *"A Scuffling of Islands" or a Nation?*

In a divided world
That don't need islands no more
Are we doomed forever,
To be at somebody's mercy.
Little keys can open up mighty doors
    – David Rudder, "The Gilded Collection 1986–1989"

The forces driving the OECS political union initiative have become more manifest since the initiative was first mooted in 1986. Nebulous portents of free trade blocs, a shifting relationship with Europe and its potentially destabilizing economic effects, and an increasingly unreceptive international environment have revealed their form and the precise ways in which they alter the landscape for small Caribbean states, and small states in general. These have taken shape in the form of the WTO, which has restructured the global economy in the interest of free trade under the hegemony of the United States and the Group of Seven; NAFTA and the proposed regional hemispheric FTAA which aims to lock CARICOM states into a reciprocal free trade regime with North and South America, with serious implications for the regional integration movement within both CARICOM and the OECS; the Cotonou partnership, which replaces the Lomé Conventions and which aims at replacing a system of nonreciprocal arrangements between developed and developing countries with reciprocal arrangements and which, ultimately, deprives CARICOM states of any special considerations.

The Caribbean's first major encounter with the restructured international environment took the form of the WTO's rejection of the European Union's revised banana regime. The regime replaced national preferential arrangements with a common system of quotas and tariffs governing banana imports into the single European market. Regional governments had worked hard to ensure that the changes necessary to bring the banana protocol in line with the requirements of the single European market would continue to provide them with the protected environment which they were convinced was necessary for their products to survive against their Latin American competitors. The WTO, in response to a challenge of the regime from the United States, Guatemala, Ecuador, Mexico and Honduras, ruled that elements, particularly the introduction of a system of licences governing the import of bananas into the market – thought to favour traditional suppliers – violated some of the provisions the General Agreement on Tariffs and Trade. Windward Islands' governments had argued consistently that the industry could not survive without protection and its collapse, given its contribution to GDP, employment and foreign exchange earnings, would have severe effects on their economies and societies. Despite this, they were initially not allowed representation before the dispute panel, because their interest in the industry fell far below the required 10 per cent of the trade, making them a minor player.

The second global trend affecting CARICOM states has been the increased regionalization of economic relations, developing apace with the globalization of trade. The region's first experience with this was the creation of NAFTA which, especially for those countries which had developed manufacturing industries based on CBI preferences, raised fears that NAFTA would erode CBI concessions, resulting in trade diversion from the region to Mexico.[1] The efforts of various CARICOM states to gain accession to NAFTA, based on the dutiful implementation of structural adjustment programmes to open up their economies, have proved unsuccessful. Instead, CARICOM states are confronting their participation in a free trade area stretching from Canada to Argentina.

There are a number of implications arising from the CARICOM region's participation in the proposed FTAA. The FTAA represents an opening up of the markets of member states to others within the arrangement, without regard to preferences arising from special considerations such as small size, which has traditionally been a feature of Caribbean international trade relations. CARICOM states' attempt to make small size central to the FTAA process through the institution of a separate negotiating group for small states was rebuffed. Instead, they had to settle for a "Consultative Group on Small Economies", restricted to monitoring negotiations and making recommendations to the negotiating council on matters of special interest to small countries.[2] Not only does the FTAA require a commitment to free trade, but it aims at implementing many WTO provisions in this regard in advance of the WTO schedule.[3] This represents a move in the opposite direction from preferences and special considerations. The regionalization process does not allow CARICOM states to opt out of the arrangement without severe costs. To sit on the sidelines is to be excluded from one of the major markets. In addition, CARICOM states are being nudged, not too gently, into embracing the FTAA. An example of this was provided by Bill Clinton's suggestion that extension of CBI II benefits be afforded only to countries actively participating in the FTAA.

The third development restructuring the international relations of CARICOM states has been the revisioning of the relationship between the European Union and its ACP counterparts. The new relationship, reflected in the Cotonou partnership agreement, moves away from the underlying philosophy of EU responsibility for the welfare and development of former colonies (underscored by aid packages and one-way access for ACP countries to EU markets) to an arrangement more suited to the philosophy of global free trade which underpins the WTO. The various protocols governing the importation of ACP commodities such as rum, rice, sugar and bananas are expected to operate within a limited life span and, even so, must be subject to a waiver under General Agreement on Tariffs and Trade regulations. The European Union expects the EU/ACP relationship which characterized the Lomé Conventions to be replaced by regional free trade areas (reciprocal Regional Economic Partnership Agreements) with former ACP countries, falling in line with the imperatives of global free trade. For the CARICOM region, this means their subsumption into a broader Latin American arrangement. The Cotonou agreement also reflects a more realistic, though less palatable, portrayal of the relationship between the ACP and the European Union, despite the title's insistence on "partnership". The inclusion of issues of "good governance", "human rights" and "democracy" as considerations influencing the disbursement of development funds points to the inequality of this relationship.[4]

The global restructuring of CARICOM's external relations reveals consistent patterns. The first is the eschewing of the concept that small size requires special considerations, and its replacement by the ideology of a level playing field existing among sovereign states, despite differences in size or resource endowment. In the WTO, as the banana case forcefully illustrated, the only provisions for deviating from WTO obligations are made with respect to the least developed countries and, even so, the provisions are for a more generous timetable in implementing WTO regulations. The pattern is also evident in the European Union's "everything but arms" package, which allows duty- and quota-free entry to all products of Least Developed Countries (except arms) including sugar, bananas and rice, phased in over a three-year period. This was done despite ACP objections that they had not been consulted as provided for under the Cotonou agreement, and fears in the Caribbean that their products may not withstand more competition.[5] The trend was also noticeable in the FTAA negotiations, which have revealed a reluctance among member states, particularly the United States, to accept smallness as a modifying condition.

The other reality to which CARICOM states are finally facing up is the fact that national decision making, even by their traditional allies in Europe, has been curtailed by the institutionalization of the WTO. WTO consistency now governs all economic relations among states. Even before the WTO, when the single European market was being negotiated, regional states found that the United Kingdom could not guarantee their banana interests against competing interests of other members of the single European market, notably Spain and Germany. This is even more the case now that the single European market has opened up to Eastern European countries, which have a different relationship to ACP countries. In relation to the WTO, the European Union was forced to modify its revised banana regime to be consistent with WTO regulations. The Cotonou agreement also reflects a refashioning of EU/ACP relations to fit the imperatives of global free trade enshrined in the WTO. The same impetus is at work in the FTAA, where countries such as the United States are keen on opening the markets of members even before the WTO requires this.

The region's experience in the sphere of international trade in goods and services has run counter to confident claims made by free trade proponents about a universal spread of benefits for all countries. From the banana issue to attempts by the Organization for Economic Cooperation and Development to blacklist offshore financial centres in the Caribbean, the region has experienced a closing, rather than an opening, of economic spaces. In both instances, their favoured economic activities have been assessed as damaging to either the sectoral interests of developed countries, or particular economic interests in those countries. In the case of their tax structures, despite not contravening existing rules of international law, they are being subjected, on pain of sanction, to rules devised by powerful Organization for Economic Cooperation and Development countries to circumscribe their operations in this area. Their attempts to compete in one of the few arenas where size does not put them at a disadvantage are deemed as harming the "interests of honest tax payers in all countries around the world", distorting trade and investment flows, and "impos[ing] constraints on governments' ability to fulfil their democratically voted mandates to provide public services and infrastructures for their citizens".[6] What is clear is that powerful Organization for Economic Cooperation and Development states, when it suits them, can freely circumvent the WTO and other international structures to develop mechanisms and rules representing their own interests to which weaker countries are forced to conform, on pain of sanctions. This suggests that for small regional states, the WTO is of limited value on issues which run afoul of the same powerful forces or countries driving economic globalization.

CARICOM Responses

CARICOM has either responded, or been forced to respond, to these developments in a number of ways. The first implication of these trends is the pressure placed on CARICOM states to redefine how they perceive themselves and their relationship with Central and South America. The first major instance of this was the establishment of CARIFORUM, which represents a broadening of the CARICOM region to include Haiti and the Dominican Republic for the purposes of the Lomé Convention. The impetus for this came from the European Union, not the CARICOM region. The second development was the formation of the Association of Caribbean States, on the initiative of CARICOM, reflecting an attempt to embrace a more inclusive definition of the Caribbean region based on common problems. The third major instance is reflected in CARICOM's responses to overtures from the Dominican Republic regarding the formation of a free trade area, indicating an appreciation of its need for allies in the wider FTAA process. An important element in the broadening of CARICOM's relations with Latin America is the region's embrace of Cuba, in the face of hostility from the US government.

The CARICOM region has also responded on the international plane by putting its weight behind efforts to reintroduce small states and the peculiarities they face into the consciousness of organizations dealing with international trade. This has taken the form of regional support for and input into the fashioning of a vulnerability index attempting to establish that small island states, in particular, face special challenges to their survival and thus must be given special considerations by the international community. This has borne fruit in the joint Commonwealth and World Bank task force findings which make a case for the special difficulties which small states confront.[7] It has also introduced a new mechanism, the Regional Negotiating Machinery, to coordinate regional responses to international developments, especially in response to the tremendous burden placed on them by involvement in simultaneous processes, such as negotiating the FTAA and the Cotonou agreement.

Internally, the CARICOM region has responded by attempting to consolidate its own integration processes with the introduction of a Single Market and Economy (CSME), in an effort to maintain a distinct identity *vis-à-vis* wider trading arrangements. The CSME, which is at various stages of implementation among member states, aims at removing restrictions on capital flows, providing services and developing enterprises within the region, and facilitating unrestricted movement among a narrow section of its population: university graduates, sportsmen, artistes, media workers and musicians. Another important element of the CSME is the establishment of a Caribbean Court of Justice, which would play a major role in arbitrating disputes within the context of the CSME, and would address the intractable issue of implementation which dogs the process.

OECS Challenges and Responses

These developments have special relevance to the members of the OECS. Among CARICOM members, OECS countries have been most immediately affected by some of the developments described above. The WTO's ruling against the European Union's revised banana regime affects them directly, with potentially devastating effects to their economies, given their heavy reliance on the industry. In addition, they also have the most to lose from the shifting of attention away from the special challenges of small size. This process is evident not only on the global level but within CARICOM, where the CSME moves away from the principle of special and differential treatment, reflected in the classification of LDCs, to equal treatment for all. In response to the proposed CSME and their involvement in free trade agreements with North and South America and possibly Europe after 2008, OECS countries announced their intention to form their own single market.

An OECS study[8] on the OECS single market and economy noted, however, that an OECS single market was of limited benefit in light of the requirements of the larger CSME, which eliminates differential provisions for OECS states. Possibilities remained, however, in the production of goods and services through joint or integrated approaches. An OECS single market and economy could also run ahead of CARICOM in removing restrictions to travel within the OECS and exempting OECS nationals from the provisions of aliens land holding regulations in member states. Such a perspective suggests that the OECS economic integration process, and probably ultimately the CARICOM process, is likely to run out of steam, given their participation in larger trading blocs which would preclude any restrictions to the CARICOM market.

Cooperation, therefore, would occur in a more limited sphere, in areas such as health, sports and education. The impetus to strengthen foreign policy coordination, one of the weakest forms of cooperation, should also be furthered given increasing pressures on their small diplomatic machinery arising from their participation in these various arrangements. The OECS region has also attempted to diversify its relationships within the wider Caribbean region by signing a memorandum of agreement with Puerto Rico in 1991, establishing closer relations with the French overseas departments of Martinique, Guadeloupe and Cayenne, and participating in France's francophone initiative. Additionally, three OECS countries have signed trade agreements with Venezuela.[9] The OECS has also strengthened its presence and negotiating capacity in Brussels with the establishment in 1993 of a joint mission to the European Union, and is considering establishing a joint mission to the WTO. Unfortunately, OECS cooperation in foreign relations has not always proceeded in the direction of cooperation. Grenada maintains its own mission in Brussels, and Antigua is considering withdrawing from the joint Brussels mission. The joint diplomatic arrangement which St Kitts–Nevis, St Vincent and St Lucia shared in London has given way to separate country missions with, as one observer noted, the same burden of tasks but performed by a smaller staff.[10] Meanwhile, the OECS continues to confront the same problems which have plagued the nearly twenty-year integration experience: "chronic shortage of funds to meet their international needs and obligations"; "shortage of appropriately trained and experienced officers" especially in foreign affairs; and "deficiency in archive and record management", also manifested in foreign affairs.[11]

Whither OECS Political Integration?

The economic developments on the international plane serve to undermine many of the economic justifications advanced for political integration in the OECS experience, and appear to lend credence to some of the initiative's detractors. The relevance of a market of five hundred thousand people, in the face of integration processes involving millions, seems limited. It is also clear, especially given the European Union's experience, that initiatives such as freedom of movement, the development of common facilities, and approaches to problems and negotiating structures in foreign affairs do not require a political union. Rather, failures to achieve these speak more to the absence of political will. This undermining of the rationale for economic integration processes among CARICOM/OECS states is problematic, given the fact that both arrangements are based on economic rather than political models of integration. The integration process is aimed at securing gains on the economic front, with little attention to the goal of a Caribbean nationhood. This was most evident in the absence of a perceived OECS or CARICOM impact on people's lives. In the type of systems developed after the Federation, the goal of a Caribbean nation was relegated to an ideal, while efforts were concentrated on economic performance. Even in the OECS initiative, union was presented primarily as a route through which to achieve the ultimate goal of true economic integration. Herein lies the contradiction. The functioning of the OECS has not been particularly "democratic". Decisions to remove tariffs, establish and protect industry, combine foreign representation – in fact the decisions underpinning the system – have been made at a bureaucratic and political level, outside the realm of popular influence. On the other hand, such popular support was considered necessary to legitimize deeper integration. In this context, political union may be seen as no more than a convenience, necessary to ensure an uncomplicated framework for bureaucratic decision and action to take place. The contradiction was evident in the fact that the difficulties in the functioning of the integration system, which forced the question of union onto the agenda, were not known or appreciated at the popular level. People had simply not been privy to the functioning of the OECS.

The most important challenge confronting the regional process, however, is the reality that the original ideology and goals underpinning the Treaty of Chaguaramas are radically different from those of the broader integration processes by which these countries are being overtaken. CARICOM developed to address the economic development of its members by providing a protected environment within which to develop a productive base, based first on import substitution, then on competitive exports. This new regional thrust, referred to as "open regionalism", has the opposite goal of liberalizing national economies, reducing governments' role in the economy and opening national markets to foreign penetration. Its aim is to open economies to full trade liberalization, at least in respect to member states, which, for the CARICOM region, would be reflected in the dissolution of barriers to all FTAA and EU members, if reciprocal Regional Economic Partnership Agreements become the preferred formula for the EU/ACP relationship. It is not an approach consciously committed to the development of small regional economies, but assumes that all will benefit if they follow the rules of the game and find the economic activities in which they have a "competitive" advantage. It is also unlikely that any latent goal of an eventual political union among CARICOM states will be promoted by this regionalism. Such a union would have to be presented in its own right, with its own justifications that go beyond the economic. This raises the question: if not in the economic sphere then where must the impetus for political union, not only among OECS states, but among CARICOM states, lie? It turns attention more fully to the less tangible grounds on which support for political integration has been expressed.

Tendencies to view the insular Caribbean as constituting a potentially viable political entity are not new, and predate the West Indies Federation and the debates preceding its formation. As early as 1852, when the islands were still firmly under the rule of different colonial powers, V. Schoelcher observed:

> Upon regarding the West Indies' position in the middle of the ocean, glancing at the map which shows them to be almost in touch with each other, one cannot help but think that they may well come together some day to form a distinct social body in the modern world. . . . They might well unite in confederation, joined by common interest, and possess a merchant fleet, an industry, arts and a literature

government, but infused with more meaningful content. Perceptions of national sovereignty in the region must shift from a preoccupation with safeguarding separateness *vis-à-vis* other countries within the region, towards an appreciation of the real threats to sovereignty which the region faces. Such threats are inherent in the limits of the region's ability to influence global trends in the direction of development defined to address the needs and aspirations of its people; to protect its integrity against drug cartels and others who view the islands as points of convenience; and to ensure that resources, especially in terms of its territorial waters and sea bed (issues which will become more important with technological advances), are exploited in the service of its own development. These measures can be achieved only within a political framework premised on a more encompassing notion of sovereignty.

The existence of territories still locked into essentially dependent economic and political relationships with former colonial powers remains one of the strongest justifications for a more politically defined regionalism, even political union. In the anglophone Caribbean such territories include Anguilla, Montserrat, the British and US Virgin Islands, and the Cayman Islands. Islands such as Anguilla and Montserrat present clear difficulties in terms of their existence as independent states. Montserrat's experience with the volcano which destroyed its economic life and which, were it not for the tenacity of Montserratians in refusing to give up on the island, would have destroyed its political structures and its viability as a place to live, suggests that viability remains a real concern for the region. A regional integration system more frontally premised on political structures would provide possibilities for addressing the peculiarities of these political arrangements, as well as providing a basis for addressing secessionist movements in other formally independent territories.

What exactly can the Caribbean gain from the embrace of political union? Owen Arthur justified his interest in Barbados pursuing a political union with OECS states on the basis that "we are essentially one Caribbean people, one Caribbean family moulded by the experience and the essential vitality of a distinctive Caribbean way of life".[17] This is an appeal to a sense of Caribbean nationhood which, while ephemeral, still holds great emotional weight, particularly at the popular level. This discussion, in focusing on political processes, has been careful not to prescribe the precise form these should take. It is important that in defining and fashioning such arrangements the attachment to formal sovereignty which remains strong in some CARICOM territories be considered, as well as the cracks which have emerged in federations in Canada, the former Soviet Union and Yugoslavia. These experiences suggest the need for creativity in forging new types of political relationships to balance the strong nationalistic and individualistic characters of Caribbean islands with the requirements for common political action. This might require the emergence of a political form, new and uniquely developed to suit the specific requirements of the region, and built to respond to challenges as they emerge.

In conclusion, in the context of a wider Caribbean union, the OECS political initiative, whittled down to a more limited Windward Islands' effort, may at first appear insignificant, especially given its failure to result in anything concrete. This would be a misreading of the deeper significance of the initiative. The initiative was successful in placing the issue of political union squarely back on the regional agenda; this was timely, given the waning appeal of the economic model which dominated the postindependence experience. It has forced Barbados to reassess its relationship with the OECS countries and to express not only an economic but a political interest in the group, more than thirty years after the collapse of attempts to politically unite the Little Eight. The consultation process launched across the Windward Islands to assess interest in a political union indicated widespread interest in and support for political union, suggesting that for many in the region, the issue of political union is not dead. The Windward Islands have thrown out a challenge to the wider CARICOM region to put the issue of political union squarely on the agenda, in a context where the economic movement has lost its centre due to a transfigured international landscape. The limited options which Caribbean governments now face suggest that governments have little to lose from throwing open the issue of integration in its totality to structured popular debate.

Notes

Chapter 1

1. Hereafter referred to as Antigua.
2. Hereafter referred to as St Kitts–Nevis.
3. Hereafter referred to as St Vincent.
4. Hereafter referred to as Dominica.
5. William G. Demas, "Consolidating Our Independence: The Major Challenge for the West Indies" (lecture delivered at the Institute of International Relations, 1986). Demas was president of the Caribbean Development Bank at the time.
6. Dominica's prime minister, Eugenia Charles, suggested that the leaders were considering the idea even before then, after a visit to Japan in 1985 by St Lucia's Prime Minister Compton, St Vincent's Prime Minister Mitchell, and Antigua's Deputy Prime Minister Lester Bird, when they were made to feel the smallness of their islands. The Japanese had informed them that it took only two hours to manufacture the volume of cars they imported annually. Since then they had spoken informally on the question of OECS unity. See "How OECS Union Idea Evolved", *Weekend Voice*, 22 August 1987.
7. This is based on Mitchell's account of how the initiative evolved. See James F. Mitchell, *Two Decades of Caribbean Unity* (Kingstown, St Vincent: Government Printing Office, 1987), 2.
8. Ibid.
9. This paper is reproduced ibid., 9.
10. Ibid.
11. V.C. Bird (prime minister of Antigua and Barbuda), welcome address at the opening ceremony of the tenth meeting of the OECS Authority, St John's, Antigua, 28–29 November 1986.
12. Compton denied that OECS union was an issue in the general elections. See "Compton Fully Behind Political Union", *Barbados Advocate*, 16 May 1987, 5.
13. See Rickey Singh, "Defeat in UWP [United Workers' Party] Victory: Big Blow to OECS Union", *Caribbean Contact*, May 1986.
14. Ibid. Also see Mitchell, *Two Decades*, 2.
15. See Mitchell, *Two Decades*, 2. McIntyre and Demas were both noted champions of Caribbean regionalism. Their role in the Caribbean integration debate is discussed in chapter 2.
16. James F. Mitchell (prime minister of St Vincent and the Grenadines), address at the opening ceremony of the eleventh meeting of the OECS Authority, Tortola, British Virgin Islands, 27 May 1987.
17. Ibid.
18. OECS, "Conclusions of the Eleventh Meeting of the Authority", Tortola, British Virgin Islands, 28–29 May 1987.
19. The communiqué is reproduced in full in *From Tortola to Kingstown: A*

Report on Eastern Caribbean Political Union (Castries: The Voice Press, *c.*1991).

20. Ronald Sanders, "Political Union in the OECS: An Opportunity Lost", *Courier* 116 (July–August 1989): 50. See also *From Tortola to Kingstown*, 5.

21. Lester Bird, interview by author, Grenada, 6 July 1989.

22. Ibid.

23. Kennedy Simmonds, interview by author, Antigua, 1 June 1989.

24. Interview with Lester Bird.

25. OECS press release, 27 November 1987.

26. Osborne was optimistic that Britain would allow Montserrat to enter the political union without a change in its position as a British colony, as had been the case in the 1958–1962 West Indies Federation.

27. John Osborne, interview by the Caribbean News Agency (CANA), in *Barbados Advocate,* 21 June 1987, 2.

28. See "Montserrat's Reservations about OECS", *Caribbean Contact,* May 1988.

29. See "Montserrat: Not without Antigua", *The Voice,* 13 April 1988, 3.

30. Bird's proposal for closer cooperation among the Leewards had led to speculation that Montserrat might withdraw from the initiative. See *CANA News Bulletin,* 16 July 1987.

31. John Osborne, interview by author, Antigua, 2 June 1989. Osborne was responding to a question on Montserrat's ability to participate in an OECS political union while still a British colony.

32. Interview with John Osborne.

33. Kennedy Simmonds, "Address by the Prime Minister, Dr the Rt Hon. Kennedy Simmonds, at the OECS Summit held in Tortola, 27 May 1987 on Closer Union" (mimeo).

34. See Sanders, "Political Union in the OECS".

35. Ibid., 50.

36. See "BVI Distanced from OECS", *BVI Beacon,* 4 June 1987.

37. H. Lavity Stoutt (chief minister of the British Virgin Islands), address at the opening ceremony of the eleventh meeting of the OECS Authority, Tortola, British Virgin Islands, 27 May 1987.

38. These include, among others, the judicial system, education and health.

39. H. Lavity Stoutt, interview by author, Antigua, 2 June 1989.

40. See OECS press release, 29 November 1988.

41. Eugenia Charles, interview by author, Dominica, 9 June 1989.

42. "Plans for OECS Unity Criticised", *Caribbean Times,* 6 August 1987.

43. Julian Hunte (leader of the opposition; leader, St Lucia Labour Party), interview by Cynthia Barrow, St Lucia, 26 May 1988.

44. See "SCOPE Meets Here", *The Voice,* 29 August 1987.

45. Ibid.

46. "SCOPE Call for Policy on OECS Unity Proposal: Regional Opposition Criticise Governments' Approach to Issue", *The Voice,* 2 September 1987.

47. "Opposition Parties Rap Move for an OECS Union", *EC News,* 4 March 1988, 3.

48. Hunte in St Lucia; Dr Ralph Gonsalves, Movement for National Unity, in St Vincent; and Tim Hector, Antigua Caribbean Liberation Movement.

49. Keohane and Hoffmann note the intensification during the 1970s and 1980s of "technology-based oligopolistic competition among increasingly internationalized firms, dependent on large-scale operations for profitability", and argue

that these changes and the competitive pressures they induced were the driving force behind the European Community's transformation to a single market. See Robert O. Keohane and Stanley Hoffmann, "Institutional Change in Europe in the 1980s", in *The New European Community: Decisionmaking and Institutional Change*, ed. R.O. Keohane and S. Hoffmann (Boulder: Westview Press, 1991), 5.

50. For a Caribbean perspective on what this would mean see Roderick G. Rainford, "Some Implications for the Caribbean of the Introduction of the Single European Market in 1992" (Port of Spain, Trinidad, 1989, mimeo); and Diane Phillip, "The OECS Countries and the Lomé Convention: An Assessment" (Kingston, Jamaica, 1989, mimeo). For a European Community perspective see Dieter Frisch, "1992 and the Developing Countries" (Bonn, 1988, mimeo).

51. The Canadian/US free trade area came into being in 1989 and gave way to NAFTA, which included Mexico, in 1993.

52. For details on the protocols and the issues involved see Paul Sutton, "The Banana Regime of the European Union, the Caribbean and Latin America", *Journal of Interamerican Studies and World Affairs* 39, no. 2 (Summer 1997): 5–36; and Keith Nurse and Wayne Sandiford, *Windward Islands Bananas: Challenges and Options under the Single European Market* (Kingston, Jamaica: Friedrich Ebert Stiftung, 1995).

53. See quotation from Richard Bernal, Jamaican ambassador to the United States, in an address to the US House of Representatives' Ways and Means Committee on Trade, in Don Marshall, *Caribbean Political Economy at the Crossroads: NAFTA and Regional Developmentalism* (London: Macmillan, 1998), 156.

54. This perspective is developed in Patsy Lewis, "Revisiting the Grenada Invasion: The OECS' Role, and Its Impact on Regional and International Politics", *Social and Economic Studies* 48, no. 3 (September 1999): 85–120.

Chapter 2

1. See chapter 14 of Gordon K. Lewis, *The Growth of the Modern West Indies* (London: MacGibbon and Kee, 1968), which gives an account of the type of regional influences which encouraged Caribbean interest in federation. It also summarizes what various interest groups expected to achieve from a political federation.

2. R.L. Watts, *New Federations: Experiments in the Commonwealth* (Oxford: Clarendon Press, 1966), 63. Giovanni Arrighi and John S. Saul project a different analysis of the dynamic contributing to the formation of interregional schemes and to the decolonization/independence movement generally. They argue that both processes, actively promoted by the United States, were beneficial to international capitalism because of the wider access to markets which regional arrangements presented, and the weakening of colonial ties which eased US access. See Arrighi and Saul, *Essays on the Political Economy of Africa* (New York: Monthly Review Press, 1953), 51–52.

3. See John Mordecai, *The West Indies: The Federal Negotiations* (London: Allen and Unwin, 1968).

4. For details on what these were, see Jesse Harris Proctor, Jr., "British West Indian Government and Co-operation in Transition 1920–1960", *Social and Economic Studies* 11 (1962): 273–304.

5. Watts, *New Federations*, 35.

6. This was expressed in a paper produced by Williams and the People's National Movement entitled "Economics of Nationhood" (Trinidad and Tobago, 1959).

7. See Anthony T. Bryan, "The CARICOM and Latin American Integration Experiences: Observations on Theoretical Origins, and Comparative Performance", in *Ten Years of CARICOM* (papers presented at the seminar Economic Integration in the Caribbean, Bridgetown, Barbados, July 1983) (Washington, DC: Inter-American Development Bank, Institute for Latin American Integration, CARICOM Secretariat, 1984), 71–94.

8. These are detailed in Patrick Emmanuel, *Approaches to Caribbean Political Integration,* Occasional Paper no. 21 (Cave Hill, Barbados: Institute of Social and Economic Research, 1987).

9. See F.G. Carnell, "Political Implications of Federalism in New States", in *Federalism and Economic Growth in Underdeveloped Countries,* by U.K. Hicks et al. (London: Allen and Unwin, 1961), 9.

10. W.A. Lewis, "The Industrialisation of the British West Indies", *Caribbean Economic Review* 2 (1950): 1–61. Lewis was revolutionary in advocating industrialization as the basis for Caribbean development. He was attacking the perspective, still prevalent in British colonial circles, that small countries such as those of the West Indies could never hope to develop manufactur-ing industries, but were destined to remain primary producers of export crops.

11. Lewis saw a complementarity between industry and agriculture in that, while industry had to be developed to allow agriculture to provide a higher standard of living, agriculture must provide a higher standard of living to boost demand for manufactured goods, in order for industry to develop.

12. Manufacturing was not to be the only absorber of surplus labour: the development of tourism, along with emigration, would play a role in this.

13. These were the United Kingdom, the United States, and Latin America, to a lesser degree.

14. This was to be modelled after the Puerto Rican development corporation.

15. For a survey of the theoretical arguments which have influenced the Latin American integration experience see David Lehmann, *Democracy and Development in Latin America: Economics, Politics and Religion in the Postwar Period* (Cambridge: Polity Press, 1990).

16. Kay noted that there were two trends in this school, "reformists and marxists", with different emphases and prescriptions. Despite this, there were common elements that defined the school. See Cristobal Kay, *Latin American Theories of Development and Underdevelopment* (London: Routledge, 1989), chapter 5.

17. See Magnus Blomstrom and Bjorn Hettne, *Development in Transition: The Dependency Debate and Beyond – Third World Responses* (London: Zed Books, 1984).

18. These include the Latin American Free Trade Association (Argentina, Chile, Brazil, Paraguay, Peru, Uruguay and Mexico) in 1960, the

Central American Common Market (El Salvador, Guatemala, Honduras and Nicaragua) in 1962, and the Andean Group in 1969. These schemes were also influenced by western European integration. See Eduardo R. Conesa, "The Integration Experience in Latin America", in *Ten Years of CARICOM* (papers presented at the seminar Economic Integration in the Caribbean, Bridgetown, Barbados, July 1983) (Washington, DC: Inter-American Development Bank, Institute for Latin American Integration, CARICOM Secretariat, 1984), 95–101.

19. European integration began with the establishment of the European Coal and Steel Community in 1952. For a detailed background to the development of European integration, see Altiero Spinelli, "The Growth of the European Movement since the Second World War", in *European Integration: Selected Readings*, ed. Michael Hodges (Harmondsworth: Penguin, 1972), 43–68.

20. For an account of the Latin American influence on Caribbean integration see Bryan, "The CARICOM and Latin American Integration Experiences", 71–94.

21. Although Demas is discussed as part of this group, it is important to note that he did not consider himself a member, nor was he considered as part of the group. He is included here because he shares common concerns and insights into the character of Caribbean economies and the need for industrialization as the basis for development, *inter alia*.

22. For critiques of their operations see Owen Jefferson, "Some Aspects of the Post-War Economic Development of Jamaica"; Edwin Carrington, "Industrialization in Trinidad and Tobago since 1950"; and Selwyn Ryan, "Restructuring of the Trinidad Economy"; all in *Readings in the Political Economy of the Caribbean*, ed. Norman Girvan and Owen Jefferson (Kingston, Jamaica: New World Group, 1971), 108–20, 143–50, and 187–203, respectively.

23. This refers to the differentiation of agriculture into modern, large-scale plantation-type production, directed at the export sector, and traditional peasant agriculture, internally directed. The former commanded resources and special consideration from the state, at the expense of the latter.

24. Alister McIntyre, "Some Issues of Trade Policy in the West Indies", *New World Quarterly* 2, no. 2 (1966), reproduced in *Readings in the Political Economy of the Caribbean*, ed. Norman Girvan and Owen Jefferson (Kingston, Jamaica: New World Group, 1971), 165–83.

25. His thesis is elaborated in William G. Demas, *The Economics of Development in Small Countries* (Montreal: McGill University Press, 1965).

26. Demas identified peculiar problems associated with small size as, *inter alia*, an obsessive urge for North American standards of consumption; the dichotomy between plantation and peasant agriculture; the dependence of export agriculture on preference and special marketing arrangements; and a great dependence on foreign capital. See Demas, *The Economics of Development in Small Countries*, 117–18. Brewster and Thomas criticized his emphasis on size, arguing that it detracted from more fundamental problems of underdevelopment. They favoured a more integrated type of regional cooperation, going

beyond the purely economic instruments of free trade and customs union, involving the integrated production of goods across the region, utilizing local resources to develop a range of heavy primary industries. See Havelock Brewster and Clive Thomas, *The Dynamics of West Indian Economic Integration,* vol. 1 of *Studies in Regional Economic Integration* (Mona, Jamaica: Institute of Social and Economic Research, 1967). See also Brewster and Thomas, "Aspects of the Theory of Economic Integration", *Journal of Common Market Studies* 8, no. 2 (December 1969): 110–31.

27. The basis of Demas's critique of Rostow was his definition of "self-sustained growth", which Demas believed could be achieved without necessarily solving problems of underdevelopment and structural unemployment. He also rejected per-capita income as an indication of development, questioning the assumption that underdeveloped countries with high per-capita income were more "developed" or nearer the takeoff point than other countries with lower per-capita income. Demas differentiated between structural transformation and high per-capita income, arguing that the former was associated with a continuous increase in real income, while high per-capita income did not necessarily indicate structural transformation.

28. This refers to the existence of high-paying manufacturing and mineral sectors in countries like Trinidad and Jamaica, alongside low-paying traditional agriculture.

29. Demas, *The Economics of Development in Small Countries,* 7–10.

30. See chapter 3 of William Demas, *Essays on Caribbean Integration and Development* (Mona, Jamaica: Institute of Social and Economic Research, 1976), where he goes into more details on the specific benefits arising from regional economic integration. He advocates "economic regionalism" as a start, because of the "unattractiveness" of a federal political solution for the Caribbean. He warned that this might not provide the solution to the Caribbean's development problems, because the region would still be too small.

31. Demas elaborated on the link between national and regional development and the need for a framework within which to coordinate both. Ibid., 117–47.

32. Norman Girvan and Owen Jefferson, "Corporate vs. Caribbean Integration", in *Readings in the Political Economy of the Caribbean,* ed. Norman Girvan and Owen Jefferson (Kingston, Jamaica: New World Group, 1971), 87–98.

33. See Kari Levitt and Lloyd Best, "Character of Caribbean Economy", in *Caribbean Economy: Dependence and Backwardness,* ed. George Beckford (Mona, Jamaica: Institute of Social and Economic Research, 1984), 34–60; and Lloyd Best, "A Model of Pure Plantation Economy", *Social and Economic Studies* 17, no. 3 (1968).

34. Bryan noted that the Latin American structuralist school influenced the New World Group, particularly in its critique of multinational corporations in the Caribbean. See Bryan, "The CARICOM and Latin American Integration Experiences".

35. Lloyd Best, "Size and Survival", in *Readings in the Political Economy of the Caribbean,* ed. Norman Girvan and Owen Jefferson (Kingston, Jamaica: New World Group, 1971), 29–34.

36. Beckford developed this to include an analysis of agricultural produc-

tion in the Caribbean, pointing out that the emphasis was still on export agriculture, where the plantations were dominant, rather than on the peasantry, whose production was for domestic consumption. He characterized the contemporary Caribbean economy as a "modification of slave plantation economy, although more diversified as a result of peasant activity". See George Beckford, *Caribbean Rural Economy* (1975; reprint, Mona, Jamaica: Institute of Social and Economic Research, 1984), 83.

37. For a more detailed summary of essential elements of the analysis of the New World Group and their contribution to Caribbean thinking see Denis Benn, *The Growth and Development of Political Ideas in the Caribbean: 1774–1983* (Mona, Jamaica: Institute of Social and Economic Research, 1987).

38. See Andrew Axline, *Caribbean Integration: The Politics of Regionalism* (London: Frances Pinter, 1979), chapter 2.

39. The development of the theory of economic integration is usually associated with Jacob Viner's writings on customs union, which provides the basis for European integration. Traditional customs union theory, which developed as a branch of neoclassical welfare economics, is primarily concerned with the effects which result from the freeing of trade among a group of countries, in terms of both the participating countries and the outside world. For an elaboration of this theory see Jacob Viner, *The Customs Union Issue* (New York: Carnegie Endowment for International Peace, 1950); Bela Balassa, *The Theory of Economic Integration* (London: Allen and Unwin, 1962); and Tibor Scitovsky, *Economic Theory and*

Western European Integration (Stanford, Calif.: Stanford University Press, 1958).

40. For a similar but more detailed critique of the New World Group see Don Marshall, *Caribbean Political Economy at the Crossroads: NAFTA and Regional Developmentalism* (London: Macmillan, 1998), 61.

41. Customs union theory was based on Viner's *Customs Union Issue*.

42. Balassa, *The Theory of Economic Integration*, 68.

43. See Axline, *Caribbean Integration*, 7.

44. Ibid.

45. See Bela Balassa, "Toward a Theory of Economic Integration", in *Latin American Economic Integration: Experience and Prospects*, ed. M.S. Wionczek (New York: Praeger, 1966), 21–33.

46. Gunnar Myrdal, in *Economic Theory and Underdeveloped Regions* (London: G. Duckworth, 1957), argued that poverty and underdevelopment were mutually reinforcing. In unions between countries or regions with different levels of development, this was manifested in "backwash" and "spread effects". Expansion in one area had "backwash effects" in others because there was a tendency for factors to flow from areas of low activity to those experiencing expansion, thus aggravating regional inequality. Certain aspects of economic theory, particularly the free play of market forces, aggravated such inequalities. See also C. Eckenstein, "Regional Integration among Unequally Developed Countries", in *Regionalism and the Commonwealth Caribbean: Special Lecture Series No. 2* (papers presented at the seminar Foreign Policies of Caribbean States, Trinidad and Tobago, April–June 1968), ed. Roy Preiswerk (St Augustine, Trinidad: Institute of International

Relations, 1969), 41–55; Hiroshi Kitamura, "Economic Theory and the Economic Integration of Underdeveloped Regions", in *Latin American Economic Integration: Experience and Prospects,* ed. M.S. Wionczek (New York: Praeger, 1966), 42–63.

47. For a contrary view see Staffan Burestain Linden, "Customs Union and Economic Development", in *Latin American Economic Integration: Experience and Prospects,* ed. M.S. Wionczek (New York: Praeger, 1966), 32–41. He believed that a customs union among underdeveloped countries had a greater number of strictly economic arguments in its favour than its counterpart among industrialized countries.

48. See Axline, *Caribbean Integration,* chapter 2.

49. Before the report was finished the group reportedly fell out with the governments. This was published as Brewster and Thomas, *Studies in Regional Economic Integration,* Volume I.

50. This is made clear in the attitudes of some of these groups, discussed in chapters 8 and 9.

51. See Michael Hodges, ed., *European Integration: Selected Readings* (Harmondsworth: Penguin, 1972).

52. The transactionalist approach, developed by Karl Deutsch, is not as useful for our purposes. It focused on the formation of communities or the interdependence of participating units, and judged the integration process on the volume of such transactions – social, economic and political.

53. The British attempts at federations included the Indian Federation of 1935, fragmented into India and Pakistan in 1947; Malaya, 1948; Rhodesia and Nyasaland, 1953; Nigeria, 1954; the West Indies, 1958; and South Arabia, 1959. The French attempts included Indochina, which fragmented into North and South Vietnam, Cambodia, and Laos; French West Africa, which included the Ivory Coast, Dahomey, Upper Volta and Niger; French Equatorial Africa which, in 1958, disintegrated into Gabon, Chad, the Congo and the Central African Republic. The Dutch attempted a federation of Indonesia that was rejected, after independence in 1950, in favour of a unitary state.

54. K.C. Wheare, "Some Pre-Requisites of Federal Government", chapter 3 of *Federal Government,* 4th ed. (London: Oxford University Press, 1963).

55. William H. Riker, *Federalism: Origin, Operation, Significance* (Boston: Little Brown, 1964).

56. Thomas A. Franck, "Why Federations Fail", in *Why Federations Fail: An Inquiry into the Requisites for Successful Federalism,* ed. Thomas A. Franck (New York: New York University Press, 1968), 167–97.

57. Ian Boxill, *Ideology and Caribbean Integration* (Kingston, Jamaica: Consortium Graduate School of Social Sciences, University of the West Indies, 1993), 31.

58. Ibid., 39.

59. David Mitrany, *A Working Peace System* (London: Royal Institute of International Affairs, 1943) and *The Functional Theory of Politics* (London: M. Robertson for the London School of Economic and Political Science, 1975).

60. Ernst B. Haas, *The Uniting of Europe* (Stanford, Calif.: Stanford University Press, 1958).

61. Ernst B. Haas and Philippe C. Schmitter, "Economics and Differential Patterns of Political Integration: Projections about Unity in Latin America", *International Organization* 18, no. 4 (Summer 1964): 705–37.

62. Ibid.
63. Automaticity results because it is nearly impossible to make isolated decisions in discrete economic sectors. Regional bureaucrats play an important role in furthering the process.
64. Negotiated integration involves a looser institutional structure with a flexible timetable for dismantling barriers. Decision making remains primarily in the hands of government delegates, and the regional secretariat is confined to technical and housekeeping tasks.
65. It also calls for a reexamination of the rate of transaction among member states and an analysis of the adaptability of the chief actors in the governmental and private spheres. This involves an examination of the ability to adapt in order to accommodate difficulties and crises, evident in the ability to redefine aims.
66. M.S. Wionczek, "Introduction: Requisites for Viable Integration", in *Latin American Economic Integration: Experience and Prospects*, ed. M.S. Wionczek (New York: Praeger, 1966), 3–18.
67. J.S. Nye, "Patterns and Catalysts in Regional Integration", *International Organization* 19, no. 4 (Autumn 1965): 70–84.
68. Ibid.
69. For a more detailed discussion of how ideology hampered cooperation in the economic sphere and in foreign affairs, see Boxill, *Ideology and Caribbean Integration*, 65–68.

Chapter 3

1. Grenada became independent in 1974, Dominica in 1978, St Lucia and St Vincent and the Grenadines in 1979, Antigua in 1981, St Kitts–Nevis in 1983.
2. For a description of these see H. Springer, *Reflection on the Failure of the West Indies Federation* (Cambridge, Mass.: Harvard University, Centre for International Affairs, 1962).
3. See James F. Mitchell, "Statement at the Opening Ceremony of the CARICOM Heads of Government Conference on June 29th, 1987 in St Lucia", in his *Two Decades of Caribbean Unity* (Kingstown, St Vincent: Government Printing Office, 1987), 19–25.
4. The Closer Union Commission that was constituted to solicit popular opinion recommended that the Leeward Islands' Federation be dissolved and united with the Windwards under a single government. See *Report of the Closer Union Commission, 1932–33*, Cmd. 4383, cited in Ann Spackman, *Constitutional Development of the West Indies 1922–1968: A Selection from the Major Documents* (Bridgetown, Barbados: Caribbean Universities Press, 1975), 284–88.
5. This is discussed in John Mordecai, *The West Indies: The Federal Negotiations* (London: Allen and Unwin, 1968), chapter 1.
6. Emmanuel counted seven reports and initiatives towards this end, including the 1972 "Tobago Declaration" by a group of West Indians including W.A. Lewis, and the recommendations of the Constitutional Commission on the West Indies Associated States and Montserrat, headed by Alister McIntyre, published in 1973. See Patrick Emmanuel, *Approaches to Caribbean Political Integration*, Occasional Paper no. 21 (Cave Hill, Barbados: Institute of Social and Economic Research, 1987).

7. Montserrat and the British Virgin Islands remained Crown Colonies, and are still British colonies.

8. See Ann Spackman, "(i) Extracts from the West Indies Associated States Supreme Court Agreement, 1967", and "(ii) Extracts from the West Indies Associated States Supreme Court Order, 1967 (S.I. 223/1967)", in *Constitutional Development of the West Indies 1922–1968: A Selection from the Major Documents* (Bridgetown, Barbados: Caribbean Universities Press, 1975), 403–13.

9. Britain still hoped for a federation with one or more of the independent countries. It therefore made the process for achieving independence more difficult by requiring not only a two-thirds majority of elected members of the legislature (as provided for if they joined with an independent Caribbean country), but an additional two-thirds majority in a referendum to alter the constitution.

10. It replaced the Regional Council of Ministers which was established between Barbados and the Leewards and Windwards after the Federation's collapse. It was an informal arrangement, its aims being "to administer certain common services and perform such other functions as may be agreed [upon] from time to time". See OECS, *Why a Political Union of OECS Countries? The Background and the Issues* (Castries, St Lucia: OECS Secretariat, 1988).

11. Spackman, "(i) Extracts from the West Indies Associated States Supreme Court Agreement, 1967" and "(ii) Extracts from the West Indies Associated States Supreme Court Order, 1967 (S.I. 223/1967)".

12. In Latin America it gave rise to the smaller Andean Group, the Latin American Free Trade Association's transformation into the Latin American Integration Association, and Honduras's withdrawal from the Central American Common Market. See Eduardo R. Conesa, "The Integration Experience in Latin America", in *Ten Years of CARICOM* (papers presented at the seminar Economic Integration in the Caribbean, Bridgetown, Barbados, July 1983) (Washington, DC: Inter-American Development Bank, Institute for Latin American Integration, CARICOM Secretariat, 1984), 95–101. The East African Common Market suffered from friction arising from Kenya's superior economic performance and larger size; see J.S. Nye, "Patterns and Catalysts in Regional Integration", *International Organization* 19 (Autumn 1965): 870–84.

13. See Anthony Payne, *The Politics of the Caribbean Community 1961–1979: Regional Integration amongst New States* (Manchester: Manchester University Press, 1980), 199. In particular, see chapters 3 and 4 for a review of CARIFTA. See also Andrew Axline, *Caribbean Integration: The Politics of Regionalism* (London: Frances Pinter, 1979), 115.

14. Payne suggested that with the experience of the Federation's collapse, they wanted their own arrangement in case CARIFTA was abandoned. See Payne, *The Politics of the Caribbean Community*.

15. The council was its principal organ, empowered to take decisions binding on member states, although it required unanimity.

16. This was a novel element in integration schemes in developing countries.

17. See Alister McIntyre, *Elements in a Sub-Regional Strategy for the Caribbean* (monograph, September

1973); and Fitzgerald Francis, "An Overview of the Economies of the English-Speaking Caribbean Countries", address by UN/OECS economic adviser at the Training Programme of the Caribbean Association of Industry and Commerce in collaboration with the Guadeloupe Chamber of Commerce and Industry, Pointe-à-Pitre, Guadeloupe, 27–29 April 1983.

18. The WISA states could have entered the European Economic Community as non-independent British colonies, which would have weakened the bargaining position of the independent Caribbean countries who now had to renegotiate their special relationship with Britain. The MDCs preferred a united front with the LDCs, and were thus more amenable to LDC demands to move the integration process beyond a free trade area. See Payne, *The Politics of the Caribbean Community*, chapter 5; and Rosina Wiltshire, "Regional Integration and Conflict in the Commonwealth Caribbean" (PhD diss., University of Michigan, 1974).

19. See Payne, *The Politics of the Caribbean Community*, 151.

20. Ibid., 154.

21. Montserrat sought special concessions because of its status as a British colony and its small size, while in Antigua, where the government had changed, the matter had become a partisan political issue. Payne, *The Politics of the Caribbean Community*, 155–56.

22. For discussions of its performance in the 1970s and 1980s, see William G. Demas, "Some Thoughts on the Caribbean Community", *Bulletin of East Caribbean Affairs* 2, no. 8 (October 1976): 1–3; Alister McIntyre, "Review of Integration Movements in the Third World

with Particular Reference to the Caribbean Community", in *Ten Years of CARICOM* (papers presented at the seminar Economic Integration in the Caribbean, Bridgetown, Barbados, July 1983) (Washington, DC: Inter-American Development Bank, Institute for Latin American Integration, CARICOM Secretariat, 1984), 14–26; George Reid, "The Evolving Structure of the CARICOM Trade Regime", *CARICOM Bulletin* 5 (1984); "CARICOM after Ten Years: The Economic Record – Cracks in the Community Show Up in a New Trade War", *Caribbean and West Indies Chronicles* (June–July 1984): 4, 6; Alister McIntyre, "The Caribbean after Grenada: Four Challenges Facing the Regional Movement" (St Augustine, Trinidad, 1984, mimeo); Anthony Payne, "The Rise and Fall of Caribbean Regionalisation", *Journal of Common Market Studies* 19, no. 3 (March 1981): 255–80; Mirlande Hippolyte-Manigat, "What Happened in Ocho Rios: Last Chance for CARICOM?", *Caribbean Review* 12, no. 2 (Spring 1983): 10–14; Karl M. Bennett, "An Evaluation of the Contribution of CARICOM to Intra-Regional Caribbean Trade", *Social and Economic Studies* 31, no. 1 (1982): 74–88.

23. Quoted in Hippolyte-Manigat, "Crisis in CARICOM or CARICOM Crisis?" (paper presented at An International Conference on the Caribbean, Mexico City, 20–25 August 1979), 2.

24. Swinburne Lestrade, *CARICOM's Less Developed Countries: A Review of the Progress of the LDC's under the CARICOM Arrangements* (Cave Hill, Barbados: Institute of Social and Economic Research, 1981).

25. An example of this was the paint factory set up in Dominica in a joint venture project with Barbadian interests, in competition with one in Antigua. Barbados was also resisting Article 56, on the grounds that such protection caused extreme dislocation to similar products that relied on access to ECCM markets. See Lestrade, *CARICOM's Less Developed Countries*, 23.

26. See WISA press release, *c.* March 1979.

27. For example, they were forced to overcome their differences and present a common front on the restructuring of the University of the West Indies, which threatened to reduce their limited control over the university.

28. See chapter 5.

29. Grenada, for example, supported the Soviet Union's intervention in Afghanistan, while this was violently opposed by the other governments.

30. This author has argued that the invasion was illegal under international law. See Patsy Lewis-Meeks, "An Analysis of the Legal Justification for the United States Invasion of Grenada on the Basis of the Invitation from the OECS" (MPhil thesis, Cambridge University, 1988).

31. This has already occurred with a trading of shares on the Barbados, Trinidad and Jamaica stock markets.

32. Although the deadline for this was July 1991 it still has not materialized, with Antigua and Jamaica, in particular, resisting it. These decisions were taken at the tenth Heads of Government meeting in Grenada, July 1989.

33. This decision was taken at the Eleventh CARICOM Summit in Kingston, Jamaica, August 1990. See "The Kingston Declaration" (*c.* August 1990, mimeo).

34. Kennedy Simmonds, address at the opening ceremony of the ninth meeting of the OECS Authority, Basseterre, St Kitts, 28–30 May 1986.

35. Herbert Blaize, address at the opening ceremony of the ninth meeting of the OECS Authority, Basseterre, St Kitts, 28–30 May 1986. Blaize died in December 1989.

36. Simmonds, address at the opening ceremony of the tenth meeting of the OECS Authority, St John's, Antigua, 28–29 November 1986.

37. John Compton, address at the eighth meeting of the OECS Authority, Kingstown, St Vincent, 28–29 November 1985.

38. Compton, address at the opening ceremony of the ninth meeting of the OECS Authority, Basseterre, St Kitts, 28–30 May 1986.

39. Blaize, address at the eighth meeting of the OECS Authority, Kingstown, St Vincent, 28–29 November 1985.

40. Compton, address at the eighth meeting of the OECS Authority.

41. Vaughan Lewis, address at the opening ceremony of the ninth meeting of the OECS Authority, Basseterre, St Kitts, 28–30 May 1986.

42. Treaty Establishing the Organization of Eastern Caribbean States, or see *International Legal Materials* 20: 1033.

43. See Article 3 of the ECCM charter, and Article 3 (2) of the OECS charter.

44. It could also meet in extraordinary sessions.

45. Montserrat withheld its participation in the Grenada invasion on this basis.

46. Percival Marie (chief of trade, economic policy and statistics, Eco-

nomic Affairs Secretariat, OECS), interview by author, Antigua, 23–24 May 1989.

47. For example, the Port Management Association of the Eastern Caribbean submitted a proposal to the Authority for a study on the vulnerability of seaports, with a view to making them less susceptible to earthquakes and hurricanes. See OECS, "Conclusions of the Tenth Meeting of the Authority", St John's, Antigua, 28–29 November 1986.

Chapter 4

1. OECS countries managed to avoid IMF-imposed devaluations like those on the currencies of Trinidad, Jamaica and Guyana, making the Eastern Caribbean dollar one of the strongest currencies in CARICOM.

2. World Bank, *Long-Term Economic Prospects of the OECS Countries*, Report no. 8058–CRG (Washington, DC, 1990), iv.

3. Ibid.

4. While there are varying definitions as to what constitutes smallness, there is convergence of analysis on the problems which derive from smallness. These include the importance of trade in small economies, a heavy reliance on foreign aid, a dearth of natural resources, vulnerability to natural disasters, and high transport costs, among others. In the anglophone Caribbean, the first comprehensive treatment of the issue was W.G. Demas's *The Economics of Development in Small Countries* (Montreal: McGill University Press, 1965). For other readings on the peculiarities associated with small size, see Benedict Burton,

ed., *Problems of Smaller Territories* (London: Institute of Commonwealth Studies, 1967); Edward Dommen and Philippe Hein, eds., *States, Microstates and Islands* (London: Croom Helm, 1985); B. Jalan, ed., *Problems and Policies in Small Economies* (London: Croom Helm, 1982); Jonathan Alford, "Security Dilemmas of Small States", *Round Table* 292 (October 1984): 377–82; Marcio Antonio Mejia-Ricart, *Crisis of Small States in the Present Economic World: A Study of the Problems of Small Underdeveloped States with Special Reference to Central America and the Caribbean Area* (London: Farm Intelligence, 1960); Martin Prachowny, *Small Open Economies: Their Structure and Policy Environment* (Lexington, Mass.: Lexington Books, 1975); E.A.G. Robinson, ed., *Economic Consequences of the Size of Nations* (London: Macmillan, 1960); August Schou, ed., *Small States in International Relations* (New York: Wiley Interscience, 1971); Percy Selwyn, ed., *Development Policy in Small Countries* (London: Croom Helm, 1975).

5. See World Bank, *Long-Term Economic Prospects*, v.

6. St Vincent's prime minister, James Mitchell, in commenting on the OECS struggle to prevent their graduation from the International Development Agency, complained that "we were about to be penalised for bringing our per capita income above US$790 per year". Mitchell, address at the opening ceremony of the eighth meeting of the OECS Authority, Kingstown, St Vincent, 28–29 November 1985.

7. OECS Economic Affairs Secretariat, *OECS Statistical Pocket Digest 1987* (St John's, Antigua: OECS Secretariat, 1987).

8. St Lucia was the largest banana producer in the OECS, exporting 45 per cent of the region's total, with Dominica being the second largest producer. See Robert Thomson, *Green Gold: Bananas and Dependency in the Eastern Caribbean* (London: Latin American Bureau, 1987), 64.

9. Ibid.

10. This figure is for 1985. It fell from 40 per cent of total export revenue in 1979. See St Vincent, Ministry of Finance and Planning, *St Vincent and the Grenadines Development Plan 1986–1988: Growth Diversification Redistribution* (Kingstown, St Vincent: Government Printing Office, 1986), 9.

11. See Thomson, *Green Gold*, 74. Thomson estimates that it supports nearly half of the population. According to the World Bank, it injects EC$1 million per week into the economy. See World Bank, *Long-Term Economic Prospects*.

12. The industry was affected by Hurricane Allen in 1980, and suffered from poor farm access roads, the loss of traditional markets, coconut mite infestation and the availability of cheaper substitutes.

13. *St Vincent and the Grenadines Development Plan 1986–1988.* Ground provisions were exported to the CARICOM market, primarily Trinidad, via the trafficker trade (p. 31).

14. Ramesh Ramsaran, *The Commonwealth Caribbean in the World Economy* (London: Macmillan, 1989), 41. The government was spearheading a diversification programme away from sugar by embarking on a land-leasing programme with land nationalized in 1975.

15. World Bank, *Long-Term Economic Prospects*, 48.

16. Neville Duncan, "Changes in International Relations: Challenges and Options for the Caribbean", in *Diplomacy for Survival: CARICOM States in a World of Change,* ed. Lloyd Searwar (Kingston, Jamaica: Friedrich Ebert Stiftung, 1991), 31.

17. Thomson, *Green Gold*, 61, 63.

18. Nutmeg and mace were the highest earners, bringing in US$14.3 million, followed by bananas at US$4.7 million, and cocoa at US$3.2 million. See Thomson, *Green Gold*, 61, 63.

19. *St Vincent and the Grenadines Development Plan 1986–1988*, 2.

20. The figures on manufacturing are taken from the *OECS Statistical Pocket Digest 1987*, 23.

21. Although the Caribbean Development Bank pointed to the negative effect of Trinidad's economic problems on its performance, the World Bank was more optimistic, describing it as being in the midst of an export boom, generated by sales to the US market. The World Bank warned, however, that in the longer term Trinidad might suffer from competition for labour, and therefore it advised a more open policy towards labour from other OECS countries.

22. The industry has suffered from the economic problems facing its major trading partners in CARICOM. See Caribbean Development Bank, *Caribbean Development Bank Annual Report 1988* (Bridgetown, Barbados: Caribbean Development Bank, 1989), 31.

23. The World Bank described Grenada's manufacturing prospects as good, due to its transportation infrastructure and wage rates. It advised improvement in investment policies and the provision of a simpler tax and regulatory environment.

24. The World Bank described agriprocessing as having limited growth potential, despite its importance to the economy at that time.

25. World Bank, *Long-Term Economic Prospects*, x.
26. Ibid., ix.
27. At its first meeting, the EAS agreed to examine the status of the industries allocated under the scheme in order to improve it (see OECS, "Report of the First Meeting of the Economic Affairs Committee of the Organization of Eastern Caribbean States", OECS/EAS Report 82/01, St Lucia, 10 November 1982). Between January and April 1983, industries in Antigua, St Lucia and Montserrat were investigated to identify constraints and difficulties associated with the scheme's implementation (see OECS, "Report of the Second Meeting of the Economic Affairs Committee of the Organization of Eastern Caribbean States", OECS/EAS Report 83/01, Dominica, 25 May 1983).
28. Interview with Percival Marie. An example of this was Dominica's establishment and protection of a boxing plant with private sector interests in Venezuela, in competition with a similar plant in St Lucia.
29. See Ramsaran, *The Commonwealth Caribbean in the World Economy*, 52.
30. World Bank, *Long-Term Economic Prospects*, xii.
31. The World Bank observed that competition for labour was likely to increase costs and reduce the competitiveness of the garment industry, while the sugar industry was expected to decline as production costs increased faster than prices in Europe. Ibid., x.
32. Ibid. The report noted that St Kitts–Nevis retained some protectionist policies against other OECS countries which should have been eliminated in January 1988.
33. The LDCs were given special concessions, involving longer periods for tax holidays and exemptions from customs duties on imported raw materials, machinery and equipment, and a lower capital investment for highly capital-intensive industries.
34. Information on the ECCM is based on an interview with Percival Marie of the EAS, Antigua, 23–24 May 1989.
35. A United Nations Development Programme/United Nations Centre for Transnational Corporations project provided the framework for developing a programme for foreign investment. It analysed policies on foreign investment and technology transfers of OECS countries, as well as laws and regulations governing foreign investment. The project sought to link the objectives of foreign investment and technology transfers to the main social and development goals and policies of member states. See UNCTAD (United Nations Conference on Trade and Development)/OECS Economic Affairs Secretariat, "A Study on the Harmonization of Foreign Investment Policies, Laws and Regulations in the Organisation of Eastern Caribbean States" (October 1988).
36. The study recommended that OECS countries strengthen the harmonization process in order to improve welfare and increase net benefits from foreign investment. This was based on a recognition of their weak bargaining power *vis-à-vis* transnational corporations.
37. See D.S. Frampton and M.J. Scholar, *Review of Customs Administration within the Organisation of Eastern Caribbean States*, Public Management and Policy Planning Project (St John's, Antigua: OECS, 1989). Moves in this direction were based on a review of customs administration called for by a meeting

of OECS comptrollers of customs in Dominica in 1985. The review team recommended the "fullest harmonization, coordination and cooperation with the Customs services" of OECS countries, with a major role for the OECS as "central facilitator and coordinator of administrative action". It called for the creation of a Central Customs Division within the OECS to coordinate customs administration, and to coordinate intelligence activities in smuggling and drug trafficking. One of the arguments in favour of harmonizing customs administration was an anticipated increase in revenue. See S. St A. Clarke, "Deepening the Customs Union Relationship in the Eastern Caribbean State" (1985, mimeo).

38. See *CANA News Bulletin,* 4 September 1987.

39. See OECS, "A Programme for Agricultural Diversification in the OECS – Identification and Promotion of Non-Traditional Export Crops with Potential for Joint Export Marketing" (November 1988). The programme was developed with the assistance of the Caribbean Development Bank and the Inter-American Institute for Cooperation on Agriculture, based on a study of agricultural diversification undertaken by these bodies.

40. For details of this programme see Harold Naylor, "OECS Tourism Technical Assistance Project Phase, Project No. 5109.20.94.125" (St Lucia, 1988).

41. The OECS had sought Lomé funding to develop a programme to make available small vessels to ply between the islands, but agreed to shelve it in favour of a wider CARICOM approach.

42. OECS, "Tenth Meeting of the Authority: Director General's Re-

port", St John's, Antigua, 28–29 November 1986, Aut 2/86(7). This programme grew out of a study of freight arrangements existing in the subregion, which sought to identify deficiencies and constraints to shipping.

43. A decision that OECS countries should seek to purchase LIAT's remaining unallocated shares was taken at the fourteenth Heads of Authority meeting in 1989.

44. OECS, "Conclusions of the Eleventh Meeting of the Authority", Tortola, British Virgin Islands, 28–29 May 1987.

45. All participating countries have island-based staff, except for Anguilla, Montserrat and the British Virgin Islands, who are served by the Antigua unit.

46. The fisheries project provided financial assistance for small projects for fishermen, and trained them in safety-at-sea procedures, as well as outboard motor diesel engine maintenance and repair. The unit had conducted a survey assessing local demand for seafood and the constraints of selling local catch in non-coastal areas, and was investigating the availability of markets in the United States, Canada and Europe.

47. "Remarks by Dr Vaughan Lewis, Director-General, OECS, at Opening of the OECS Fisheries Workshop, July 30–August 1, 1986", in OECS, "Workshop for the Formulation of a Regional Management and Development Programme for Fisheries of the OECS Region: Report of Proceedings" (Castries, St Lucia, 30 July–1 August 1986).

48. See "Unity Pledged at OECS", *BVI Beacon,* 3 December 1987.

49. See OECS, "Report of Proceedings of the Workshop for the Formulation of a Regional Management

and Development Programme for Fisheries of the OECS Region".

50. Grenada was the only country with integrated biological and socioeconomic statistics, fisheries infrastructure, and incentives. While St Lucia had an overall development programme, it suffered from an inadequate knowledge of the resource base, poor fishing methods and techniques by fishermen, poor distribution and marketing structures, and poor control over foreign fishing.

51. The dispute centred on whether Aves Island, which belonged to the Venezuelans, was a rock or an island. Under the Law of the Sea Convention, designation as an island would entitle it to a two-hundred-mile limit, but if classified as a rock, it would be entitled to only twelve miles. Venezuela claimed that it was an island, the implication of which was to substantially reduce the Exclusive Economic Zone of nearly all OECS countries.

52. This was facilitated by the establishment of the Public Management and Policy Planning Project at the EAS, funded by the United States Agency for International Development.

53. For instance, the Public Management and Policy Planning Project conducted a study on the enforcement of import duties, reviewed consumption tax control and enforcement, and executed a project on tax reform for the Dominican government; prepared income tax audit manuals for the Dominican and St Lucian governments; provided technical support for the establishment of a computerized system of programme and performance budgeting for St Kitts–Nevis; and assisted the Grenadian government in developing a public sector investment programme to 1990.

For an example, see Larry Odum, "Dominica Income Tax Auditing Final Report" (Antigua, 28 January 1987); and OECS, Public Management and Policy Planning Project, "Seminar on the Tax System of Dominica" (Layou River Hotel, Dominica, 5–6 November 1986).

54. The decision for a wider role for the secretariat was based on an EAS presentation made to the second meeting of the Economic Affairs Committee of the OECS in August 1983, which sought to apprise member states of the EAS's capability to assist in public sector planning and management.

55. Income tax was abolished after the US invasion of Grenada in 1983, and was replaced by the value-added tax. In early 1991 the new National Democratic Congress government reintroduced income tax, while retaining the value-added tax under the guise of a debt levy tax. See James Ferguson, *Grenada: Revolution in Reverse* (London: Latin American Bureau, c.1990).

56. OECS, "Tenth Meeting of the Authority: Director General's Report".

57. The effect of tourism on the environment was receiving increasing attention. The World Bank noted that there had already been some degradation of the OECS environment, particularly the pollution of the sea by the many beach-front hotels which exist. World Bank, *Long-Term Economic Prospects*, viii.

Chapter 5

1. Grenada was the first of the group to gain its independence, in 1974.

2. The closest the United States came to showing an appreciation for the region's economic difficulties was the launching of the CBI in 1983;

yet even this had a strategic component, reflected in the exclusion of Nicaragua, Grenada, Cuba and Guyana, considered outside of its political influence. For details on the CBI see, "Caribbean Basin Recovery Act", *Business America,* August 1983, 6–8.

3. See Henry S. Gill, "The Foreign Policy of the Grenada Revolution", *Bulletin of Eastern Caribbean Affairs* 7, no. 1 (March–April 1981). For an analysis of the factors which gave rise to the revolution and of its character see Brian Meeks, "Social Formation and People's Revolution: A Grenadian Study" (PhD diss., University of the West Indies, 1988).

4. It also involved negotiating a contract with the Soviet Union for the purchase of nutmeg, and entering an arrangement with Indonesia – which produced 75 per cent of the world's nutmeg, to Grenada's 25 per cent – to stabilize production, and hence prices. The Grenada airport was a major thorn in the side of the US president, Ronald Reagan, who was convinced that it had the potential for military use by the Soviet Union.

5. For details on United States–Grenada relations during the revolution see Chris Searle, *Grenada: The Struggle Against Destabilization* (London: Writers and Readers Publishers Cooperative Society, 1983).

6. Percival Marie (chief of trade, EAS), interview by author, Antigua, 23–24 May 1989.

7. WISA Heads of Government meeting, press release, 20 March 1979 (mimeo).

8. Ibid.

9. In April 1981, an attempt was made to overthrow the Charles government in Dominica by former prime minister, Patrick John, in collaboration with American and Canadian mercenaries. In December, a coup attempt was made by members of the Dominica Defence Force, which was disbanded. See Ivelaw L. Griffith, "Image as Reality: The Security Perceptions of English Caribbean Elites" (paper presented at the Fourteenth Annual Conference of the Caribbean Studies Association, Barbados, 23–26 May 1989).

10. Quoted from Resource Center, *Focus on the Eastern Caribbean: Bananas, Bucks and Boots* (Alburquerque: Resource Center, 1984), 25, and in Tom Barry, Beth Wood, and Deb Preusch, *The Other Side of Paradise: Foreign Control in the Caribbean* (New York: Grove Press, 1984), 206.

11. Gary P. Lewis viewed the security threat to the Eastern Caribbean as deriving from "linked external support for internal political challenge". The threat was likely to come from "both extremes of left and right", and the external culprits were likely to be Cuba and Libya. See Gary P. Lewis, "Prospects for a Regional Security System in the Eastern Caribbean" *Journal of International Studies* 15, no. 1, 77.

12. See David A. Simmons, "Militarization of the Caribbean: Concerns for National and Regional Security", *International Journal* 40 (Spring 1985): 355. Simmons viewed this tendency among regional leaders to define internal threats as external as "[an excuse] for their inability to cope with the social and economic problems afflicting the area". They were thus happy to join the United States' anticommunist bandwagon.

13. The Eastern Caribbean states' interest in security began even before

they were independent, with attempts to form a security force. Earliest attempts grew out of Britain's refusal, during the period of Associated Statehood, to involve itself in quelling disturbances in Dominica and Antigua in 1967, on the basis that these were internal. As a result, interest developed in the formation of a military force to quell internal uprisings. Attempts among the WISA group to form a regional defence force in the late 1960s broke down over issues of ultimate authority, and general logistical difficulties arising from their separation by sea. See Simmons, "Militarization of the Caribbean", 354–57. While nothing came of this attempt, Antigua formed its own defence force, in seeming contravention of the Associated Statehood arrangement.

14. Article 8 of the OECS charter.
15. "The Declaration of St George" (Grenada, 16 July 1979, mimeo). Signed by the governments of Grenada, Dominica and St Lucia, the declaration recognized "the principles of mutual respect for sovereignty and territorial integrity, non-interference in each other's internal affairs, equality and regional solidarity".
16. Memorandum of Understanding Between the Government of Antigua and Barbuda, the Government of Barbados, the Government of the Commonwealth of Dominica, the Government of St Lucia, and the Government of St Vincent and the Grenadines Relating to Security and Military Cooperation, 1982, part 1. Printed in *Caribbean Monthly Bulletin* (supplement) 17, nos. 11–12 (November–December 1983).
17. Cited in Resource Center, *Focus on the Eastern Caribbean*, 25.

18. It also provided for joint procurement of arms, equipment and uniforms, and required participating countries to revive and update laws on their territorial waters and exclusive economic zones, and those relating to armed forces visiting the participating countries – an attempt to facilitate the RSS's operations.
19. A conference on the security problems of small Caribbean states defined the threats to their security as emanating from a "susceptibility to mercenary attacks, or in the case of multi-island states, to secessionist tendencies, and more recently to a modern manifestation of mercenary interests – the increasing infiltration and penetration of their societies by powerful drug-trafficking groups". See Lloyd Searwar, executive summary to "Peace, Development and Security in the Caribbean Basin: Perspectives to the Year 2000 – A Conference Report" (report, Canadian Institute for International Peace and Security, no. 4, 1987).
20. See William C. Gilmore, *The Grenada Intervention: Analysis and Documents* (London: Mansell, 1984), 97.
21. Ibid. Also see "Did Washington Ghost-Write Scoon's Appeal?", *New Statesman*, 11 November 1983; Ellen Ray and Bill Schaap, "US Crushed Caribbean Jewel", *Covert Action*, no. 20 (1984); Patsy Lewis-Meeks, "An Analysis of the Legal Justification for the United States Invasion of Grenada on the Basis of the Invitation from the OECS" (MPhil thesis, Cambridge University, 1988).
22. See Lewis, "Prospects for a Regional Security System", 80. His proposal amounted to the formation of an Eastern Caribbean army

designed to reduce the risk of governments falling prey to their own armies.

23. Ibid., 80, 81. Mitchell stated that his government had "no intention of releasing one cent for the creation of a regional army or [of wasting] money on security matters in preference for a basic needs programme"; Compton declared that "we never agreed to participate in a regional army. We are not going to send men to be billeted in Barbados"; and Charles asserted, "I was never fully convinced of the need for a regional army." See Humberto Garcia Muniz, *Boots, Boots, Boots: Intervention, Regional Security and Militarization in the Caribbean 1979–1986* (Rio Piedras, Puerto Rico: Proyecto Caribeño de Justicia y Paz, 1986), 14.

24. Adams's proposed Caribbean Defence Force envisaged a key role for the Special Services Unit, which was to be deployed in cases where the local police could not contain internal disturbances. If the Special Services Unit itself failed, then the Caribbean Defence Force would be deployed. See Muniz, *Boots, Boots, Boots,* 13–14.

25. The coast guard gave the governments the capability to respond quickly in one another's defence, although its value in the fight against drug trafficking and in safeguarding the waters of the region from exploitation is also obvious.

26. The training of the Special Services Unit was described as follows: "There is a US special forces training team on each island. Each team consists of eight men, except for St Vincent and the Grenadines where there is a six-man team and Jamaica, which has a twelve-man team. At least twenty-five men are located at the headquarters team. Training sessions last for six weeks and 'include becoming familiar with the new weapons, learning to shoot straight . . . map reading and basic military field operations and procedures'. . . . The graduates from the programme are to replace the so-called Caribbean Peacekeeping force that followed the United States into Grenada . . . . All of the newly trained troops are to operate 'under one command and would move to any island which shows signs of revolutionary crisis'." Bernard Diederich, "The End of West Indian Innocence: Arming the Police", *Caribbean Review* 13, no. 2 (Spring 1984): 10–13, quoted in Hilbourne Watson, "Imperialism, National Security, and State Power in the Commonwealth Caribbean: Issues in the Development of the Authoritarian State", in *Militarization in the Non-Hispanic Caribbean,* ed. Dion E. Phillip and Alma H. Young (Boulder: Lynne Rienner, 1986), 17–41.

27. In Grenada, it was used to seize the equipment of a radio station and arrest its owner, Stanley Charles. This provoked a demonstration. See Muniz, *Boots, Boots, Boots,* 15 (quoting from *Caribbean Insight* 8, no. 8 [August 1985]: 1).

28. Watson viewed the establishment of the Special Services Unit as a strategy aimed at reducing the need for future direct military invasions and occupation by US forces. He observed that Commonwealth Caribbean leaders now shared Washington's view that well-armed and well-trained armies were the only security against left-wing "subversion" or revolutionary upheavals. "National security" was therefore the theme of the new regional security strategy. See Watson, "Imperi-

alism, National Security, and State Power", 17–41.

29. Stuart Nanton (parliamentary secretary, Prime Minister's Office; deputy executive secretary, CDU), interview by author, St Vincent, 12 July 1989.

30. The background to this was the division of the ruling New National Party on the eve of elections between the New National Party, led by Keith Mitchell who was elected its chairman, and The National Party, which was formed when Prime Minister Herbert Blaize lost control of his New National Party. Blaize died shortly after, leaving Ben Jones, who replaced him as prime minister, to take over the leadership of The National Party. The CDU actively supported Mitchell's New National Party.

31. See James Ferguson, *Grenada: Revolution in Reverse* (London: Latin American Bureau, *c.*1990), 56–63.

32. Catherine A. Sunshine, *The Caribbean: Survival, Struggle and Sovereignty*, 2d ed. (Washington, DC: Ecumenical Program on Central America and the Caribbean, 1988), 134.

33. Searwar, executive summary,vi.

34. The fisheries unit was directly involved in this, and had some success in capturing some of these vessels, whose catch were seized and crew fined. Interview with Percival Marie.

35. The OECS was contemplating an agreement with the United States to pursue suspected drug traffickers in OECS waters.

36. Patrick Emmanuel observed that their capacity to act in concert, in defending their interests against Venezuela over their Exclusive Economic Zone and against threats to their marine resources, will be the "best single guide to their level of genuine community of interests in the immediate future". See Patrick Emmanuel, "Community within a Community: The OECS Countries", in *Ten Years of CARICOM* (papers presented at the seminar Economic Integration in the Caribbean, Bridgetown, Barbados, July 1983) (Washington, DC: Inter-American Development Bank, Institute for Latin American Integration, CARICOM Secretariat, 1984), 210.

37. This argument is developed in Patsy Lewis, "Revisiting the Grenada Invasion: The OECS' Role, and Its Impact on Regional and International Politics", *Social and Economic Studies* 48, no. 3 (1999)· 85–120.

38. The report attributed the lo⁻·e nrolment in secondary schools, in evidence everywhere except St Kitts–Nevis, to the eleven-plus system and a shortage of places. Interestingly, it notes that in all the countries many more females than males were enrolled, except in St Kitts–Nevis, which had abolished the eleven-plus system. This seems to suggest that the exams favoured girls, who performed better at that level than boys.

39. See "Ministers End Meeting Here: OECS Moves to Develop Tertiary Education", *The Voice*, 30 March 1988, 2.

40. Information on the Eastern Caribbean Drug Service scheme is based on documents from the Eastern Caribbean Drug Service unit, such as: OECS, "Establishment of the ECDS" (Castries, St Lucia, mimeo), and OECS, "An Overview of the ECDS" (Castries, St Lucia, mimeo); an interview with Eastern Caribbean Drug Service director Sherita Gregoire (interview by author, St Lucia, 14 June 1989),

and OECS, "Twelfth Meeting of the Authority, Director General's Report", paper no. 2, Aut 2/87. Antigua and the British Virgin Islands did not participate initially. The British Virgin Islands entered the scheme in 1988, and Antigua and the Turks and Caicos Islands later expressed interest in participating.

41. The programme developed from a CARICOM health ministers conference which identified the problems facing the OECS as "short supply of drugs, disorganised warehouses, limited or non-existent inventory management systems, obsolete products, untrained staff, unreliable transport, fiscal constraints and cost containment". See *Organisation of Eastern Caribbean States Eastern Caribbean Drug Service (ECDS) Bulletin* 1, no. 1 (September 1988).

42. Joseph "Reds" Pereira (OECS sports coordinator), interview by author, St Lucia, 14 June 1989.

43. John Douglas Barrymore Renwick (head, OECS legal unit), interview by author, St Lucia, 14 June 1989.

44. OECS, "Twelfth Meeting of the Authority, Director General's Report".

45. See chapter 4.

46. See Kathy Ann Brown, "Now That the Ship Has Docked: A Postscript to the Shiprider Debate", *CARICOM Perspectives*, 1997, 48–54; Stephen Vasciannie, "Political and Policy Aspects of the Jamaican/US Shiprider Negotiations", *Caribbean Quarterly* 43, no. 3 (1997): 34–53; W. Holger Henke, "Drugs in the Caribbean: The Shiprider Controversy and the Question of Sovereignty", *European Review of Latin America and Caribbean Studies*, no. 64 (1998): 27–47.

47. This involved reviewing some 162 multilateral treaties from 1956 to 1977, on a wide range of subjects, and 250 bilateral treaties.

48. For instance, Lewis revealed that only one OECS country had acceded to the Vienna Convention on Treaties.

49. OECS countries refused to readmit Grenada to the court before the trials involving persons convicted of killing Grenada's Prime Minister Maurice Bishop in 1983 were over. Under the OECS system, final appeal rested with the privy council. However, the Grenadian court, set up after the 1979 revolution, was the end of the appeal process. The implications were that if the Grenadian court system was to be reintegrated into the subregional system, those convicted of Bishop's murder would be able to lodge an appeal with the privy council. Their case had been fought on the basis that the Grenadian court was illegal, since it was not based on the 1973 constitution (which had the privy council as the final court of appeal), reinstated in 1983 after the US invasion.

50. Byron Blake (economics and industry division, CARICOM secretariat), interview by author, Jamaica, 15 May 1989.

51. Ibid.

52. For instance, Marie suggested that the European Community played an important role in fostering cooperation by insisting that OECS present more viable projects covering the area. Interview with Percival Marie.

53. OECS, "Report of the Fourteenth Meeting of Officials of the Authority", Castries, St Lucia, 22 November 1988.

54. This trend was also evident in the attempt by the West Indies Jaycees organization to seek affiliation with the OECS. The request was denied

on the grounds that the organization did not acknowledge such a relationship. See ibid.

55. Vaughan Lewis (director-general, OECS), interview by author, St Lucia, 11 June 1989.

56. OECS, "Organisation of Eastern Caribbean States Summary of Decisions of the Fifteenth Meeting of the Authority", St John's, Antigua and Barbuda, 1–2 June 1989.

57. Ibid. A suggestion was made for a centralized monitoring and financing mechanism at either of the secretariats, to prepare OECS budgets and establish accounts by participating states at the East Caribbean Central Bank, which would make payments on their behalf.

58. James Mitchell, interview by author, Antigua, 2 June 1989. He revealed that the OECS had an EC$8 million deficit.

59. John Compton, interview by author, St Lucia, 13 June 1989.

60. Ibid.

61. "Compton: Act Now on OECS Union", *Weekend Voice*, 26 November 1988.

62. Interview with James Mitchell.

63. "Mitchell and Forde Both Want Unity", *Vincentian*, 9 September 1988.

Chapter 6

1. W.G. Demas, *Seize the Time: Towards OECS Political Union* (St Michael, Barbados: n.p., 1987), based on an address at the inauguration of the National Advisory Committee of St Vincent and the Grenadines on Political Unity in the Eastern Caribbean, Barbados, 20 July 1987.

2. James Mitchell, "Thoughts on an East Caribbean Union", in *Two Decades of Caribbean Unity* (Kingstown, St Vincent: Government Printing Office, 1987), 9–17 (extracts from paper presented to Heads of Government of OECS, November 1986).

3. John Compton, interview by author, St Lucia, 13 June 1989.

4. "Compton Again Puts Case for a Union: Sees 'Difficult Times' Ahead for Islands", *The Voice*, 25 November 1989.

5. "Call for Political Union", *Barbados Advocate*, 2 June 1987, 5.

6. Dominica's Prime Minister Eugenia Charles also identified the Windward Islands Banana Growers' Association as an example of the success of subregional action, arguing that there would have been no banana industry in the Windward Islands without the association. Eugenia Charles, interview by author, Dominica, 9 June 1989.

7. Interview with John Compton.

8. *CANA News Bulletin*, 20 July 1987.

9. Mitchell, "Thoughts on an East Caribbean Union".

10. William Demas, *The Economics of Development in Small Countries: With Special Reference to the Caribbean* (Montreal: McGill University Press, 1965).

11. Demas, *Seize the Time*.

12. For example, fish and minerals from their Exclusive Economic Zone.

13. Alister McIntyre (vice chancellor, University of the West Indies), interview by author, Jamaica, 12 April 1989.

14. Demas, *Seize the Time*.

15. He cited Grenada's experience in 1989 of receiving only two-thirds of a promised EC$18 million in budgetary support from the United States, the remaining third coming late in the year.

16. *CANA News Bulletin*, 20 July 1987.

17. Mitchell, address at the opening ceremony of the eleventh meeting of the OECS Authority, Tortola, British Virgin Islands, 27 May 1987.
18. Ibid.
19. Demas, *Seize the Time*.
20. "Compton Again Puts Case for a Union".
21. Ibid.
22. Ben Jones, interview by author, Grenada, July 1989.
23. Mitchell, interview by author, Antigua, 2 June 1989.
24. Mitchell, "Thoughts on an East Caribbean Union".
25. Demas, *Seize the Time*.
26. McIntyre suggested that this was an important issue for the OECS countries, particularly St Vincent with its many islands. Interview with Alister McIntyre.
27. James F. Mitchell, *Two Decades of Caribbean Unity* (Kingstown, St Vincent: Government Printing Office, 1987), 2.
28. "Foreign Affairs Minister Cenac on OECS Union: Isolation Makes No Sense", *Weekend Voice*, 23 April 1988, 1, 14. This elevation of security as a key consideration behind the initiative is puzzling, since Compton had disclaimed the relevance of security as a factor motivating the initiative. He had stated emphatically that the OECS countries had no security concerns: "This is not fashionable now. Who is going to invade you? . . . The whole question of security concerns was put to bed in 1983" (interview with John Compton). However, the privileging of security suggests that, to some, cold war considerations remained valid.
29. Charles viewed the police force as an area that could be greatly enhanced by a political union. Interview with Eugenia Charles.
30. Interview with John Compton.
31. CANA News Bulletin, 20 July 1987.
32. Mitchell, "Thoughts on an East Caribbean Union", 11.
33. Interview with Eugenia Charles.
34. Rosina Wiltshire, "Regional Integration and Conflict in the Commonwealth Caribbean" (PhD diss., University of Michigan, 1974).
35. "Summit Hears Regional Concerns", *Vincentian*, 16 October 1986. Mitchell was addressing the opening of the Commonwealth summit in Vancouver.
36. Interview with John Compton.
37. Interview with Eugenia Charles. Charles asked: "Who are we in the Caribbean to think that we can paddle our own canoe and make any sort of impression on the world if we sit by ourselves?"
38. Charles Maynard (minister of tourism, trade, industry and agriculture, Dominica), interview by author, Dominica, 9 June 1989.
39. See Arthur Lewis, *The Agony of the Eight* (Barbados: Advocate Commercial Printery, 1965).
40. Although the OECS countries were based on a two-party system of government, it was the norm for one party to dominate at elections. For example, Grenada was ruled by Eric Gairy almost continuously for nearly thirty years, and in St Vincent in 1989, Mitchell's party won all the seats in the general elections. This left Mitchell in a position where he was not constitutionally bound to advise the Governor General to appoint a leader of the opposition, since the constitution provides for a leader of the opposition on the basis of his ability to command the second largest block of seats in the house of representatives.
41. Lewis, *The Agony of the Eight*. Lewis was arguing for a federal rather

than a unitary state, but the argument is still valid under either form of union. This is evident from the fact that when these arguments are used today, no one links them to the federal as opposed to the unitary form; rather, they are used generally to support the idea of union.

42. For example, in St Vincent it resulted in the disintegration of the United People's Movement, an alliance of three left-wing groups formed to contest the 1979 general elections.

43. We must note that, aside from the issue of whether Cuba could or could not put up a credible defence in the face of US intervention, Cuba clearly had no desire to do so after the murder of Maurice Bishop.

44. This perspective is further developed in Patsy Lewis, "Revisiting the Grenada Invasion: The OECS' Role, and Its Impact on Regional and International Politics", *Social and Economic Studies* 48, no. 3 (1999): 85–120.

45. See Mitchell, "Statement at the Opening Ceremony of the CARICOM Heads of Government Conference on June 29th, 1987 in St Lucia", in *Two Decades of Caribbean Unity* (Kingstown, St Vincent: Government Printing Office, 1987), 20.

46. "Call for Political Union", *Barbados Advocate*, 2 June 1987, 5.

47. This was equally expressed by Mitchell when he suggested to Alister McIntyre that St Vincent had exhausted its options. Interview with Alister McIntyre.

48. J.S. Nye, "Patterns and Catalysts in Regional Integration", *International Organization* 19, no. 4 (Autumn 1965): 870–84.

Chapter 7

1. For example, the trade union movement was left out of negotiations surrounding the formation of the West Indies Federation, which were dominated by nominated legislators. See John Mordecai, *The West Indies: The Federal Negotiations* (London: Allen and Unwin, 1968), 36.

2. The Federation of Rhodesia and Nyasaland provided an extreme example of this, with the franchise restricted to a small white oligarchy. Consequently, the interests of self-governing white settlers were well represented in the negotiations, while black people in Northern Rhodesia and Nyasaland – British protectorates – were forced to rely on the British to "represent" their interests. R.L. Watts, *New Federations: Experiments in the Commonwealth* (Oxford: Clarendon Press, 1966), 28.

3. Mordecai, *The West Indies*, 44.

4. The Jamaicans' decision appeared to indicate that, while agreement among political leaders and the Colonial Office was sufficient to bring the Federation into being, it could not survive without popular support.

5. See Earl Huntley, "RCA Update", in *Caribbean Integration: The OECS Experience Revisited,* ed. Neville Duncan (Kingston, Jamaica: Friedrich Ebert Stiftung, 1995), 111–12.

6. The character of this type of relationship is captured in Singham's study of Eric Gairy's relationship with the Grenadian population. See A.W. Singham, *The Hero and the Crowd in a Colonial Polity* (New Haven: Yale University Press, 1968).

7. The Grenada revolution introduced into Commonwealth Caribbean politics the philosophy that governments could be changed by direct popular action outside of the parliamentary framework. Its potency was evident in the series of demonstrations and disturbances against governments in Dominica and St Lucia between 1979 and 1980.

8. David Butler and Austin Ranney, eds., *Referendums: A Comparative Study of Practice and Theory* (Washington, DC: American Enterprise Institute for Public Policy Research, 1978).

9. Prime Minister Charles of Dominica, for instance, said that if her people rejected the idea, she would not pursue it. Eugenia Charles, interview by author, Dominica, 9 June 1989.

10. Butler and Ranney, *Referendums*.

11. See "OECS Union to Get a Push: Several Task Forces Go to Work Next Month", *The Voice*, 12 December 1987.

12. Letter from Prime Minister Kennedy Simmonds, 1 September 1987, Ref. No. PM/018/3.

13. "Report of the National Advisory Committee on OECS Closer Political Union", St Kitts, 14 June 1988, PRO/O/005.

14. Ibid.

15. Dr William Herbert, the committee's chairman, was founder of the ruling People's Action Movement, as well as ambassador plenipotentiary. At the time of the committee's establishment, his Anguilla-based bank was being accused in certain quarters in London and the United States of laundering drug money. The main opposition party, the St Kitts–Nevis Labour Party, objected to Herbert's chairing the committee until he was in a position to clear his name. The People's Action Movement, in an alliance with the Nevis Reformation Party, controlled eight of the eleven seats (six plus two), the Labour Party had two, and the recently formed Concerned Citizens Movement had one.

16. The leader of the Labour Party and of the opposition, Denzil Douglas, said that before the appointment was made public his party had expressed its disapproval with his choice of chairman. Denzil Douglas, interview by author, St Kitts, 6 June 1989.

17. Dr Kennedy Simmonds (prime minister, St Kitts–Nevis), interview by author, Antigua, 1 June 1989.

18. Simmonds said that after the Tortola meeting, he met with the opposition, briefed them on what had occurred in Tortola, and informed them of his intention to form a national committee, to which they agreed. Interview with Kennedy Simmonds.

19. The opposition's behaviour is probably also linked to the fact that Herbert was the founder of the ruling party.

20. Compton was a strong supporter of a WISA union, declaring that he was not prepared to lead "a mere 100,000 people into independence". See A.E. Thorndike, "Concept of Associated Statehood" (PhD diss., University of London, 1980).

21. Rickey Singh, "Defeat in UWP [United Workers' Party] Victory, Big Blow to OECS Union", *Caribbean Contact*, May 1986. Following the elections on 6 April, which gave Compton a one-seat lead, he again called elections on 30 April, with the same result. However, his hand was strengthened when one of the opposition members, Neville Cenac, crossed the floor.

22. Ibid.

23. Ibid.

24. "Compton Fully Behind Political Union", *Barbados Advocate*, 16 May 1987. Compton was speaking on the Caribbean News Agency's monthly *Caribbean Conference* radio call-in programme.

25. "St Lucia Cabinet Drafting Terms for National Consultative Body: OECS Unity Plan still on Schedule", *EC News*, 21 August 1987. The Movement for National Unity charged that the initiative had slowed because of the absence of clear direction from the Heads of Government.

26. CANA News Bulletin, 7 August 1987. Compton was speaking at a press conference in Kingston, Jamaica, after a luncheon given in his honour by the Jamaica branch of the Commonwealth Parliamentary Association.

27. "Compton: 'Act Now on OECS Union' ", *Weekend Voice*, 26 November 1988. He was addressing the opening ceremony of a two-day OECS summit in St Lucia.

28. This was probably a reference to Montserrat, the only OECS member still a British colony. It might also refer to the British Virgin Islands (also a British colony) which, although not a full member of the OECS, might be persuaded to join in the event of an OECS union.

29. "Compton: 'Act Now on OECS Union' ".

30. Farrel Charles (member, Independent Committee for OECS Unity), interview by author, St Lucia, 13 June 1989.

31. Dwight Venner (director of finance, Ministry of Finance, St Lucia; president of the East Caribbean Central Bank; member, Independent Committee for OECS Unity), interview by author, St Lucia, 12 June 1989.

32. Ibid.

33. Julian Hunte (leader of the opposition, St Lucia; leader, St Lucia Labour Party), interview by Cynthia Barrow, 26 May 1988.

34. The antagonistic relationship between Compton and Hunte was long-standing, dating from the 1950s. Compton, who was a minister in the St Lucia Labour Party government in 1957, defected from the government and set up the opposition People's Progressive Party. He formed the United Workers' Party in 1962 and badly beat the St Lucia Labour Party government (eight seats to two) in the 1962 elections. See Thorndike, "Concept of Associated Statehood", 311–16.

35. Interview with Eugenia Charles.

36. This seems to suggest that union was not a priority in Dominica.

37. Charles initially sought a common platform with Douglas from which to launch the debate. Douglas's response, Charles said, was favourable, although he had to raise the matter with his party executive. He never returned with a response. Interview with Eugenia Charles.

38. Mike Douglas (leader of the opposition; leader, Dominica Labour Party), interview by author, Dominica, 7 June 1989.

39. Edison James (leader, United Workers' Party; general manager, Banana Marketing Corporation), interview by author, Dominica, 7 June 1989. The United Workers' Party was formed on 2 July 1988.

40. The government's failure to seek alliance with James's party was probably influenced by the trend in Caribbean politics for two dominant parties, which means that third parties are generally ignored. Interestingly, the United Workers' Party became the parliamentary opposition, after winning more seats

than Douglas's Dominica Labour Party in the 1990 general elections.

41. She listed among these the Rotary Club, the Dominica Association of Industry and Commerce, and the Dominica Employers' Federation. Interview with Eugenia Charles.

42. This is supported by Ninian Marie, chairman of the manufacturing subcommittee of the Dominica Association of Industry and Commerce, and executive member of the Council of East Caribbean Manufacturers. Ninian Marie, interview by author, Dominica, 8 June 1989.

43. Francis Emmanuel (director, Musson Trading Company; president, Dominica Employers' Federation), interview by author, Dominica, 8 June 1989.

44. Louis Benoit (president, Waterfront and Allied Workers' Union) and Heric Augustus (executive member, Waterfront and Allied Workers' Union), interviews by author, Dominica, 8 June 1989.

45. Rawlings Jemmott (president-general, National Workers' Union), interview by author, Dominica, 8 June 1989.

46. Bernard Nicholas (general secretary, Dominica Trade Union), interview by author, Dominica, 7 June 1989.

47. Louis Benoit of the Waterfront and Allied Workers' Union provides an example of this: "The only way people would support it is for the sake of the party in power or the prime minister. . . . I would support it because I realise that Eugenia Charles is not going to live anywhere else, she has to live here . . . But I can't support it on the facts because I don't know enough about it. Being a fan of Eugenia, [*sic*] I would support anything she says". Interview with Louis Benoit.

48. Danny Williams, the committee's chairman, said that the committee was formed after a meeting of former and current parliamentarians, in mid-1987, called by Prime Minister Blaize. At that meeting, "certain" parliamentarians were suggested for membership. Danny Williams, interview by author, Grenada, 11 June 1989.

49. Interview with Danny Williams. At the time of the interview Williams was Grenada's attorney-general and minister of health.

50. The political party which had dominated Grenadian politics since adult suffrage in 1951, until it was overthrown by the New Jewel Movement in 1979. It was led by Sir Eric Matthew Gairy.

51. The National Democratic Congress went on to win the March 1990 elections and, in alliance with members of Blaize's former cabinet, to form the government.

52. Williams pointed to the existence of a Civic Awareness Society comprising "prominent" Grenadians, who had declared themselves to be nonpolitical, which took on the promotion of the idea through radio call-in programmes.

53. The party of deposed former prime minister, Eric Gairy.

54. A party formed after the revolution's collapse by some former members of the New Jewel Movement who supported Maurice Bishop.

55. Hugh Dolland (president, Grenada Chamber of Industry and Commerce), interview by author, Grenada, 11 July 1989.

56. Anslem DeBourg (president, Commercial and Industrial Workers Union; president, Grenada Trade Union Council), Grenada, 4 July 1989.

57. Eric Pierre (Seamen and Water-front Workers' Union), interview by author, Grenada, 10 July 1989.

58. The Grenada Chamber of Industry and Commerce hosted a symposium in November 1987 at which OECS bureaucrats, including the director-general, Vaughan Lewis, participated. The Trade Union Council, in addition to the seminar already mentioned, hosted another in conjunction with the CCL, attended by government and opposition representatives.

59. George Brizan of the Grenada Democratic Party, and Francis Alexis who entered a political alliance with Blaize's Grenada National Party to form the New National Party, left the alliance within the first two years of the government. Additionally, Blaize was unpopular with trade unions because of his threat to cut a significant portion of the civil service to satisfy an IMF structural adjustment programme, and his initial refusal to honour a pay agreement concluded with the civil service.

60. "Mitchell Praised for Leadership", *EC News*, 21 August 1987. This took place at the New Democratic Party's annual convention.

61. "Mitchell and Forde Both Want Unity", *Vincentian*, 9 September 1988.

62. Stuart Nanton (parliamentary secretary, Prime Minister's Office; deputy executive secretary, CDU), interview by author, St Vincent, 12 July 1989.

63. The opposition then would have been the St Vincent Labour Party, which is no longer the official opposition. The St Vincent Labour Party was known to be hostile to the initiative.

64. Interview with Stuart Nanton.

65. Noel Venner (secretary, National Advisory Committee on Political Union in the Eastern Caribbean), interview by author, St Vincent, 14 July 1989. Information concerning the committee's operations is generally based on this interview. Between 1987 and 1988 the committee met monthly, with an average attendance of thirteen or fourteen.

66. Up to July 1989 when these interviews were done, there had been no further meetings.

67. The 1989 general elections gave Mitchell a landslide victory, with his party winning all the seats. This left the country without an official opposition in parliament, as the constitution provides no clear guidelines for such a situation.

68. Adrian Saunders (leader, United People's Movement), interview by author, St Vincent, 14 July 1989.

69. St Vincent National Advisory Committee on Political Union in the Eastern Caribbean, circular on its terms of reference (rev. 1 December 1987).

70. Renison Howell (vicar-general of the Roman Catholic Church of St Vincent and the Grenadines; chairman, St Vincent and the Grenadines Christian Council), interview by author, St Vincent, 12 July 1989.

71. Noel Jackson, general secretary of the National Workers' Movement and chairman of the Joint Workers' Council, said his union pulled out of the National Advisory Committee because they were dissatisfied with the way it was formed, and with the unreceptive atmosphere of its meetings. He had attended two meetings. Noel Jackson, interview by author, St Vincent, 12 July 1989.

72. Interview with Noel Venner.

73. The National Youth Council used its organizational structure, of a

national executive and general meetings – the latter held thrice yearly – to transmit information on responses. Additionally, it provided documents on unity at its office. Angela Patrick (field officer, National Youth Council, and former executive member, National Alliance of Development Organizations) and Geoffrey Samuels (administrative coordinator, Caribbean Federation of Youth), interview by author, St Vincent, 14 July 1989.

74. Fitzroy Jones (public relations officer, St Vincent Union of Teachers), interview by author, St Vincent, 13 July 1989.

75. The St Vincent Union of Teachers representative reported to his executive, who decided whether or not to support National Advisory Committee decisions. The executive then reported to the general membership "on a regular basis". Jackson noted that the general membership tended to endorse the executive's recommendations because they felt "that was what they elected the executive to do".

76. Colin Williams, general secretary of the Commercial, Technical and Allied Workers' Union, complained that the union's representative did not report back to them (interview by author, St Vincent, 13 July 1989). Nelcia Robinson, coordinator of the Committee for the Development of Women, said that the group did not receive reports from the National Council of Women – to whom they were affiliated – which was represented on the National Advisory Committee (interview by author, St Vincent, 14 July 1989). The Committee for the Development of Women itself had been invited to sit on the National Advisory Committee but had declined to do so.

77. The St Vincent Committee was the only consultative body which had, readily available in its office, documents on union including speeches from various leaders on union, booklets produced by the OECS secretariat, the terms of reference of the committee, and a list of the organizations and persons represented on it.

78. Rotaract Club of St Kitts, report to the chairman of the National Advisory Committee on OECS Closer Union, St Kitts, 25 May 1988.

79. Interview with Eugenia Charles.

80. Butler and Ranney, *Referendums*.

81. Movement for National Unity leader, Ralph Gonsalves, observed that the government had nothing to lose from tabling a bill in parliament, as its parliamentary majority would have ensured its passage while allowing for opposition involvement. Ralph Gonsalves, interview by author, St Vincent, 13 July 1989.

82. James Mitchell, interview by author, Antigua, 2 June 1989.

83. See following chapters.

84. In Jamaica, although the referendum showed over 40 per cent support for maintaining the Federation, the established wisdom has been that Jamaicans are permanently opposed to it, thus making any notion of unity a politically dead issue. An example of this was Prime Minister Manley's declaration, at the CARICOM Heads of Government Conference in Grenada in 1989, that while he supported an initiative for a regional parliament, Jamaica could participate only if this did not require any encroachment on its sovereignty.

85. St Lucia in 1987, St Vincent in 1988, Dominica in 1989, and Grenada in 1990.

86. This led Fitzroy Jones of the St Vincent Union of Teachers to observe that more community-based discussion was needed with the leadership of political parties to explain issues raised by political union.

87. Gordon Lewis points to the "West Indian popular psychology" which "encouraged the politicization of everything", and which was held to be one of the factors contributing to the breakup of the West Indies Federation. Gordon K. Lewis, *The Growth of the Modern West Indies* (London: MacGibbon and Kee, 1968), 369.

Chapter 8

1. Bradley T. Carrot (president of the senate, and advisor to the Antigua Trades and Labour Union), interview by author, Antigua, 26 May 1989.

2. Arthur Lewis, *The Agony of the Eight*, reprinted in *Journal of Eastern Caribbean Studies* 23, no. 1 (1998): 10.

3. He represented Antigua in the federal house of representatives of the West Indies Federation.

4. In his "Thoughts on an East Caribbean Union", Mitchell had expressed support for a unitary state. See James Mitchell, "Thoughts on an East Caribbean Union", in *Two Decades of Caribbean Unity* (Kingstown, St Vincent: Government Printing Office, 1987), 9–17.

5. Orland U. Lindsay (archbishop of the West Indies, and bishop of the North Eastern Caribbean and Aruba), interview by author, Antigua, 30 May 1989.

6. Interview with Bradley Carrot.

7. Ibid.

8. Lester Bird (deputy prime minister of Antigua), interview by author, Antigua, 6 July 1989.

9. The United National Democratic Party was the result of a merger of two political parties – the National Democratic Party and the United People's Movement – in 1984, after the ruling Antigua Labour Party had swept the polls and won all the seats. The United National Democratic Party was led by Dr Ivor Heath.

10. Although for Antigua Caribbean Liberation Movement leader Tim Hector, this goes beyond CARICOM countries to include a broader pan-Caribbean vision.

11. Tim Hector (leader, Antigua Caribbean Liberation Movement), interview by author, Antigua, 24 May 1989.

12. Baldwin Spencer (deputy leader, United National Democratic Party; leader of the opposition; assistant general secretary and first vice-president, Antigua Workers Union), interview by author, Antigua, 31 May 1989.

13. Interview with Tim Hector.

14. The Antigua Trades and Labour Union was formed in 1939 in the wake of the labour unrest which swept the region in the mid-1930s. Prime Minister Vere Bird was one of its founding members, and was its president from 1940 to 1968. The Antigua Trades and Labour Union gave rise to the Antigua Labour Party, which contested and won the first general elections based on universal adult suffrage in 1951. In 1946 the union had successfully secured the election of five of its members to the legislature in general elections based on restricted franchise.

15. The Antigua Workers Union was formed in 1967 after a split in the

Antigua Trades and Labour Union that saw the departure of some of its leading members.

16. Interview with Baldwin Spencer.

17. Interview with Bradley Carrot.

18. Peter Harker (chairman, Council of Eastern Caribbean Manufacturers; president, Antigua–Barbuda Manufacturers' Association), interview by author, Antigua, 26 May 1989.

19. Interview with Orland Lindsay.

20. Interview with Lester Bird.

21. Interview with Orland Lindsay.

22. Interview with Tim Hector.

23. Interview with Baldwin Spencer.

24. Interview with Lester Bird.

25. Ibid.

26. Ibid.

27. Ibid.

28. Interview with Tim Hector.

29. "Report of the National Advisory Committee on OECS Closer Political Union", St Kitts–Nevis, 14 June 1988, PRO/O/005.

30. Kennedy Simmonds (prime minister of St Kitts), interview by author, Antigua, 1 June 1989.

31. This threat obviously has not been carried out, since Nevis remains in the St Kitts–Nevis federation.

32. Denzil Douglas (leader of the opposition, St Kitts–Nevis; leader, St Kitts–Nevis Labour Party), interview by author, St Kitts, 6 June 1989.

33. Dr William Herbert (chairman, National Advisory Committee on OECS Closer Union; founder of the People's Action Movement), interview by author, St Kitts, 6 June 1989.

34. Ibid.

35. Ibid.

36. Ibid.

37. Before the initiative was formally announced, Herbert, along with Demas and Ramphal, met to discuss the possibilities for furthering OECS political cooperation. Interview with William Herbert.

38. Ibid.

39. Ibid.

40. Interview with Denzil Douglas.

41. St Kitts–Nevis Labour Party, "A New Way Forward with Labour", manifesto, 1988.

42. "Plans for OECS Unity Criticised", *Caribbean Times*, 6 August 1987.

43. Ricky Skeritt (president/executive director, St Kitts–Nevis Chamber of Industry and Commerce), interview by author, St Kitts, 5 June 1989.

44. George T. Warren (secretary of the St Kitts–Nevis Manufacturers' Association), "On OECS Closer Union", letter to William Herbert, 29 January 1988.

45. St Kitts Jaycees, "Report on Concerns on OECS Unification Raised at a Meeting Held 7 January 1988" (paper presented to the National Advisory Committee on OECS Closer Union, St Kitts, n.d.).

46. Interview with Ricky Skeritt.

47. Warren, "On OECS Closer Union".

48. Ibid.

49. St Kitts Jaycees, "Report on Concerns on OECS Unification".

50. Ibid.

51. Warren, "On OECS Closer Union".

52. Interview with Ricky Skeritt.

53. Ibid.

54. St Kitts Jaycees, "Report on Concerns on OECS Unification".

55. Business and Professional Women's Club of St Kitts, report to the National Advisory Committee on OECS Closer Union, St Kitts, 12 April 1988.

56. Inter-Ministerial Council of the Ministry of Women's Affairs, report to the National Advisory Committee on OECS Closer Union, St Kitts, 7 April 1988.

57. St Kitts–Nevis Secretaries Association, report to the National Advisory Committee on OECS Closer Union, St Kitts, 14 January 1988.

58. The association wished "to keep its own identity, . . . and would not want to lose this identity to become part of an OECS Secretaries Association as a member of the newly formed Caribbean Secretaries Association".

59. St Kitts Lions Club, "Position on Current Proposals for a Political Union of the OECS Territories", presented to the National Advisory Committee on OECS Closer Union, St Kitts, 26 May 1988.

60. St Kitts Christian Council, statement on OECS union to the National Advisory Committee on OECS Closer Union (n.d.).

61. Nevis Co-operative Credit Union Limited, "The Proposed OECS Closer Union", report to the chairman of the National Advisory Committee on OECS Closer Union, St Kitts, 27 May 1988.

62. Rotaract Club of St Kitts, report to the chairman of the National Advisory Committee on OECS Closer Union, St Kitts, 25 May 1988.

63. Interview with William Herbert.

64. Ibid.

65. Lester Bird commented that under the Federation, Antigua was to be developed as an area for cattle breeding. He contrasted this with its present prosperity. Interview with Lester Bird.

66. See chapter 2.

67. Carrot detected some hostility towards Antiguans from the Windward Islands. Interview with Bradley Carrot.

68. See above. Interview with Lester Bird.

Chapter 9

1. In Grenada, trade unions and political parties were strongly represented in the interview process for this book, but no social groups were interviewed. This was not by design, but was due to difficulty of access to representatives in the limited time available.

2. Jones was minister of agriculture and fisheries in the new government, but has since resigned.

3. It is interesting to note that the political union initiative was not an issue in the general elections. Even the ruling National Party made no mention of it in its election manifesto.

4. In 1989 the New National Party split in into two factions, with Blaize's rival, Keith Mitchell, controlling the larger section of the party, leaving Blaize to form The National Party with the smaller faction. Attempts were made to interview Mitchell even before the split, but these proved unsuccessful.

5. Ben Jones (deputy prime minister and minister of foreign affairs), interview by author, Grenada, 7 July 1989.

6. Danny Williams (minister of health and attorney-general), interview by author, Grenada, 11 July 1989.

7. George Brizan (deputy leader, National Democratic Congress), interview by author, Jamaica, 12 April 1989.

8. "Unity Gets 'Yes' Vote in Grenada", *EC News*, 27 November 1987, 15, and *CANA News Bulletin*, 15 July 1987.

9. The Grenada United Labour Party was deposed in 1979 by the New Jewel Movement, after having dominated Grenada's political life since adult suffrage was achieved in 1951. Grenada United Labour Party founder Eric Gairy, who was in the United States when the revolution occurred and had remained there, returned after the 1983 invasion and reentered political life. His

party, which has its support mainly in the rural areas and among agricultural workers, had a strong showing in the 1990 elections. Although Gairy himself did not run in the elections, he was unquestionably still the major force behind the party's thinking.

10. Ben Jones, in his interview, said that the Grenada United Labour Party's position, as relayed to the parliamentarians' committee, was that Grenada's strategic location made it of value to the United States, which meant that it did not need to seek union with other OECS countries, as it could get favours from the United States.

11. A reference to the Grenada revolution which ousted him from power.

12. The Maurice Bishop Patriotic Movement, named after Prime Minister Maurice Bishop, was formed after his death in 1983 by a faction of the New Jewel Movement. It was a split in the New Jewel Movement, the party which had seized power in 1979 and had formed the People's Revolutionary Government of which Bishop was head, which led to his death and the subsequent US invasion in October 1983.

13. Einstein Louison (deputy leader, Maurice Bishop Patriotic Movement), interview by author, Grenada, 11 July 1989. Louison was a major in the Grenada People's Revolutionary Army, which was disbanded after the US invasion.

14. The Trade Union Council was the umbrella organization for most of the trade unions in Grenada. Affiliated to it were seven unions: the Grenada Union of Teachers, the Public Workers Union, the Bank and General Workers Union, the Seamen and Waterfront Workers Union, the Taxi Owners and Drivers Association, the Commercial and Industrial Workers Union, and the Technical and Allied Workers Union.

15. Trade Union Council president DeBourg felt this was necessary to transform people's nationalist perception of themselves into a regionalist one.

16. The Commercial and Industrial Workers' Union, formed in 1956, had 890 members drawn from factories, stores and commercial houses. It is one of the smaller trade unions, reflecting the small size of the commercial sector in Grenada. The largest workplace represented had one hundred members. When the Commercial and Industrial Workers' Union was formed in 1956, it had only sixty members.

17. He believed that the absence of popular involvement contributed to the Federation's failure. Eric Pierre (Seamen and Waterfront Workers' Union), interview by author, Grenada, 10 July 1989.

18. Elections have since been held and Matthew Stephens no longer holds this position.

19. Anslem DeBourg (president, Grenada Trade Union Council), interview by author, Grenada, 4 July 1989.

20. He suspected that some of them supported union because they were lured by the possibility of becoming the first OECS prime minister.

21. See chapter 4, note 28.

22. Interview with Eric Pierre.

23. A reference to St Vincent's prime minister, James Mitchell.

24. Interview with Eric Pierre. He gave the example of the Grenadian police force, which had benefited from people from Barbados and other islands.

25. Hugh Dolland (president, Grenada Chamber of Industry and Commerce), interview by author, Grenada, 11 July 1989.
26. Adrian Redhead (executive director, Grenada Chamber of Industry and Commerce), interview by author, Grenada, 11 July 1989.
27. Auslyn Williams (president, Grenada Manufacturers' Association), interview by author, Grenada, 5 July 1989. Williams is a garment manufacturer.
28. A reference to the Single Europe Act which took effect in 1992.
29. A reference to the US/Canada free trade agreement.
30. "Unity Gets 'Yes' Vote in Grenada", 15.
31. Interviews with Redhead and Williams.
32. "Unity Gets 'Yes' Vote in Grenada", 15.
33. Ibid.
34. The United Workers' Party is Dominica's youngest political party, having been formed in July 1988. It went on to win more seats than the traditional opposition, the Dominica Labour Party.
35. Michael Douglas (leader of the opposition; leader, Dominica Labour Party), interview by author, Dominica, 7 June 1989.
36. Edison James (leader, United Workers' Party), interview by author, Dominica, 7 June 1989.
37. Interview with Michael Douglas.
38. This is probably a reference to James Mitchell's, "Thoughts on an East Caribbean Union", in *Two Decades of Caribbean Unity* (Kingstown, St Vincent: Government Printing Office, 1987), 9–17.
39. He argued that, unlike the writing of the independence constitution where the British acted as referees, there was no clear "referee" to guarantee that opposition views were equally represented in any new constitution.
40. He charged that in the previous local government elections, his party had won six of eight seats which should have assured them a majority in the local council. This was thwarted when the government nominated five members to the council, thus giving them a lead of seven members. Such incidents led to an absence of "mutual trust".
41. Interview with Michael Douglas.
42. Louis Benoit had been president of the Waterfront and Allied Workers' Union for nineteen years. Louis Benoit, interview by author, Dominica, 8 June 1989.
43. Heric Augustus was an executive member of Waterfront and Allied Workers' Union and an executive member of the port section of the union. Heric Augustus, interview by author, Dominica, 8 June 1989.
44. The Waterfront and Allied Workers' Union represented dock and clerical workers. With a membership of four thousand, it was the largest trade union in Dominica.
45. Rawlings Jemmott was the president-general of the National Workers' Union. Rawlings Jemmott, interview by author, Dominica, 8 June 1989.
46. The National Workers' Union, formed in 1977, was one of the youngest trade unions in Dominica. It had some fifteen hundred members, mainly from the telecommunications sector. It also represented workers in the timber and furniture industries, mining, engineering, surveying and construction sectors, tobacco factories, agricultural estates, and hotel security guards. Rawlings Jemmott, address to the Sixth Caribbean Trade Union Conference, Santo Domingo, 18–21 April 1989.

47. Interview with Rawlings Jemmott.
48. The Dominica Trade Union, formed in 1944, is Dominica's oldest trade union. Its membership, which came primarily from the agricultural sector, numbered 850, making it the smallest of the three trade unions represented. At its peak, in the 1960s, it numbered 9,000.
49. A reference to the scheduled date for the formation of a single market among members of the European Community.
50. Bernard Nicholas (general secretary, Dominica Trade Union), interview by author, Dominica, 7 June 1989.
51. A reference to the boxing plant dispute between Dominica and St Lucia and the airline row between St Vincent and St Lucia.
52. He mentioned an incident where a group of farmers were declared *persona non grata* in Dominica, and pointed to the difficulties which Rastafarians experienced in entering Dominica.
53. This scepticism was reflected in his comment that although he had heard that OECS leaders had decided that people from the OECS countries could travel within the subregion without passports, he was unwilling to take the chance because he did not trust them. Interview with Louis Benoit.
54. Interview with Rawlings Jemmott.
55. Another reference to the RSS.
56. The United States was the main supporter of the RSS, and the US military held joint manoeuvres with the RSS in the Caribbean.
57. Jemmott, address to the Sixth Caribbean Trade Union Conference.
58. He remarked that St Lucian workers had complained that Compton had threatened to reduce their wages, in line with those of the other OECS countries. Whether or

not this was true, it did reflect anxiety over the possible negative effects of union.
59. Francis Emmanuel (president, Dominica Employers' Federation), interview by author, Dominica, 8 June 1989.
60. Ninian Marie (chairman, manufacturing subcommittee of the Dominica Association of Industry and Commerce; executive member, Council of East Caribbean Manufacturers), interview by author, Dominica, 8 June 1989. Marie was also managing director of a Dominican paint company, Harris Paints.
61. In a conversation after the interview, Emmanuel expressed scepticism about the governments' commitment to forming a political union, in light of the barriers, such as alien landholding acts and work permit requirements, which OECS citizens faced in member countries.
62. The National Council of Women had some ninety-three groups throughout Dominica, ranging in membership from ten to over one thousand. (The latter number represents trade unions which were affiliated to the National Council of Women.) These groups also ranged from agricultural workers to girl guides.
63. Small Projects Assistance Team was a nongovernmental organization based mainly in rural Dominica, working with marginalized groups such as small farmers, the unemployed, small businesses, youth and women.
64. Neva Edwards (managing director, Dominica Social Centre; president, Dominica National Council of Women), interview by author, Dominica, 8 June 1989.
65. Joey Peltier (member, Small Projects Assistance Team), interview by author, Dominica, 7 June 1989.

66. Interview with Michael Douglas.
67. Interview with Ninian Marie.
68. Ibid.
69. Brian Alleyne (minister of legal affairs and attorney-general of Dominica), interview by author, Dominica, 9 June 1989.
70. Ibid. Alleyne explained that arable land was a relatively scarce commodity in Dominica, given its mountainous, heavily forested topography.
71. Interview with Joey Peltier.
72. Rickey Singh, "Defeat in UWP [United Workers' Party] Victory, Big Blow to OECS Union", *Caribbean Contact,* May 1986.
73. He was speaking shortly after his party's defeat by a narrow one-seat margin in two general elections in April 1987.
74. "Hunte Says OECS Unity Plans Too Hasty", *Caribbean Contact,* 4 July 1987. Hunte was addressing a press conference in St Lucia at the venue where the CARICOM Heads of Government conference was taking place.
75. "Hunte Says Let Unity Wait: Lessons in Integration Must Come First", *EC News,* 8–9 April 1988, 2.
76. Ibid.
77. He called for a firmer commitment to OECS trading and an end to disputes, such as those over the boxing plants and airlines, which made a "mockery" of OECS integration. Julian Hunte, interview by Cynthia Barrow, 26 May 1988.
78. "SLP [St Lucia Labour Party] Is Opposed to a Political Federation", *The Voice,* 13 April 1988, 3. Josie was speaking in an interview with the Caribbean News Agency.
79. This led the writer of the article to suggest that this represented a "change" in the St Lucia Labour Party's position which had appeared to support the initiative it-

self, but to object to the government's approach in involving the opposition. In my opinion, this represented less a shift than a more emphatic phrasing of the St Lucia Labour Party's position at the time.
80. Julian Hunte, interview by Cynthia Barrow.
81. "Hunte: OECS Unity in Six Years", *EC News,* 10–11 July 1989, 1. Hunte was speaking at a two-day party summit at which he presented a statement of his party's position on union.
82. Hunte had also resisted Compton's bid for independence in the late 1970s, and had called for a referendum. Thorndike noted that his response reflected more his deep hostility towards Compton than a rejection of independence. See A.E. Thorndike, "Concept of Associated Statehood" (PhD diss., University of London, 1980).
83. "Hunte Says OECS Unity Plans Too Hasty".
84. This suspicion of the governments, fuelled by their membership in the CDU, was also voiced by Josie, who charged that the initiative was "manufactured from outside and [had] nothing to do with the people on the ground". See "SLP [St Lucia Labour Party] Is Opposed to a Political Federation", 3.
85. "SLP [St Lucia Labour Party] Is Opposed to a Political Federation", 3.
86. Julian Hunte, interview by Cynthia Barrow. Hunte was referring to Mitchell's "Thoughts on an East Caribbean Union", which set out his position for supporting the initiative and detailed the kind of union he would like to see.
87. See Ralph Gonsalves, "At the Cross-Roads", *Vincentian,* October 1987.
88. George Odlum (leader, Progressive Labour Party), interview by author,

St Lucia, 15 June 1989. The Progressive Labour Party was formed in 1981 after Odlum broke away from the ruling St Lucia Labour Party.

89. "Soufriere Youth Say No to Casino but Need More Information on OECS Union", *Crusader,* 29 January 1988. The discussion was held at the Soufriere town hall and was organized by the Progressive Labour Party Youth Arm.

90. Interview with George Odlum.

91. Ibid.

92. "CCL Affiliates Meet in Barbados: Local Unions Back OECS Union Plan", *Weekend Voice,* 10 October 1987.

93. Hilford Deterville (president, Seamen and Waterfront and General Workers' Trade Union; member of the opposition; member, St Lucia Labour Party), interview by author, St Lucia, 16 June 1989. Deterville was also an executive member of the CCL, sitting on the administrative council

94. He pointed out that he had participated in the drafting of the CCL resolution that supported the initiative.

95. Interview with Hilford Deterville.

96. David Demacque (president, St Lucia Civil Service Association; director of agriculture, Ministry of Agriculture), interview by author, St Lucia, 16 June 1989.

97. Demacque said this suspicion was fuelled by Compton's claims that the initiative sought to reduce the administrative costs of the islands, and by government's concerns about the "large chunk from public expenditure" which supported the public services. Reservations were also fuelled by a circular letter from Compton to government ministers, linking Liberia's financial problems at the time to the effects on public finances of a large public service.

98. He did concede that the leaders were made to feel "small and tiny" abroad and therefore needed a "bigger backing" to get respect from the international community.

99. Craig Barnard (president, St Lucia Hoteliers Association), interview by author, St Lucia, 16 June 1989.

100. A.F. Valmont (ex-president, chamber of commerce; managing director, A.F. Valmont and Company Ltd; managing director, Windward Islands Gas Ltd; managing director, Valmont Accounts Development Ltd, St Lucia), interview by author, St Lucia, 15 June 1989.

101. Farrel Charles (member, Independent Committee for OECS Political Union), interview by author, St Lucia, 13 June 1989.

102. "OECS Unity: Where to from Here?", *The Voice,* 6 February 1988, 12. He was speaking at the awards ceremony of a local company, Bryden and Partners.

103. A reference to the Special Services Unit within the RSS.

104. Gregory Downs (acting general manager, St Lucia Banana Growers' Association), interview by author, St Lucia, 13 June 1989.

105. The St Lucia Banana Growers' Association, a statutory body, brought banana growers together and provided support services.

106. The Windward Islands Banana Association was the regional grouping responsible for coordinating the industry. It was responsible for introducing technological innovations to the industry and improving production practices in the field.

107. Castries is the capital of St Lucia.

108. The National Youth Council, formed in 1985, had one hundred member organizations. It grouped together all youth organizations in St Lucia. It operated on a district basis, with fifteen district branches

and one student branch. Each district council had a number of youth organizations (religious, sports, political, community), while the student branch represented student councils of various schools. The National Youth Council was not politically affiliated, but had affiliated to it the youth arms of various political parties, excluding the ruling party.

109. "Soufriere Youth Say No".
110. The St Vincent Labour Party was the official opposition party before the 1989 general elections, in which it lost its seats to Mitchell's New Democratic Party.
111. Adrian Saunders (leader, United People's Movement), interview by author, St Vincent, 14 July 1989.
112. While acknowledging that there was a certain urgency to the issue of an OECS union, St Vincent Labour Party leader Vincent Beache was concerned that it was being pursued with "inordinate haste". See "Plan for OECS Union Criticised", *Caribbean Times*, 6 August 1987.
113. Stanley ("Stalky") John (public relations officer, St Vincent Labour Party), interview by author, St Vincent, 12 July 1989. Another St Vincent Labour Party member, John Thompson, described the initiative as an attempt to achieve union through a "shotgun marriage". *CANA News Bulletin*, 28 July 1987.
114. Ralph Gonsalves (leader, Movement for National Unity), interview by author, St Vincent, 13 July 1989.
115. Saunders's suspicions were based on Mitchell's conviction that if union did not happen then, it never would. Interview with Adrian Saunders.
116. "OECS Not People Oriented: Mitchell's Policies Attacked", *Caribbean Contact*, February 1986.

117. He argued that inter-island conflicts (as reflected in the dispute between St Vincent and St Lucia over air rights for airlines, none of which was locally owned) would be better resolved if a central administration existed. Blazer Williams, deputy leader of the Movement for National Unity, also agreed that union was necessary as governments lacked the "political will" to strengthen OECS cooperation. Blazer Williams, interview by author, St Vincent, 12 July 1989.
118. The Commercial, Technical and Allied Workers' Union was the largest union in St Vincent.
119. The St Vincent Union of Teachers represented all government-employed teachers, including those in primary schools and training colleges.
120. The National Workers' Movement represented workers in the industrial, agricultural, commercial, hotel and tourism sectors. It was not affiliated to the CCL, but to the Caribbean Workers Council (with headquarters in Guyana), and the Latin American Confederation of Workers. It was also affiliated to the World Confederation of Labour. The National Workers' Movement had 950 members, which made it one of the smaller unions.
121. Noel Jackson (general secretary, National Workers' Movement; chairman, Joint Workers' Council), interview by author, St Vincent, 12 July 1989. The Joint Workers' Council was an umbrella organization of trade unions in St Vincent.
122. He charged that rights such as freedom of association and collective bargaining, accepted by International Labour Organization conventions, were not accepted by Mitchell, who refused to speak to

or recognize some unions. He noted that in implementing a recent administrative reform programme, the government refused to consult the Public Service Union, which represented the affected workers.

123. Colin Williams (general secretary, Commercial, Technical and Allied Workers' Union), interview by author, St Vincent, 13 July 1989.

124. Fitzroy Jones (public relations officer and president of the Kingstown branch, St Vincent Union of Teachers), interview by author, St Vincent, 13 July 1989.

125. "Regional Trade Unionists Want to See OECS Unity Broaden [*sic*]", *Vincentian*, 2 September 1988.

126. Mitchell described these in his Tortola speech as the "yes butters and not yetters".

127. While not admitting to sharing these views himself, Jackson commented that people were suspicious of the United States' support for the RSS, which suggested to them that the United States had "a game plan for the whole political union".

128. "Chamber Elects New Executive and Supports OECS Unity", *Vincentian*, c. 25 March 1988.

129. Noel Venner (secretary, National Advisory Committee on Political Union in the Eastern Caribbean), interview by author, St Vincent, 14 July 1989.

130. The St Vincent National Youth Council had affiliated to it a total of forty-five youth and community groups, ranging from sports and culture to self-employed groups. The National Youth Council served to link these groups, to develop programmes to strengthen their organizational structure, and to provide leadership training.

131. The National Council of Women was the umbrella organization for women's groups, and had approxi-

mately fifteen such groups affiliated to it.

132. Angela Patrick (field officer, National Youth Council; former executive member of the National Alliance of Development Organizations [1988]) and Geoffrey Samuels (administrative coordinator, Caribbean Federation of Youth), interview by author, St Vincent, 14 July 1989.

133. Ibid.

134. Nelcia Robinson (coordinator, Committee for the Development of Women; past president, National Council of Women [1984–1986]), interview by author, St Vincent, 14 July 1989. The Committee for the Development of Women, a nongovernmental organization, is an affiliate of the National Council of Women. It was formed in 1984 and is largely dedicated to research.

135. Renison Howell (vicar-general of the Roman Catholic Church of St Vincent and the Grenadines; chairman, St Vincent and the Grenadines Christian Council), interview by author, St Vincent, 12 July 1989. He was the Roman Catholic Church's representative on the National Advisory Committee.

136. The Antilles Episcopal Conference, which Father Howell described as the "bishop's body", governed the Catholic diocese in the Caribbean.

137. Father Howell said that this was due to internal difficulties the council was facing, which meant that it did not play as forceful a role as it had in the past.

138. Interview with Angela Patrick.

139. This interview cannot be taken as representative of the position of the main women's group, the National Council of Women. Although the Committee for the Development of Women was not politically affiliated, Robinson was a member of

the United People's Movement, which did not support the initiative.

140. Ian Boxill, *Ideology and Caribbean Integration* (Kingston, Jamaica: Consortium Graduate School of Social Sciences, University of the West Indies, 1993), 91.

Chapter 10

1. See A.E. Thorndike, "Concept of Associated Statehood" (PhD diss., University of London, 1980).

2. He outlined the basis on which the opposition parties rejected the 1971 Grenada Declaration: "(1) The secrecy, indecent haste and total disregard of public opinion. (2) The exclusion of the opposition from the discussions leading to the signing of the Declaration. (3) The imposition of a completed plan for political union without prior public consultation. (4) The fact that the proposed grouping seemed designed solely to entrench the position of certain political leaders then in Government. (5) That in all deliberations on regional matters adequate representation should have been given to opposition parties." See "Pat Emmanuel Says Unity Calls for Greater Political Will", *Vincentian,* 23 October 1987.

3. Rosina Wiltshire, "Regional Integration and Conflict in the Commonwealth Caribbean" (PhD diss., University of Michigan, 1974).

4. Ibid., 25.

5. Most of these governments were involved in one way or another in the US invasion of Grenada. Compton and Charles were at the forefront of the decision to "invite" the United States to invade Grenada, and Blaize benefited after the fact by winning the Americans' backing to form the first elected post-invasion

government. Mitchell, although then in opposition, also supported the invasion. The CDU represented a consolidation of pro–United States/anti-Soviet sentiments in the wake of the Grenada invasion. During the Grenada revolution, the ruling New Jewel Movement had organized seminars of regional left-wing parties, which broke down when the revolution collapsed in 1983.

6. James Mitchell, "Thoughts on an East Caribbean Union", in *Two Decades of Caribbean Unity* (Kingstown, St Vincent: Government Printing Office, 1987), 11.

7. These governments habitually refused entry to politicians from other islands whose political perspectives they did not share. Grenada, under the Herbert Blaize regime, was notorious for this.

8. The St Lucian cabinet had refused to allow opposition members to attend a meeting on the initiative in St Lucia. In its defence, a cabinet statement said that "it viewed this as a matter on which there should be a common OECS policy and accordingly, government is consulting with the OECS governments to ensure uniformity of approach and reciprocity of treatment of visiting political figures". See *CANA News Bulletin,* 3 August 1987.

9. His parliamentary position was further strengthened after the 1989 general elections, which returned him with control over all the seats and no opposition.

10. Blaize came to power through a coalition of three political parties, his Grenada National Party, Francis Alexis's National Democratic Party, and Brizan's National Democratic Congress, which made up the New National Party under Blaize's leadership. During his

term, both Alexis and Brizan left the government, thus strengthening the number of people in opposition who held seats in parliament. This exodus continued in 1989, when Keith Mitchell effectively managed to usurp political power in the New National Party from Blaize, forcing him to form a new party, The National Party. For a while, in 1989, Blaize's government was threatened by a vote of no confidence, which Mitchell mooted. His government was saved by Brizan's reluctance to support the motion. In addition, Blaize's government was facing mounting unpopularity among the public as a result of its economic policies, particularly its retrenchment programmes within the civil service along IMF guidelines.

11. Not all left-wing parties were in SCOPE. For example, the Maurice Bishop Patriotic Movement in Grenada was not a member. The parties in question were Gonsalves's Movement for National Unity in St Vincent, Odlum's Progressive Labour Party in St Lucia, and Hector's Antigua Caribbean Liberation Movement in Antigua.

12. Odlum remarked on the irony which resulted in some of these "parliamentary" opposition parties, for example, Beache's St Vincent Labour Party and Douglas's Dominica Labour Party, losing their status as parliamentary opposition in elections.

13. George Odlum (leader, Progressive Labour Party), interview by author, St Lucia, 5 June 1989.

14. Ibid.

15. See Mitchell, "Thoughts on an East Caribbean Union".

16. Regional journalist Rickey Singh berated Mitchell for falling back on anticommunist hysteria in his response to the opposition parties.

See Rickey Singh, "Prime Minister James Mitchell's 'Red' Eye OECS Search for Political Unity", in *From Tortola to Kingstown: A Report on Eastern Caribbean Political Union* (St Lucia: The Voice Press, c.1991), 27.

17. Because the unions interviewed were all of a similar category, it is difficult to determine what positions might be taken by unions from other categories.

18. The most clear example of this was in Grenada, where some of the Trade Union Council officials were formerly members of the New Jewel Movement, which had initiated the Grenada revolution. See A.W. Singham, *The Hero and the Crowd in a Colonial Polity* (New Haven: Yale University Press, 1968), 311, 312. Singham provides an insight into the relationship between political parties and trade unions: "In most of the West Indian countries the party organization does not depend on a strong core of dues-paying members, for this function is performed by the trade union."

19. Dominica had undertaken a structural adjustment programme between 1987 and 1991 (see United Nations, Economic Commission for Latin America and the Caribbean, *Review of Caribbean Economic and Social Performance in the 1980s and 1990s* [Port of Spain, Trinidad: Caribbean Development and Cooperation Committee, 1999], 3); and St Vincent was involved in an exercise to reform the public sector. See chapter 9, notes 98 and 122.

20. The historical role of the trade union movement in contributing to the development of national identities in various Caribbean states, as well as to a West Indian identity, is well known. The new trade unions

recognized their commonality on a regional basis and were strong advocates of a West Indies Federation. Although the trade union movement was initially at the forefront of the move for federation, it was marginalized in later discussions, with more focus given to politicians and the private sector. Nevertheless, the trade union movement was proud of its heritage of regionalism and, indeed, some of the manifestos of individual trade unions pledged support for a Caribbean nation.

21. See "Now CCL Backing Planned OECS Union", *Barbados Advocate*, 2 October 1987, 2; or "Draft Statement on the OECS Political Union", *Labour Spokesman*, 14 October 1987, 3.

22. CCL, presentation to the tenth meeting of the CARICOM Heads of Government, Grenada, 3–7 July 1989. It congratulated the OECS governments on their decision, taken earlier in May, to ease travel restrictions on OECS citizens.

23. The role of the sector in shaping the CARICOM treaty is detailed by Anthony Payne in *The Politics of the Caribbean Community 1961–1979: Regional Integration amongst New States* (Manchester: Manchester University Press, 1980), 68–70. Payne shows that the CARICOM treaty was modelled along the lines of a paper presented by the Incorporated Chambers of Industry and Commerce which placed a heavier emphasis on economic considerations, in preference to the more *dirigiste* approach advocated by Brewster and Thomas.

24. See *OECS Made: Magazine and Buyer's Guide* 1, no. 1 (*c.* September 1988).

25. See *Latin American Monitor* (London) 7, no. 9 (November 1990): 836.

26. Singham, *The Hero and the Crowd*, 329.

27. Wiltshire, "Regional Integration and Conflict in the Commonwealth Caribbean", 17.

28. The Caribbean Conference of Churches is a broad-based ecumenical grouping of the major Christian churches in the Caribbean.

29. "Churches Back Union", *Barbados Advocate*, 2 October 1987, 9.

30. "Churchmen Want Human Rights Guarantees in Constitution: OECS Bishops Back Move for Union", *The Voice*, 28 November 1987, 7. See also "OECS Unity: Statement by Catholic Bishops", *Vincentian*, 11 December 1987, 7, 12.

31. These were Archbishop Kelvin Felix of St Lucia, Bishop Sydney Charles of Grenada, Bishop Arnold Boghaert of Dominica, Bishop Anthony Dixon of Barbados and Bishop Lester Guilly, former apostolic administrator of the archdiocese of Castries.

32. "OECS Unity: Statement by Catholic Bishops", 7, 12.

33. Allan Kirton, "Integration from Within", *Caribbean Contact*, August 1987, 3.

34. *The Voice*, 28 November 1987.

35. Ibid.

36. *CANA News Bulletin*, 11 September 1987.

37. "Church in the Province of the West Indies", journal of the Twenty-ninth Provincial Synod, Guyana, 2–6 November 1986.

38. He was speaking in Dominica at a series of talks organized by the University of the West Indies extramural centre and the University of the West Indies Guild of Graduates on the union initiative. See *CANA News Bulletin*, 11 September 1987.

39. Linden Lewis, "The Social Reproduction of Youth in the Caribbean", in *Essays on Youth in the*

Caribbean, ed. Linden Lewis and
Richard C. Carter (Cave Hill, Barbados: Institute of Social and Economic Research, 1995), 1–34.

40.   *St Vincent and the Grenadines Development Plan 1986–1988: Growth Diversification Redistribution* (St
Vincent, 1986).

41.   This was probably a reference to
the Caribbean Youth Federation
which was revived in October
1986, and which had among its
goals "to improve regional integration through education, social, cultural and sporting programmes
among the youth of the Caribbean". The federation's members
included the National Youth Councils of most OECS countries – Grenada, Montserrat, St Kitts, Nevis,
St Lucia and St Vincent. See Lewis, "The Social Reproduction of
Youth in the Caribbean", 29.

42.   West Indian Commission, *Time for
Action: The Report of the West Indian
Commission* (Black Rock, Barbados:
West Indian Commission, 1992),
335.

43.   Ernst B. Haas and Philippe Schmitter, "Economic and Differential
Patterns of Political Integration:
Projections about Unity in Latin
America", *International Organization* 18, no. 4 (Summer 1964):
705–37.

44.   Earl Huntley, "Reuniting the Caribbean: Towards OECS Political
Union" (St Lucia, February 1988,
mimeo).

45.   Dwight Venner (director of finance, Ministry of Finance, St Lucia), interview by author, St Lucia,
12 June 1989.

46.   Interview with Dwight Venner; William Demas (president, Trinidad
and Tobago Central Bank; former
president, Caribbean Development
Bank; former CARICOM secretary-
general), interview by author, Trini-

dad, 27 June 1989; Earl Huntley
(permanent secretary, Ministry of
Foreign Affairs, St Lucia), interview by author, St Lucia, 15 June
1989; Randolph Cato (permanent
secretary, Ministry of Finance and
Planning), interview by author, St
Vincent, 13 July 1989.

47.   Huntley, Lazare, Lewis and Marie.

48.   First articulated by Arthur Lewis in
The Agony of the Eight (Barbados:
Advocate Commercial Printery,
1965), this rationale for union was
solidly accepted by proponents of
union.

49.   Interview with Dwight Venner.

50.   He illustrated this by pointing out
that although Prime Minister Charles represented the Windward Islands in negotiations relating to the
banana industry, she had to constantly refer back to the other prime
ministers since she had no power to
take decisions on their behalf.
Vaughan Lewis (director-general,
OECS), interview by author, St Lucia, 11 June 1989.

51.   Percival Marie (chief of trade,
EAS), interview by author, Antigua, 23–24 May 1989.

52.   University of the West Indies vice
chancellor Alister McIntyre was
asked by the OECS leaders supporting the initiative to head a task
force to study its feasibility, but it
never got off the ground.

53.   Vaughan Lewis, "Time and Tide:
Changing Orientation Towards
Caribbean Integration", *Social and
Economic Studies* 48, no. 4 (1999): 93.

54.   "The Palm Island Statement", reproduced in *From Tortola to Kingstown,* 36.

55.   Ibid.

56.   OECS, "Political Unification of the
Windward Islands of the OECS",
press release, 19 September 1990,
reproduced in *From Tortola to Kingstown,* 37.

57. "Annex to Agreement Establishing a Constituent Regional Assembly of the Windward Islands", reproduced in *From Tortola to Kingstown*, 41–42.

58. Ibid., 41.

59. "The Palm Island Statement", 35.

60. "Annex to Agreement Establishing a Constituent Regional Assembly of the Windward Islands", 41–42.

61. From Tortola to Kingstown, 46.

62. *From Tortola to Kingstown*, 45.

63. "Annex to Agreement Establishing a Constituent Regional Assembly of the Windward Islands", 41.

64. Government press conference, HTS TV, St Lucia, 15 June 1998; quoted in Patsy Lewis, "Not Seizing the Time: The Consultative Process in the OECS Political Union Initiative", *Pensamiento Propio*, no. 8 (October–December 1998): 66. See also Earl Huntley, "RCA Update", in *Caribbean Integration: The OECS Experience Revisted* (Kingston, Jamaica: Friedrich Ebert Siftung), 111–12, for a discussion of the RCA report.

65. "Report of the First Meeting of the Regional Constituent Assembly of the Windward Islands on Political Union", St Vincent and the Grenadines, 14–18 January 1991, 58; quoted in Lewis, "Not Seizing the Time", 68.

66. George Brizan, deputy leader of the National Democratic Congress, which formed the 1990 government, had said that the party was willing to examine the possibilities of union, with the other Heads of Government, if it won the elections.

67. In the Windward Islands this concern was also voiced by Hunte and Josie of the St Lucia Labour Party. Josie commented that St Lucia had not yet exhausted the limits of nationhood, and Hunte agreed that the loss of the country's ability to vote in international forums would be significant.

68. "Mitchell and Forde Both Want Unity", *Vincentian*, 9 September 1988.

69. Owen S. Arthur, "Prospects for Caribbean Political Unity", *Journal of Eastern Caribbean Studies* 23, no. 1 (March 1998): 27–34.

70. Singham's treatise on Caribbean political relationships, although developed to describe Eric Gairy's role in Grenadian politics, aptly describes the character of Vere Bird's influence in Antiguan politics. See Singham, *The Hero and the Crowd*, 302–30.

71. K.C. Wheare, *Federal Government*, 4th ed. (London: Oxford University Press, 1963), 40.

72. Arthur, "Prospects for Caribbean Political Unity", 29.

73. Lewis, "Not Seizing the Time", 69.

Chapter 11

Chapter title: The quote is borrowed from Gordon Rohlehr, "A Scuffling of Islands: The Dream and Reality of Caribbean Unity in Poetry and Song", in *New Caribbean Thought: A Reader*, ed. Brian Meeks and Folke Lindahl (Kingston, Jamaica: University of the West Indies Press, 2001), 265–306. Rohlehr uses "scuffling" "to suggest the link between economic necessity, the desperate struggle to survive ('scuffling') and the insular conflicts ('scuffling') in another sense of the word that have attended all efforts at Caribbean integration" (p. 265).

1. See Hilbourne A. Watson, "Global Restructuring and the Prospects for Caribbean Competitiveness: With a Case Study from Jamaica", in *The Caribbean in the Global Political Economy*, ed. Hilbourne A. Watson (Boulder: Lynne Rienner Publish-

ers, 1994), 67–90; Henry S. Gill, "NAFTA: Challenges for the Caribbean Community", in *New Dynamics in Trade and Political Economy*, ed. Anthony T. Bryan (Florida: North–South Centre, 1995), 27–54; Emilio Pantojas-Garcia, "Trade Liberalization and the Peripheral Postindustrialization: The Caribbean in the New Hemispheric Order" (paper presented to the Fourth International Caribbean Studies Seminar, Cartagena de las Indias, Colombia, 2–6 August 1999); Henry S. Gill, "Defining a Caribbean Position on NAFTA" (first draft of paper presented at the Fourth Conference of the Association of Caribbean Economists, Curaçao, 22–25 June 1993).

2. See Norman Girvan, "Caribbean–Latin American Relations and the FTAA", in *CARICOM, Central America and the Free Trade Agreement of the Americas* (Kingston, Jamaica: Friedrich Ebert Siftung, 1998), 4.

3. Jose M. Salazar, OAS chief trade advisor, notes that the FTAA differs from the WTO in a number of ways: while the WTO promotes free trade by a gradual reducing of barriers, the FTAA has this as its immediate objective; the FTAA addresses a more comprehensive array of issues, such as competition policy, investment, and government procurement, not yet fully included in the WTO. See Greater America Business Coalition, "The Trade Agenda: Where Is It and Where Is It Going?", 2 March 2000, http://www.sice.oas.org/geograph/western/Agda_jmse.asp.

4. "The Cotonou Agreement", http://europa.eu.int/comm/development/cotonou/agreement/agr_01.htm. The connection made between political processes and trade or financial assistance suggests a relationship of power. This is particularly the case when benefits flow in a one-way direction from rich EU countries to recipient developing countries. In other words, while EU members can act by withholding support when they determine that recipients have violated norms of good governance, democracy, corruption and so on, ACP countries have no basis for making a similar determination about a donor country, or for responding in kind.

5. Jamaica's minister of foreign trade, Anthony Hylton, argues that in keeping with procedures in the Joint Declaration on Market Access (Annex, xxiii) the European Union should have conducted an impact assessment on ACP commodities arising from the opening of market access to LDCs. He noted that the LDC market access was potentially most damaging to the rice and rum sectors. Anthony Hylton (minister of foreign trade, Ministry of Foreign Affairs and Foreign Trade, Jamaica), "EU/ACP Post-Lomé Arrangements: Implications for the Caribbean", address at the Sir Arthur Lewis Institute for Social and Economic Studies Seminar Series, University of the West Indies, Mona, Jamaica, 1 November 2000.

6. Seiichi Kondo (deputy secretary-general, OECD), opening speech at High Level Consultations on Organization for Economic Cooperation and Development Harmful Tax Competition, 8 January 2001, Barbados. See http://www.oecd.org/da/harm_tax/harmtax.htm.

7. World Bank/Commonwealth Secretariat, *Small States: Meeting Challenges in the Global Economy*, report of the Commonwealth Secretariat/World Bank Joint Task Force on

Small States (London: Commonwealth Secretariat, 2000).

8. OECS, "The OECS Single Market
and Economy: Issues Related to its
Future Direction" (December
1999).

9. Jessica Byron, "The Foreign Policy
Reorientation of the OECS Countries and the Restructuring of their
Foreign Policy Institutions", consultant's report commissioned by
the OECS Secretariat, December
1999 56.

10. Ibid., 54

11. Ibid., 50, 51, 53.

12. V. Schoelcher, *Les Colonies Fran-
caises* (Paris, 1852), quoted in Gordon K. Lewis, *The Growth of the
Modern West Indies* (London:
MacGibbon and Kee, 1968), 415.

13. W.G. Demas, "Consolidating Our
Independence: The Major Chal-
lenge for the West Indies", quoted
in Patrick Emmanuel, *Approaches to
Caribbean Political Integration,* Oc-
casional Paper no. 21 (Cave Hill,
Barbados: Institute of Social and
Economic Research, 1987), 3.

14. Stuart Hall, "Negotiating Carib-
bean Identities", in *New Caribbean
Thought: A Reader,* ed. Brian Meeks
and Folke Lindahl (Kingston,
Jamaica: University of the West
Indies Press, 2001), 24–25.

15. Vaughan A. Lewis, "Regional and
International Integration and
Modes of Governance: The Caribbean Case" (paper presented at the
conference Governance in the Contemporary Caribbean: The Way
Forward, Sir Arthur Lewis Institute
of Social and Economic Studies, St
Augustine, Trinidad, 14–16 March
2001), 4.

16. A belated attempt was made by Barbados and Jamaica to connect the
shiprider treaties with broader issues confronting the region such as
the banana dispute, arms trafficking and deportees. See Ivelaw Griffith, *Drugs and Security in the
Caribbean: Sovereignty under Siege*
(University Park, Penn.: Pennsylvania State University Press, 1997),
193–94.

17. Owen Arthur, "Prospects for Carib-
bean Political Unity", *Journal of
Eastern Caribbean Studies* 23, no. 1
(March 1998): 29.

Bibliography

Primary Sources

Official Papers

Bird, Vere C. Welcome address at the opening ceremony of the tenth meeting of the OECS Authority, St John's, Antigua, 28–29 November 1986.

Blaize, Herbert. Address at the eighth meeting of the OECS Authority, Kingstown, St Vincent, 28–29 November 1985.

——. Address at the opening ceremony of the ninth meeting of the OECS Authority, Basseterre, St Kitts, 28–30 May 1986.

Business and Professional Women's Club of St Kitts. Report to the National Advisory Committee on OECS Closer Union, St Kitts, 12 April 1988.

CCL (Caribbean Congress of Labour). Presentation to the tenth meeting of the CARICOM Heads of Government, Grenada, 3–7 July 1989.

Collister, Roy. President, Caribbean Association of Industry and Commerce. Presentation to the CARICOM Heads of Government, 4 July 1989. Excerpt.

Compton, John. Address at the eighth meeting of the OECS Authority, Kingstown, St Vincent, 28–29 November 1985.

——. Address at the opening ceremony of the ninth meeting of the OECS Authority, Basseterre, St Kitts, 28–30 May 1986.

"The Declaration of St George". Grenada, 16 July 1979. Mimeo.

ECCM Charter. St George's, Grenada, June 1968.

Frampton, D.S., and M.J. Scholar. *Review of Customs Administration within the Organisation of Eastern Caribbean States.* Public Management and Policy Planning Project. St John's, Antigua: OECS, 1989.

Inter-Ministerial Council of the Ministry of Women's Affairs. Report to the National Advisory Committee on OECS Closer Union, St Kitts, 7 April 1988.

Lewis, Vaughan. Address at the opening ceremony of the ninth meeting of the OECS Authority, Basseterre, St Kitts, 28–30 May 1986.

Memorandum of Understanding Between the Government of Antigua and
Barbuda, the Government of Barbados, the Government of the Commonwealth
of Dominica, the Government of St Lucia, and the Government of St Vincent
and the Grenadines Relating to Security and Military Co-operation, 1982. Part
1. Printed in *Caribbean Monthly Bulletin* (supplement) 17, nos. 11–12
(November–December 1983).

Mitchell, James F. Address at the opening ceremony of the eighth meeting of the
OECS Authority, Kingstown, St Vincent, 28–29 November 1985.

———. Address at the opening ceremony of the eleventh meeting of the OECS
Authority, British Virgin Islands, 27 May 1987.

Naylor, Harold. "OECS Tourism Technical Assistance Project Phase, Project No.
5109.20.94.125". St Lucia, 1988.

Nevis Co-operative Credit Union Limited. "The Proposed OECS Closer Union".
Report to the chairman of the National Advisory Committee on OECS Closer
Union, St Kitts, 27 May 1988.

OECS. "Report of the First Meeting of the Economic Affairs Committee of the
Organization of Eastern Caribbean States". St Lucia, 10 November 1982.
OECS/EAS Report 82/01.

———. "Report of the Second Meeting of the Economic Affairs Committee of the
Organization of Eastern Caribbean States". Dominica, 25 May 1983.
OECS/EAS Report 83/01.

———. "Conclusions of the Third Meeting of the Authority". Dominica, 27 May
1983.

———. "Workshop for the Formulation of a Regional Management and
Development Programme for Fisheries of the OECS Region: Report of
Proceedings". Castries, St Lucia, 30 July–1 August 1986.

———. "Conclusions of the Tenth Meeting of the Authority". St John's, Antigua,
28–29 November 1986.

———. "Tenth Meeting of the Authority: Director General's Report". St John's,
Antigua, 28–29 November 1986. Aut 2/86(7).

———. "Conclusions of the Eleventh Meeting of the Authority". Tortola, British
Virgin Islands, 28–29 May 1987.

———. "Twelfth Meeting of the Authority, Director General's Report". Castries,
St Lucia, 26–27 November 1987. Paper no. 2, Aut 2/87.

———. "Export Development Agency (ECSEDA) Project Document". Antigua,
March 1988.

———. "Report of the Twelfth Meeting of the Economic Affairs Committee".
St Vincent, 29 September 1988.

———. "Report of the Fourteenth Meeting of Officials of the Authority". Castries,
St Lucia, 22 November 1988.

————. "A Programme for Agricultural Diversification in the OECS: Identification and Promotion of Non-Traditional Export Crops with Potential for Joint Export Marketing". Annex, November 1988.

————. "Organisation of Eastern Caribbean States Summary of Decisions of the Fifteenth Meeting of the Authority", St John's, Antigua and Barbuda, 1–2 June 1989.

————. "Establishment of the ECDS". Castries, St Lucia. Mimeo.

————. "An Overview of the ECDS". Castries, St Lucia. Mimeo.

————. OECS Natural Resources Management Project (NRMP). "Report of Activities in OECS Member Countries for Period October 1, 1987 to March 31, 1988". OECS-NRMP Working Paper 8. Castries, OECS Secretariat, August 1988.

————. OECS Public Management and Policy Planning Project. "Seminar on the Tax System of Dominica". Layou River Hotel, Dominica, 5–6 November 1986.

"Report of the National Advisory Committee on OECS Closer Political Union". St Kitts, 14 June 1988. PRO/O/005.

Rotaract Club of St Kitts. Report to the chairman of the National Advisory Committee on OECS Closer Union, St Kitts, 25 May 1988.

Simmonds, Kennedy. Address at the opening ceremony of the ninth meeting of the OECS Authority, Basseterre, St Kitts, 28–30 May 1986.

————. Address at the opening ceremony of the tenth meeting of the OECS Authority, St John's, Antigua, 28–29 November 1986.

————. "Address by the Prime Minister, Dr the Rt Hon. Kennedy Simmonds, at the OECS Summit held in Tortola, 27 May 1987 on Closer Union". Mimeo.

————. Letter to author, 1 September 1987. Ref. no. PM/018/3.

St Kitts Christian Council, statement on OECS union to the National Advisory Committee on OECS Closer Union (n.d.).

St Kitts Jaycees. "Report on Concerns on OECS Unification Raised at a Meeting Held 7 January 1988". Paper presented to the National Advisory Committee on OECS Closer Union. St Kitts, n.d.

St Kitts–Nevis Labour Party. "A New Way Forward with Labour". Manifesto. 1988.

St Vincent. Ministry of Finance and Planning. *St Vincent and the Grenadines Development Plan 1986–1988: Growth Diversification Redistribution*. Kingstown, St Vincent: Government Printing Office, 1986.

St Vincent National Advisory Committee on Political Union in the Eastern Caribbean. Circular on its terms of reference. Rev. 1 December 1987.

Stoutt, H. Lavity. Address at the opening ceremony of the eleventh meeting of the OECS Authority, Tortola, British Virgin Islands, 27 May 1987.

Treaty of Basseterre (establishing the Organization of Eastern Caribbean States). Basseterre, St Kitts, 18 June 1981.

UNCTAD [United Nations Conference on Trade and Development]/OECS Economic Affairs Secretariat, OECS. "A Study on the Harmonization of Foreign Investment Policies, Laws and Regulations in the Organisation of Eastern Caribbean States". October 1988.

Warren, George T. Secretary, St Kitts–Nevis Manufacturers' Association. "On OECS Closer Union". Letter to William Herbert, 29 January 1988.

Interviews

Allard, Derek. President, Grenada Bank and General Workers Union, and member of the executive, Trade Union Council. Interview by author. Grenada, 4 July 1989.

Allen, Errol. Deputy director, Eastern Caribbean Central Bank. Interview by author. St Kitts, 5 June 1989.

Alleyne, Brian. Minister of legal affairs and attorney-general of Dominica. Interview by author. Dominica, 9 June 1989.

Augustus, Heric. Executive member, Waterfront and Allied Workers' Union. Interview by author. Dominica, 8 June 1989.

Benoit, Louis. President, Waterfront and Allied Workers' Union. Interview by author. Dominica, 8 June 1989.

Bernard, Craig. President, St Lucia Hoteliers Association. Interview by author. St Lucia, 16 June 1989.

Bird, Lester. Deputy prime minister of Antigua and Barbuda. Interview by author. Grenada, 6 July 1989.

Blake, Byron. Director, economics and industry division, CARICOM secretariat. Interview by author. Jamaica, 15 May 1989.

Brizan, George. Deputy leader, Grenada National Democratic Congress. Interview by author. Jamaica, 12 April 1989.

Carrot, Bradley. Advisor, Antigua Trades and Labour Union. Interview by author. Antigua, 26 May 1989.

Cato, Randolph. Permanent secretary, Ministry of Finance and Planning, St Vincent. Interview by author. St Vincent, 13 July 1989.

Charles, Eugenia. Prime minister of Dominica. Interview by author. Dominica, 9 June 1989.

Charles, Farrel. Member, Independent Committee for OECS Political Union. Interview by author. St Lucia, 13 June 1989.

Compton, John. Prime minister of St Lucia and leader, United Workers' Party. Interview by author. St Lucia, 13 June 1989.

DeBourg, Anslem. President, Commercial and Industrial Workers' Union and Grenada Trade Union Council. Interview by author. Grenada, 4 July 1989.

Demacque, David. President, St Lucia Civil Service Association and director of agriculture, Ministry of Agriculture. Interview by author. St Lucia, 16 June 1989.

Demas, William. President, Trinidad and Tobago Central Bank; former president, Caribbean Development Bank; and former CARICOM secretary-general. Interview by author. Trinidad, 27 June 1989.

Deterville, Hilford. President, St Lucia Seamen and Waterfront and General Workers' Trade Union and member, St Lucia Labour Party. Interview by author. St Lucia, 16 June 1989.

Dolland, Hugh. President, Grenada Chamber of Industry and Commerce. Interview by author. Grenada, 11 July 1989.

Dominique, Joseph. News director, Radio Antilles, Montserrat. Interview by author. Antigua, 1 June 1989.

Douglas, Denzil. Leader, St Kitts–Nevis Labour Party, and leader of the opposition. Interview by author. St Kitts, 6 June 1989.

Douglas, Michael. Leader, Dominica Labour Party, and leader of the opposition. Interview by author. Dominica, 7 June 1989.

Downs, Gregory. Acting general manager, St Lucia Banana Growers' Association. Interview by author. St Lucia, 13 June 1989.

Edwards, Neva. Managing director, Dominica Social Centre, and president, National Council of Women. Interview by author. Dominica, 8 June 1989.

Emmanuel, Francis. President, Dominica Employers' Federation, and director, Musson Trading Company. Interview by author. Dominica, 8 June 1989.

Emmanuel, Jimmy. Director, OECS Special Projects. Interview by author. St Lucia, 14 June 1989.

Emmanuel, Patrick. Institute of Social and Economic Research, University of the West Indies, Barbados. Interview by author. Barbados, 20 June 1989.

Esquivel, Manuel. Prime minister of Belize. Interview by author. Grenada, 6 July 1989.

Fraser, Adrian. Caribbean People's Development Agency. Interview by author. St Vincent, 13 July 1989.

Gairy, Eric. Founder, Grenada United Labour Party. Interview by author. Grenada, 11 July 1989.

Gonsalves, Ralph. Leader, St Vincent Movement for National Unity. Interview by author. St Vincent, 13 July 1989.

Goodwin, George. OECS Economic Affairs Secretariat. Interview by author. St Lucia, 23 May 1989.

Gregoire, Sherita. Director, Eastern Caribbean Drug Service. Interview by author. St Lucia, 14 June 1989.

Harker, Peter. Chairman, Council of Eastern Caribbean Manufacturers; president, Antigua–Barbuda Manufacturers' Association. Interview by author. Antigua, 26 May 1989.

Hector, Tim. Leader, Antigua Caribbean Liberation Movement. Interview by author. Antigua, 24 May 1989.

Herbert, William. Chairman, National Advisory Committee on OECS Closer Union, and founder of the People's Action Movement. Interview by author. St Kitts, 6 June 1989.

Howell, Renison. Vicar-general, Roman Catholic Church of St Vincent and the Grenadines; chairman, St Vincent and the Grenadines Christian Council. Interview by author. St Vincent, 12 July 1989.

Hunte, Julian. Leader of the opposition, and leader, St Lucia Labour Party. Interview by Cynthia Barrow. 26 May 1988.

Huntley, Earl. Permanent secretary, Ministry of Foreign Affairs, St Lucia. Interview by author. St Lucia, 15 June 1989.

Jackson, Noel. General secretary, National Workers' Movement, and chairman, Joint Workers' Council, St Vincent. Interview by author. St Vincent, 12 July 1989.

James, Canute. Caribbean News Agency. Interview by author. Grenada, 7 July 1989.

James, Edison. Leader, Dominica United Workers' Party. Interview by author. Dominica, 7 June 1989.

Jemmott, Rawlings. President-general, Dominica National Workers' Union. Interview by author. Dominica, 8 June 1989.

John, Stanley ("Stalky"). Public relations officer, St Vincent Labour Party. Interview by author. St Vincent, 12 July 1989.

Johnson, Anthony. President, St Kitts Youth Council. Interview by author. St Kitts, 6 June 1989.

Jones, Ben. Deputy prime minister of Grenada. Interview by author. Grenada, July 1989.

Jones, Fitzroy. Public relations officer and president of the Kingstown branch, St Vincent Union of Teachers. Interview by author. St Vincent, 13 July 1989.

Joseph, Keith. President, Amateur Athletic Association; advisor to the Olympic Association; chairman, OECS Athletics Association; lecturer in Sports Administration, International Olympic Committee. Interview by author. St Vincent, 14 July 1989.

Lazare, Alick. Fiscal advisor to the Government of Dominica, and former financial secretary. Interview by author. Dominica, 8 June 1989.

Lewis, Vaughan. Director-general, OECS. Interview by author. St Lucia, 11 June 1989.

Lindsay, Orland U. Anglican Archbishop of the West Indies, and bishop of the
North Eastern Caribbean and Aruba. Interview by author. Antigua, 30 May
1989.

Louison, Einstein. Deputy leader, Maurice Bishop Patriotic Movement. Interview
by author. Grenada, 11 July 1989.

Marie, Ninian. Chairman, manufacturing subcommittee, Dominica Association of
Industry and Commerce; executive member, Council of East Caribbean
Manufacturers; managing director, Harris Paints. Interview by author.
Dominica, 8 June 1989.

Marie, Percival. Chief of trade, economic policy, external economic relations and
statistics, OECS Economic Affairs Secretariat. Interview by author. Antigua,
23–24 May 1989.

Maynard, Charles. Minister of tourism, trade, industry and agriculture, Dominica.
Interview by author. Dominica, 9 June 1989.

McIntyre, Alister. Vice chancellor, University of the West Indies. Interview by
author. Jamaica, 12 April 1989.

Michel, Mario. Former president, St Lucia National Youth Council. Interview by
author. St Lucia, 12 June 1989.

Mitchell, James. Prime minister of St Vincent. Interview by author. Antigua, 2 June
1989.

Nanton, Stuart. Parliamentary secretary, Prime Minister's Office; deputy executive
secretary, CDU. Interview by author. St Vincent, 12 July 1989.

Nicholas, Bernard. General secretary, Dominica Trade Union. Interview by author.
Dominica, 7 June 1989.

Odlum, George. Leader, St Lucia Progressive Labour Party. Interview by author.
St Lucia, 15 June 1989.

Osborne, John. Chief minister of Montserrat. Interview by author. Antigua, 2 June
1989.

Patrick, Angela. Field officer, St Vincent National Youth Council; former executive
member, National Alliance of Development Organizations (1988). Interview by
author. St Vincent, 14 July 1989.

Peltier, Joey. Member, Small Projects Assistance Team, Dominica. Interview by
author. Dominica, 7 June 1989.

Pereira, Joseph. OECS sports coordinator. Interview by author. St Lucia, 14 June
1989

Pierre, Eric. Grenada Seamen and Waterfront Workers' Union. Interview by
author. Grenada, 10 July 1989.

Redhead, Adrian. Executive director, Grenada Chamber of Industry and
Commerce. Interview by author. Grenada, 11 July 1989.

Renwick, John Douglas Barrymore. Head, OECS legal unit. Interview by author. St Lucia, 14 June 1989.

Robinson, Nelcia. Coordinator, Committee for the Development of Women, and past president, St Vincent National Council of Women. Interview by author. St Vincent, 14 July 1989.

Samuels, Geoffrey. Administrative coordinator, St Vincent National Youth Council; administrative coordinator, Caribbean Federation of Youth. Interview by author. St Vincent, 14 July 1989.

Sandiford, Erskine. Prime minister of Barbados. Interview by author. Grenada, 7 July 1989.

Saunders, Adrian. Leader, St Vincent United People's Movement, Interview by author. St Vincent, 14 July 1989.

Simmonds, Kennedy. Prime minister of St Kitts–Nevis. Interview by author. Antigua, 1 June 1989.

Singh, Rickey. Caribbean News Agency. Interview by author. Grenada, 7 July 1989.

Skeritt, Ricky. President, St Kitts–Nevis Chamber of Industry and Commerce. Interview by author. St Kitts, 5 June 1989.

Sorhaindo, Crispin A. Head, CARICOM Review Committee. Interview by author. Grenada, 7 July 1989.

Spencer, Baldwin. Deputy leader, Antigua United National Democratic Party; leader of the opposition; and assistant secretary and first vice-president, Antigua Workers Union. Interview by author. Antigua, 31 May 1989.

Stephens, Matthew. First vice-president, Grenada Technical and Allied Workers' Union. Interview by author. Grenada, 4 July 1989.

Stoutt, H. Lavity. Chief minister of the British Virgin Islands. Interview by author. Antigua, 2 June 1989.

Thomas, Clive Y. Lecturer, University of Guyana, Interview by author. Jamaica, 14 April 1989.

Valmont, A.F. Ex-president, St Lucia Chamber of Commerce; managing director, A.F. Valmont and Company Ltd; managing director, Windward Islands Gas Ltd; managing director, Valmont Accounts Development Ltd. Interview by author. St Lucia, 15 June 1989.

Venner, Dwight. Director of finance, Ministry of Finance, St Lucia. Interview by author. St Lucia, 12 June 1989.

Venner, Noel. Secretary, St Vincent National Advisory Committee on Political Union in the Eastern Caribbean. Interview by author. St Vincent, 14 July 1989.

Williams, Auslyn. President, Grenada Manufacturers' Association. Interview by author. Grenada, 5 July 1989.

Williams, Blazer. Deputy political leader, St Vincent Movement for National Unity. Interview by author. St Vincent, 12 July 1989.

Williams, Colin. General secretary, St Vincent Commercial, Technical and Allied
　　Workers' Union. Interview by author. St Vincent, 13 July 1989.
Williams, Danny. Minister of health and attorney-general of Grenada. Interview by
　　author. Grenada, 11 July 1989.

Newspapers and Periodicals

Barbados Advocate, 16 May–2 October 1987
Business America, 8 August 1983
CANA News Bulletin, 15 July–11 September 1987
Caribbean Contact, February 1986–August 1987
Caribbean Times, 6 August 1987
Catholic Chronicle, September 1979
Crusader, 1 August 1987–16 April 1988
Gleaner (Jamaica), 15 June 1987
Daily Nation (Barbados), 16 August 1990
EC [Eastern Caribbean] News, 21 August 1987–11 July 1989
Labour, 30 April 1988
Labour Spokesman, 14 October 1987
New Chronicle, 5 June 1987
Vincentian (St Vincent), 16 October 1986–9 September 1988
The Voice (St Lucia), 22 August 1987–25 Novemeber 1989
Weekend Voice (St Lucia), 10 October 1987–26 November 1988

Secondary Sources

Books and Articles

Alderson, Stanley. *Yea or Nay? Referenda in the United Kingdom.* London: Cassell,
　　1975.
Alford, Jonathan. "Security Dilemmas of Small States". *Round Table* 292 (October
　　1984).
Andic, Fuat, Suphan Andic, and Douglas Dosser. *A Theory of Economic Integration
　　for Developing Countries.* London: Allen and Unwin, 1971.
Arrighi, Giovanni, and John S. Saul. *Essays on the Political Economy of Africa.* New
　　York: Monthly Review Press, 1953.
Arthur, Owen S. "Prospects for Caribbean Political Unity". *Journal of Eastern
　　Caribbean Studies* 23, no. 1 (March 1998).
Axline, Andrew. *Caribbean Integration: The Politics of Regionalism.* London: Frances
　　Pinter, 1979.

Balassa, Bela. *The Theory of Economic Integration*. London: Allen and Unwin, 1962.

———. "Toward a Theory of Economic Integration". In *Latin American Economic Integration: Experience and Prospects,* edited by M.S. Wionczek. New York: Praeger, 1966.

Barry, Tom, Deb Preusch, and Beth Wood. *The Other Side of Paradise: Foreign Control in the Caribbean*. New York: Grove Press, 1984.

Beckford, George L., ed. *Caribbean Economy: Dependence and Backwardness*. Mona, Jamaica: Institute of Social and Economic Research, 1984.

———. *Caribbean Rural Economy*. 1975; reprint, Mona, Jamaica: Institute of Social and Economic Research, 1984.

Benn, Denis. *The Growth and Development of Political Ideas in the Caribbean: 1774–1983*. Mona, Jamaica: Institute of Social and Economic Research, 1987.

Bennett, Karl M. "An Evaluation of the Contribution of CARICOM to Intra-Regional Caribbean Trade". *Social and Economic Studies* 31, no. 1 (1982).

———. "The CBI and its Implications for CARICOM Exports". *Social and Economic Studies* 36, no. 2 (1989).

Bernal, Richard, Mark Figueroa, and Michael Witter. "Caribbean Economic Thought: The Critical Tradition". *Social and Economic Studies* 33, no. 2 (1984).

Best, Lloyd. "A Model of Pure Plantation Economy". *Social and Economic Studies* 17, no. 3 (1968).

———. "Size and Survival". In *Readings in the Political Economy of the Caribbean,* edited by Norman Girvan and Owen Jefferson. Kingston, Jamaica: New World Group, 1971.

Blomstrom, Magnus, and Bjorn Hettne. *Development in Transition: The Dependency Debate and Beyond – Third World Responses*. London: Zed Books, 1984.

Boxill, Ian. *Ideology and Caribbean Integration*. Kingston, Jamaica: Consortium Graduate School of Social Sciences, University of the West Indies, 1993.

Brewster, Havelock, and Clive Thomas. *Studies in Regional Economic Integration*. Vol. 1, *The Dynamics of West Indian Economic Integration*. Mona, Jamaica: Institute of Social and Economic Research, 1967.

———. "Aspects of the Theory of Economic Integration". *Journal of Common Market Studies* 8, no. 2 (December 1969).

Brown, Kathy Ann. "Now That the Ship Has Docked: A Postscript to the Shiprider Debate". *CARICOM Perspectives,* 1997.

Bryan, Anthony T. "The CARICOM and Latin American Integration Experiences: Observations on Theoretical Origins, and Comparative Performance". In *Ten Years of CARICOM*. Papers presented at the seminar Economic Integration in the Caribbean, Bridgetown, Barbados, July 1983. Washington, DC:

Inter-American Development Bank, Institute for Latin American Integration, CARICOM Secretariat, 1984.

Bulmer-Thomas, Victor. *The Political Economy of Central America since 1920.* Cambridge: Cambridge University Press, 1987.

Burton, Benedict, ed. *Problems of Smaller Territories.* London: Institute of Commonwealth Studies, 1967.

Butler, David, and Austin Ranney, eds. *Referendums: A Comparative Study of Practice and Theory.* Washington, DC: American Enterprise Institute for Public Policy Research, 1978.

BVI Development Planning Unit. *BVI National Account Statistics 1984–1989,* no. 2. Tortola, BVI: Development Planning Unit, *c.*1990.

Byron, Jessica. "The Foreign Policy Reorientation of the OECS Countries and the Restructuring of their Foreign Policy Institutions". Consultant's report commissioned by the OECS Secretariat. December 1999.

The Caribbean Community in the 1980s. Report by a Group of Caribbean Experts. Georgetown, Guyana: CARICOM Secretariat, 1981.

Caribbean Development Bank. *Caribbean Development Bank Annual Report 1988.* Bridgetown, Barbados: Caribbean Development Bank, 1989.

CARICOM. "The Kingston Declaration". Eleventh CARICOM Summit, Kingston, Jamaica, August 1990. Mimeo.

Carnell, F.G. "Political Implications of Federalism in New States". In *Federalism and Economic Growth in Underdeveloped Countries,* by U.K. Hicks et al. London: Allen and Unwin, 1961.

Carrington, Edwin. "Industrialization in Trinidad and Tobago since 1950". In *Readings in the Political Economy of the Caribbean,* edited by Norman Girvan and Owen Jefferson. Kingston, Jamaica: New World Group, 1971.

"Church in the Province of the West Indies". *Journal of the Twenty-Ninth Provincial Synod,* Guyana, 2–6 November 1986.

Clarke, S. St A. "Deepening the Customs Union Relationship in the Eastern Caribbean State". 1985. Mimeo.

Conesa, Eduardo R. "The Integration Experience in Latin America". In *Ten Years of CARICOM.* Papers presented at the seminar Economic Integration in the Caribbean, Bridgetown, Barbados, July 1983. Washington, DC: Inter-American Development Bank, Institute for Latin American Integration, CARICOM Secretariat, 1984.

Demas, William G. *The Economics of Development in Small Countries.* Montreal: McGill University Press, 1965.

———. *Essays on Caribbean Integration and Development.* Mona, Jamaica: Institute of Social and Economic Research, 1976.

————. "Some Thoughts on the Caribbean Community". *Bulletin of East Caribbean Affairs* 2, no. 8 (October 1976).

————. "Consolidating Our Independence: The Major Challenge for the West Indies". Lecture delivered at the Institute of International Relations. Trinidad and Tobago, 1986.

————. *Seize the Time: Towards OECS Political Union.* St Michael, Barbados: n.p., 1987.

Dommen, Edward, and Philippe Hein, eds. *States, Microstates and Islands.* London: Croom Helm, 1985.

Duncan, Neville. "Changes in International Relations: Challenges and Options for the Caribbean". In *Diplomacy for Survival: CARICOM States in a World of Change,* edited by Lloyd Searwar. Kingston, Jamaica: Friedrich Ebert Stiftung, 1991.

Eckenstein, C. "Regional Integration among Unequally Developed Countries". In *Regionalism and the Commonwealth Caribbean: Special Lecture Series No. 2* (papers presented at the seminar Foreign Policies of Caribbean States, Trinidad and Tobago, April–June 1968), edited by Roy Preiswerk. St Augustine, Trinidad: Institute of International Relations, 1969.

Emmanuel, Patrick. "Community within a Community: The OECS Countries". In *Ten Years of CARICOM.* Papers presented at the seminar Economic Integration in the Caribbean, Bridgetown, Barbados, July 1983. Washington, DC: Inter-American Development Bank, Institute for Latin American Integration, CARICOM Secretariat, 1984.

————. *Approaches to Caribbean Political Integration.* Occasional Paper no. 21. Cave Hill, Barbados: Institute of Social and Economic Research, 1987.

Ferguson, James. *Grenada: Revolution in Reverse.* London: Latin American Bureau, c.1990.

Francis, Fitzgerald. "An Overview of the Economies of the English-Speaking Caribbean Countries". Address by UN/OECS economic adviser at the Training Programme of the Caribbean Association of Industry and Commerce in collaboration with the Guadeloupe Chamber of Commerce and Industry, Pointe-à-Pitre, Guadeloupe, 27–29 April 1983. Mimeo.

Franck, Thomas A. "Why Federations Fail". In *Why Federations Fail: An Inquiry into the Requisites for Successful Federalism,* edited by Thomas A. Franck. New York: New York University Press, 1968.

Frank, A. Gunder. *Capitalism and Underdevelopment in Latin America.* New York: Modern Reader Paperbacks, 1969.

Frisch, Dieter. "1992 and the Developing Countries". Bonn, 1988. Mimeo.

From Tortola to Kingstown: A Report on Eastern Caribbean Political Union. Castries: The Voice Press, c.1991.

Gill, Henry S. "The Foreign Policy of the Grenada Revolution". *Bulletin of Eastern Caribbean Affairs* 7, no. 1 (March–April 1981).

———. "Defining a Caribbean Position on NAFTA". First draft of paper presented at the Fourth Conference of the Association of Caribbean Economists. Curaçao, 22–25 June 1993.

———. "NAFTA: Challenges for the Caribbean Community". In *New Dynamics in Trade and Political Economy*, edited by Anthony T. Bryan. Florida: North–South Centre, 1995.

Gilmore, William C. *The Grenada Intervention: Analysis and Documents*. London: Mansell, 1984.

Girvan, Norman. "Caribbean–Latin American Relations and the FTAA". In *CARICOM, Central America and the Free Trade Agreement of the Americas*. Kingston, Jamaica: Friedrich Ebert Siftung, 1998.

Girvan, Norman, and Owen Jefferson. "Corporate vs. Caribbean Integration". In *Readings in the Political Economy of the Caribbean*, ed. Norman Girvan and Owen Jefferson. Kingston, Jamaica: New World Group, 1971.

———, eds. *Readings in the Political Economy of the Caribbean*. Kingston, Jamaica: New World Group, 1971.

Gonsalves, Ralph. "At the Cross-Roads", *Vincentian*, October 1987.

Griffith, Ivelaw L. "Image as Reality: The Security Perceptions of English Caribbean Elites". Paper presented at the Fourteenth Annual Conference of the Caribbean Studies Association, Barbados, 23–26 May 1989.

———. *Drugs and Security in the Caribbean: Sovereignty under Siege*. University Park, Penn.: Pennsylvania State University Press, 1997.

Grimond, J.O., and Brian Neve. *The Referendum*. London: Collings, 1975.

Haas, Ernst B. *The Uniting of Europe*. Stanford, Calif.: Stanford University Press, 1958.

Haas, Ernst B., and Philippe C. Schmitter. "Economics and Differential Patterns of Political Integration: Projections about Unity in Latin America". *International Organization* 18, no. 4 (Summer 1964).

Hall, Stuart. "Negotiating Caribbean Identities". In *New Caribbean Thought: A Reader*, edited by Brian Meeks and Folke Lindahl. Kingston, Jamaica: University of the West Indies Press, 2001.

Hansen, Roger D. *Central America: Regional Integration and Economic Development*. National Planning Association Studies in Development Progress, no. 1. Washington DC: National Planning Association, 1967.

Henke, W. Holger. "Drugs in the Caribbean: The Shiprider Controversy and the Question of Sovereignty". *European Review of Latin America and Caribbean Studies*, no. 64 (1998).

Hicks, U.K., et al. *Federalism and Economic Growth in Underdeveloped Countries: A Symposium*. London: Allen and Unwin, 1961.

Hippolyte-Manigat, Mirlande. "Crisis in CARICOM or CARICOM Crisis?" Paper presented at An International Conference on the Caribbean, Mexico City, 20–25 August 1979. Mimeo.

—————."What Happened in Ocho Rios: Last Chance for CARICOM?" *Caribbean Review* 12, no. 2 (Spring 1983).

Hodges, Michael, ed. *European Integration: Selected Readings.* Harmondsworth: Penguin, 1972.

Huntley, Earl. "Reuniting the Caribbean: Towards OECS Political Union". St Lucia, February 1988. Mimeo.

—————. "RCA Update". In *Caribbean Integration: The OECS Experience Revisited,* edited by Neville Duncan. Kingston, Jamaica: Friedrich Ebert Stiftung, 1995.

Hylton, Anthony. "EU/ACP Post-Lomé Arrangements: Implications for the Caribbean". Address at the Sir Arthur Lewis Institute for Social and Economic Studies Seminar Series. University of the West Indies, Mona, Jamaica, 1 November 2000

Jacobs, Ian, and W. Richard Jacobs. *Grenada: The Route to Revolution.* La Havana: Casa de las Americas, 1980.

Jalan, B., ed. *Problems and Policies in Small Economies.* London: Croom Helm, 1982.

Jefferson, Owen. "Some Aspects of the Post-War Economic Development of Jamaica". In *Readings in the Political Economy of the Caribbean,* edited by Norman Girvan and Owen Jefferson. Kingston, Jamaica: New World Group, 1971.

Kay, Cristobal. *Latin American Theories of Development and Underdevelopment.* London: Routledge, 1989.

Keohane, Robert O., and Stanley Hoffmann. "Institutional Change in Europe in the 1980s". In *The New European Community: Decisionmaking and Institutional Change,* edited by R.O. Keohane and S. Hoffmann. Boulder: Westview Press, 1991.

Khan, Zorina B. "Overview on the Sociology of Tourism in Developing Countries". *Bulletin of Eastern Caribbean Affairs* 9, no. 2 (March–June 1983).

Kirton, Allan. "Integration from Within". *Caribbean Contact,* August 1987.

Kitamura, Hiroshi. "Economic Theory and the Economic Integration of Underdeveloped Regions". In *Latin American Economic Integration: Experience and Prospects,* edited by M.S. Wionczek. New York: Praeger, 1966.

Lehmann, David. *Democracy and Development in Latin America: Economics, Politics and Religion in the Postwar Period.* Cambridge: Polity Press, 1990.

Lestrade, Swinburne. *CARICOM'S Less Developed Countries: A Review of the Progress of the LDC's under the CARICOM Arrangements.* Cave Hill, Barbados: Institute of Social and Economic Research, 1981.

Levitt, Kari, and Lloyd Best, "Character of Caribbean Economy". In *Caribbean Economy: Dependence and Backwardness,* edited by George Beckford. Mona, Jamaica: Institute of Social and Economic Research, 1984.

Lewis, Arthur. *The Agony of the Eight.* Barbados: Advocate Commercial Printery, 1965.

Lewis, Gary P. "Prospects for a Regional Security System in the Eastern Caribbean". *Journal of International Studies* 15, no. 1.

Lewis, Gordon K. *The Growth of the Modern West Indies.* London: MacGibbon and Kee, 1968.

Lewis, Linden. "The Social Reproduction of Youth in the Caribbean". In *Essays on Youth in the Caribbean,* edited by Linden Lewis and Richard C. Carter. Cave Hill, Barbados: Institute of Social and Economic Research, 1995.

Lewis, Patsy. "Not Seizing the Time: The Consultative Process in the OECS Political Union Initiative". *Pensamiento Propio,* no. 8 (October–December 1998).

———. "Revisiting the Grenada Invasion: The OECS' Role, and Its Impact on Regional and International Politics". *Social and Economic Studies* 48, no. 3 (1999).

Lewis-Meeks, Patsy. "An Analysis of the Legal Justification for the United States Invasion of Grenada on the Basis of the Invitation from the OECS". MPhil thesis, Cambridge University, 1988.

Lewis, Sybil, and Thomas G. Matthews, eds. *Caribbean Integration: Papers on Social, Political, and Economic Integration.* Papers from the Third Caribbean Scholars' Conference, Georgetown, Guyana, 4–9 April 1966. Rio Piedras, Puerto Rico: Institute of Caribbean Studies, University of Puerto Rico, 1967.

Lewis, Vaughan. "Time and Tide: Changing Orientation Towards Caribbean Integration". *Social and Economic Studies* 48, no. 4 (1999).

———. "Regional and International Integration and Modes of Governance: The Caribbean Case". Paper presented at the conference Governance in the Contemporary Caribbean: The Way Forward, Sir Arthur Lewis Institute of Social and Economic Studies, St Augustine, Trinidad, 14–16 March 2001.

Lewis, Vaughan, ed. *Size, Self-Determination and International Relations: The Caribbean.* Mona, Jamaica: Institute of Social and Economic Research, 1976.

Lewis, W.A. "The Industrialisation of the British West Indies". *Caribbean Economic Review* 2 (1950).

Linden, Staffan Burestain. "Customs Union and Economic Development". In *Latin American Economic Integration: Experience and Prospects,* edited by M.S. Wionczek. New York: Praeger, 1966.

Maingot, Anthony P. "A New Caribbean Politics for a New World Economy". *Hemisphere* 1, no. 1 (Fall 1988).

Mandle, Jay R. *Big Revolution, Small Country: The Rise and Fall of the Grenada Revolution*. Lanham, Md.: North–South Publishers, 1985.

Marshall, Don. *Caribbean Political Economy at the Crossroads: NAFTA and Regional Developmentalism*. International Political Economy Series. London: Macmillan, 1998.

Martin, Megan. *Volcanoes and Hurricanes: Revolution in Central America and the Caribbean*. London: Cardinal Enterprises, 1982.

Martin, Tony, ed. *In Nobody's Backyard I: The Revolution in Its Own Words*. Dover, Mass.: Majority Press, 1985.

McIntyre, Alister. "Some Issues of Trade Policy in the West Indies". *New World Quarterly* 2, no. 2 (1966).

———. *Elements in a Sub-Regional Strategy for the Caribbean*. September 1973. Monograph.

———. "The Caribbean after Grenada: Four Challenges Facing the Regional Movement". St Augustine, Trinidad, 1984. Mimeo.

———. "Review of Integration Movements in the Third World with Particular Reference to the Caribbean Community". In *Ten Years of CARICOM*. Papers presented at the seminar Economic Integration in the Caribbean, Bridgetown, Barbados, July 1983. Washington, DC: Inter-American Development Bank, Institute for Latin American Integration, CARICOM Secretariat, 1984.

McIntyre, Arnold. *The Economies of the Organisation of Eastern Caribbean States in the 1970s*. Cave Hill, Barbados: Institute of Social and Economic Research, 1986.

Meeks, Brian. "Social Formation and People's Revolution: A Grenadian Study". PhD diss., University of the West Indies, 1988.

Meeks, Brian, and Folke Lindahl, eds. *New Caribbean Thought: A Reader*. Kingston, Jamaica: University of the West Indies Press, 2001.

Mejia-Ricart, Marco Antonio. *Crisis of Small States in the Present Economic World: A Study of the Problems of Small Underdeveloped States with Special Reference to Central America and the Caribbean Area*. London: Farm Intelligence, 1960.

Mitchell, James F. "Thoughts on an East Caribbean Union". Extracts from paper presented to Heads of Government of OECS, November 1986. Mimeo.

———. *Two Decades of Caribbean Unity*. Kingstown, St Vincent: Government Printing Office, 1987.

Mitrany, David. *A Working Peace System*. London: Royal Institute of International Affairs, 1943.

———. *The Functional Theory of Politics*. London: M. Robertson for the London School of Economic and Political Science, 1975.

Mordecai, John. *The West Indies: The Federal Negotiations*. London: Allen and Unwin, 1968.

Morgan, D.J. *The Official History of Colonial Development*. Vol. 5, *Guidance Towards Self-Government in British Colonies 1941–1971*. London: Macmillan, 1980.

Muniz, Humberto Garcia. *Boots, Boots, Boots: Intervention, Regional Security and Militarization in the Caribbean 1979–1986*. Rio Piedras, Puerto Rico: Proyecto Caribeño de Justicia y Paz, 1986.

Myrdal, Gunnar. *Economic Theory and Underdeveloped Regions*. London: G. Duckworth, 1957.

Nye, J.S. "Patterns and Catalysts in Regional Integration". *International Organization* 19, no. 4 (Autumn 1965).

Nurse, Keith, and Wayne Sandiford. *Windward Islands Bananas: Challenges and Options under the Single European Market*. Kingston, Jamaica: Friedrich Ebert Stiftung, 1995.

OECS. *Caribbean Cooperation and Integration: The OECS Experience*. Castries, St Lucia: OECS Secretariat, 1987.

———. Economic Affairs Secretariat, *OECS Statistical Pocket Digest 1987*. St John's, Antigua: OECS Secretariat, 1987.

———. *Economic Integration: The OECS Experience*. Castries, St Lucia: OECS Secretariat, 1988.

———. *Forms of Political Union: A Discussion Paper on a Union to Suit Our Needs: Federation? Confederation? Unitary State? Another Form?* Castries, St Lucia: OECS Secretariat, 1988.

———. *Organisation of Eastern Caribbean States Eastern Caribbean Drug Service (ECDS) Bulletin* 1, no. 1 (September 1988).

———. Questions and Answers on OECS Political Unity. Castries, St Lucia: OECS Secretariat, 1988.

———. Why a Political Union of OECS Countries? The Background and the Issues. Castries, St Lucia: OECS Secretariat, 1988.

———. "The OECS Single Market and Economy: Issues Related to Its Future Direction". December 1999.

OECS Made: Magazine and Buyer's Guide 1, no. 1 (*c*. September 1988).

Orantes, Isaac Cohen. *Regional Integration in Central America*. Lexington, Mass.: Heath, 1972.

Pantojas-Garcia, Emilio. "Trade Liberalization and the Peripheral Postindustrialization: The Caribbean in the New Hemispheric Order". Paper presented to the Fourth International Caribbean Studies Seminar. Cartagena de las Indias, Colombia, 2–6 August 1999.

Payne, Anthony. *The Politics of the Caribbean Community 1961–1979: Regional Integration amongst New States*. Manchester: Manchester University Press, 1980.

———. "The Rise and Fall of Caribbean Regionalisation". *Journal of Common Market Studies* 19, no. 3 (March 1981).

Percy, Selwyn, ed. *Development Policy in Small Countries*. London: Croom Helm, 1975.

Phillip, Diane. "The OECS Countries and the Lomé Convention: An Assessment". Kingston, Jamaica, 1989. Mimeo.

Prachowny, Martin. *Small Open Economies: Their Structure and Policy Environment.* Lexington, Mass.: Lexington Books, 1975.

Preiswerk, Roy, ed. *Regionalism and the Commonwealth Caribbean: Special Lecture Series No. 2.* Papers presented at the seminar Foreign Policies of Caribbean States, Trinidad and Tobago, April–June 1968. St Augustine, Trinidad: Institute of International Relations, 1969.

Pryer, Frederick L. *Revolutionary Grenada: A Study in Political Economy.* New York: Praeger, 1986.

Rainford, Roderick G. "Some Implications for the Caribbean of the Introduction of the Single European Market in 1992". Port of Spain, Trinidad, 1989. Mimeo.

Ramsaran, Ramesh. *The Commonwealth Caribbean in the World Economy.* London: Macmillan, 1989.

Ray, Ellen, and Bill Schaap. "US Crushed Caribbean Jewel". *Covert Action,* no. 20 (1984).

Reid, George. "The Evolving Structure of the CARICOM Trade Regime". *CARICOM Bulletin* 5 (1984).

Resource Center. *Focus on the Eastern Caribbean: Bananas, Bucks and Boots.* Alburquerque: Resource Center, 1984.

Riker, William H. *Federalism: Origin, Operation, Significance.* Boston: Little Brown, 1964.

Robinson, E.A.G., ed. *Economic Consequences of the Size of Nations.* London: Macmillan, 1960.

Rodney, Walter. *How Europe Underdeveloped Africa.* London: Bogle–L'Ouverture Publishers, 1972.

Rohlehr, Gordon. "A Scuffling of Islands: The Dream and Reality of Caribbean Unity in Poetry and Song". In *New Caribbean Thought: A Reader,* edited by Brian Meeks and Folke Lindahl. Kingston, Jamaica: University of the West Indies Press, 2001.

Ryan, Selwyn. "Restructuring of the Trinidad Economy". In *Readings in the Political Economy of the Caribbean,* edited by Norman Girvan and Owen Jefferson. Kingston, Jamaica: New World Group, 1971.

Sanders, Ronald. "Political Union in the OECS: An Opportunity Lost". *Courier* 116 (July–August 1989).

Sandford, Gregory, and Richard Vigilante. *Grenada: The Untold Story.* Lanham, Md.: Madison Books, 1984.

Schou, August, ed. *Small States in International Relations.* New York: Wiley Interscience, 1971.

Scitovsky, Tibor. *Economic Theory and Western European Integration.* Stanford, Calif.: Stanford University Press, 1958.

Searle, Chris. *Grenada: The Struggle Against Destabilization*. London: Writers and Readers Publishers Cooperative Society, 1983.

Searle, Chris, and Merle Hodge. *Is Freedom We Making*. St Georges, Grenada: Government Information Service, 1981.

Searwar, Lloyd. Executive summary to *"Peace, Development and Security in the Caribbean Basin: Perspectives to the Year 2000 – A Conference Report"*. Report. Canadian Institute for International Peace and Security, no. 4, 1987.

Sheppard, Jill. *Marryshow of Grenada: An Introduction*. Bridgetown, Barbados: Lechworth Press, 1987.

Simmons, David A. "Militarization of the Caribbean: Concerns for National and Regional Security". *International Journal* 40 (Spring 1985).

Singh, Ricky. "Defeat in UWP [United Workers' Party] Victory: Big Blow to OECS Union". *Caribbean Contact*, May 1986.

———. "Prime Minister James Mitchell's 'Red' Eye OECS Search for Political Unity". In *From Tortola to Kingstown: A Report on Eastern Caribbean Political Union*. St Lucia: The Voice Press, *c.*1991.

Singham, A.W. *The Hero and the Crowd in a Colonial Polity*. New Haven: Yale University Press, 1968.

Spackman, Ann. *Constitutional Development of the West Indies 1922–1968: A Selection from the Major Documents*. Bridgetown, Barbados: Caribbean Universities Press, 1975.

Spinelli, Altiero. "The Growth of the European Movement since the Second World War". In *European Integration: Selected Readings*, edited by Michael Hodges. Harmondsworth: Penguin, 1972.

Springer, H. *Reflection on the Failure of the West Indies Federation*. Cambridge, Mass.: Harvard University, Centre for International Affairs, 1962

Sunshine, Catherine. *The Caribbean: Survival, Struggle and Sovereignty*, 2d ed. Washington, DC: Ecumenical Program on Central America and the Caribbean, 1988.

Sutton, Paul. "The Banana Regime of the European Union, the Caribbean and Latin America". *Journal of Interamerican Studies and World Affairs* 39, no. 2 (Summer 1997).

———, ed. *Europe and the Caribbean*. London: Macmillan, 1991.

Ten Years of CARICOM. Papers Presented at a Seminar on Economic Integration in the Caribbean, Bridgetown, Barbados, July 1983. Washington, DC: Inter-American Development Bank, Institute for Latin American Integration, CARICOM Secretariat, 1984.

Thomas, Clive. *The Poor and the Powerless: Economic Policy and Change in the Caribbean*. London: Monthly Review Press, 1988.

Thomson, Robert. *Green Gold: Bananas and Dependency in the Eastern Caribbean.* London: Latin American Bureau, 1987.

Thorndike, A.E. "Concept of Associated Statehood". PhD diss., University of London, 1980.

Thorndike, Tony. "National Identity and Secession: The Case of Nevis". Paper presented at the Caribbean Studies Association Conference, Curaçao, 7–10 May 1980.

————. "Europe and the Caribbean: Threat and Opportunity". Port of Spain, Trinidad, 1990. Mimeo.

United Nations Development Programme. *UNDP Human Development Report.* New York: United Nations Development Programme, 1991.

United Nations. Economic Commission for Latin America and the Caribbean. *Review of Caribbean Economic and Social Performance in the 1980s and 1990s.* Port of Spain, Trinidad: Caribbean Development and Cooperation Committee, 1999.

United Nations Institute for Training and Research. *Status and Problems of Very Small States and Territories.* New York: United Nations, 1969.

Valenta, Jiri, and Herbert J. Ellison. *Grenada and Soviet/Cuban Policy: Internal Crisis and US/OECS Intervention.* Boulder: Westview Press 1986.

Vasciannie, Stephen. "Political and Policy Aspects of the Jamaican/US Shiprider Negotiations". *Caribbean Quarterly* 43, no. 3 (1997).

Viner, Jacob. *The Customs Union Issue.* New York: Carnegie Endowment for International Peace, 1950.

Wallace, Elisabeth. *The British Caribbean: From the Decline of Colonialism to the End of Federation.* Toronto: University of Toronto Press, 1977.

Watson, Hilbourne. "Imperialism, National Security, and State Power in the Commonwealth Caribbean: Issues in the Development of the Authoritarian State". In *Militarization in the Non-Hispanic Caribbean,* edited by Dion E. Phillip and Alma H. Young. Boulder: Lynne Rienner, 1986.

————, ed. *The Caribbean in the Global Political Economy.* Boulder: Lynne Rienner, 1994.

Watts, R.L. *New Federations: Experiments in the Commonwealth.* Oxford: Clarendon Press, 1966.

West Indian Commission. *Time for Action: The Report of the West Indian Commission.* Black Rock, Barbados: West Indian Commission, 1992.

Wheare, K.C. *Federal Government,* 4th ed. London: Oxford University Press, 1963.

Wiltshire, Rosina. "Regional Integration and Conflict in the Commonwealth Caribbean". PhD diss., University of Michigan, 1974.

Wiltshire-Brodber, Rosina. *Caribbean Integration: Performance and Promise.* Unrevised working papers, Trinidad and Tobago, September 1986.

Wionczek, M.S. "Introduction: Requisites for Viable Integration". In *Latin American Economic Integration: Experience and Prospects,* edited by M.S. Wionczek. New York: Praeger, 1966.

World Bank. *World Development Report 1989: Financial Systems and Development World Development Indicators.* Oxford: Oxford University Press, 1989.

————. *Long-Term Economic Prospects of the OECS Countries.* Report no. 8058–CRG. Washington, DC: World Bank, 1990.

World Bank/Commonwealth Secretariat. *Small States: Meeting Challenges in the Global Economy.* Report of the Commonwealth Secretariat/World Bank Joint Task Force on Small States. London: Commonwealth Secretariat, 2000.

Index

www.ingramcontent.com/pod-product-compliance
Lightning Source LLC
Chambersburg PA
CBHW021811270326
41932CB00007B/133